BRING MAGIC INTO THE NEW...

For some people, magic is something that was done in the past by ancient wizards, and the only way to do magic now is by copying them and their actions. Not only is this idea incorrect, it would probably astound the ancient magicians if they heard it!

The magicians of 1000 or even 100 years ago were, first and foremost, *experimenters.* These men and women tried new things and interpreted the actions of those who had gone before in new ways—the ways of their times.

Magic should not become static and unchanging. It should be reinterpreted in new ways for each generation. Certainly we should *learn* from the past, but we should recreate magic, using the latest scientific and philosophical techniques and methods.

This is what Donald Tyson has done in his book *The New Magus.* It is a practical framework on which a student can base his or her personal system of magic.

This book is filled with practical, usable magical techniques and rituals which anyone from any magical tradition can use. It includes instructions on how to design and perform rituals, create and use sigils, do invocations and evocations, do spiritual healings, learn rune magic, use god-forms, create telesmatic images, discover your personal guardian, create and use magical tools and much more. You will learn how *YOU* can be a *New Magus!*

The New Age is based on ancient concepts that have been put into terms, or *metaphors,* that are appropriate to life in our world today. That makes *The New Magus* the book on magic for today.

If you have found that magic seems illogical, overcomplicated and not appropriate to your lifestyle, *The New Magus* is the book for you. It will change your ideas of magic forever!

About Donald Tyson

DONALD TYSON was born at midnight on Jan. 14, 1954 in the city of Halifax, Nova Scotia, Canada. His father (deceased) was an officer in the Royal Canadian Mounted Police, and was the son of a Saskatchewan store owner who emigrated from England. His mother is the daughter of a Cape Breton coal miner who came from Yorkshire. He has one older sister and one younger brother.

Attending university locally, he graduated magna cum laude with a major in English literature and a minor in philosophy. He then went on to complete course requirements for a master's degree in literature, but found the atmosphere of graduate studies stupefying and decided to pursue a writing career rather than produce a thesis.

Short stories and articles of his have appeared in magazines such as *Fate*, *Black Belt*, and *Twilight Zone*. He has also written radio and TV drama for the Canadian Broadcasting Corp.

Purposely avoiding any affiliation with political or social movements, he belongs to no religion, group, organization, or society and divorces himself from fads, styles, fashions, and "isms" of all kinds because he believes the perceptions of the individual are tacitly subordinated by the truisms of any cult or body he voluntarily enters, that the act of joining is an act of surrender.

His serious interest in the occult began with an old deck of Tarot cards. Without knowing anything about the Tarot, he began to play with the cards, idly arranging them into patterns. To his surprise, these patterns revealed meanings. Intrigued, he began research into the Tarot that ultimately led to an intense study of all branches of the occult.

To Write to the Author

We cannot guarantee that every letter written to the author can be answered, but all will be forwarded. Both the author and the publisher appreciate hearing from readers, learning of your enjoyment and benefit from this book. Llewellyn also publishes a bi-monthly news magazine with news and reviews of practical esoteric studies and articles helpful to the student, and some readers' questions and comments to the author may be answered through this magazine's columns if permission to do so is included in the original letter. The author sometimes participates in seminars and workshops, and dates and places are announced in *The Llewellyn New Times*. To write to the author, or to ask a question, write to:

Donald Tyson
c/o THE LLEWELLYN NEW TIMES
P.O. Box 64383-825, St. Paul, MN 55164-0383, U.S.A.
Please enclose a self-addressed, stamped envelope for reply, or $1.00 to cover costs.

ABOUT LLEWELLYN'S HIGH MAGICK SERIES

Practical Magick is performed with the aid of ordinary, everyday implements, is concerned with the things of the Earth and the harmony of Nature, and is considered to be the magick of the common people. *High Magick*, on the other hand, has long been considered the prerogative of the affluent and the learned. Some aspects of it certainly call for items expensive to procure and for knowledge of ancient languages and tongues, though that is not true of all High Magick. There was a time when, to practice High Magick, it was necessary to apprentice oneself to a Master Magician, or *Mage*, and to spend many years studying and, later, practicing. Throughout the Middle Ages there were many high dignitaries of the Church who engaged in the practice of High Magick. They were the ones with both the wealth and the learning.

High Magick is the transformation of the Self to the Higher Self. Some aspects of it also consist of rites designed to conjure spirits, or entities, capable of doing one's bidding. Motive is the driving force of these magicks and is critical for success.

In recent years there has been a change from the traditional thoughts regarding High Magick. The average intelligence today is vastly superior to that of four or five centuries ago. Minds attuned to computers are finding a fascination with the mechanics of High Magical conjurations (this is especially true of the mechanics of Enochian Magick).

The Llewellyn High Magick Series has taken the place of the Mage, the Master Magician who would teach the apprentice. "Magick" is simply making happen what one desires to happen—as Aleister Crowley put it: "The art, or science, of causing change to occur in conformity with will." The Llewellyn High Magick Series shows how to effect that change and details the steps necessary to cause it.

Magick is a tool. High Magick is a potent tool. Learn to use it. Learn to put it to work to improve your life. This series will help you do just that.

Other Books by Donald Tyson

Rune Magic

Llewellyn's High Magick Series

THE NEW MAGUS

Ritual Magic
as a Personal Process

Donald Tyson

1988
Llewellyn Publications
St. Paul, Minnesota, 55164-0383, U.S.A.

International Standard Book Number: 0-87542-825-8
Library of Congress Catalog Number: 87-45746

First Edition, 1988
First Printing, 1988
Second Printing, 1988

Cover Design: Donald Tyson
Book Design: Terry Buske
Illustrations: Donald Tyson

Produced by Llewellyn Publications
Typography and Art property of Chester-Kent, Inc.

Published by
LLEWELLYN PUBLICATIONS
A Division of Chester-Kent, Inc.
P.O. Box 64383
St. Paul, MN 55164-0383, U.S.A.
Printed in the United States of America

1988
Llewellyn Publications
St. Paul, Minnesota, 55164-0383, U.S.A.

About The Cover

1. The wheel represents the Spirit that moves on the face of the waters. It is white because the Spirit is the source of all emanations and the highest purity. In a lower sense it is the Tao or Prana or Chi or Ki or Vril or Om—the Quintessence, usually called Light. It is three units of measurement to symbolize perfection.

2. The hub of the wheel is assigned to Mercury, planet of the Magus and of the center of the universe where dualities meet. It is hollow and can be passed through.

3. The six spokes of the wheel are the six directions of space: Up, Down, North, South, East, and West.

4. The six colors represent the six planets that form male and female pairs:

Yellow–Sun–Male	Red–Mars–Male	Orange–Jupiter–Male
Purple–Moon–Female	Green–Venus–Female	Blue–Saturn–Female

5. The upward-pointing red triangle stands for primal Fire, the impulse to action, the masculine force. The Father. Elemental Fire. It is six units of measure on each side.

6. The downward-pointing blue triangle stands for primal Water, that which is acted upon, the female ground. The Mother. Elemental Water. It is also six units per side.

7. The yellow circle embraces and unites the opposites, transcending them by creating a new generation of being. It is androgenous, the Child principle. Elemental Air. Its inner circle is seven units of measure—the limit of the planets—its outer circle nine units. Circle of the Zodiac.

8. The black square is the matter of the universe. The circle surrounded by the square symbolizes divine Will made manifest. The mystical squaring of the circle. Elemental Earth. The square is ten units across.

9. The silver background is primal Chaos upon which the Light acts.

CONTENTS

Part Two: MICROCOSM

Preface

A SHORT EXPLANATION is necessary for the ordering of the planets on the hexagram, chakras, and Tree of Life. This is at variance with the long-accepted arrangement and results from a basic shift of emphasis away from the Sun to Mercury as the central influence of planetary magic.

There are good rationales for a Sun-central pattern, which is why it has endured for so many centuries. The Sun is the most beautiful heavenly body, its power the most overt. It is the only "planet" that can directly be felt, producing life-giving warmth and chastizing the unwary with sunburn and sun-blindness .

All the Magi of old were astrologers. They observed the planets and ordered them by their apparent motions. The Moon was quickest, Saturn slowest, and the Sun of median speed. Therefore the Sun was assigned the central planetary sphere.

Modern astronomy did nothing to upset this Sun centrality. The Sun is observed by telescope and calculated by mathematics to reside at the center of the solar system, fixed in relation to the other bodies that revolve around it. Again it is distinguished as singularly different, more important, and central.

The difficulty with a Sun-central arrangement is that it results in an imbalance among the other six planets that cannot be corrected by rearranging them in contrasting pairs around the Sun. In fact, balanced pairs are impossible. No other planet except the Sun adequately balances the Moon, and no planet at all can successfully balance Mercury, which is solitary and unique among the wandering bodies.

The Sun may be central astronomically, but it can never be central magically because it is by its nature unbalanced. It is blazingly masculine xii / New Magus

where neutrality is demanded. It is yellow, and to be neutral, it must
be colorless. It has an observable sphere, allowing it to balance in this
respect only another observable sphere.

Philosophically the Sun is at the the extreme masculine active
end of a linear scale and balances its heavenly mate, the Moon, which
is at the extreme passive feminine end. Between them lie the remaining five planets, also arranged in pairs about a theoretical center.
Jupiter is the masculine mate of feminine Saturn. Mars is the masculine mate of feminine Venus.

But Mercury has no mate, for the simple reason that it embodies
both masculine and feminine elements within itself. As a magical
symbol, Mercury is balanced and complete. Because of this balance, it
neither needs to be nor will tolerate being paired to any other
planet.

As is explained in the chapter on the hexagram, the astrological
symbols of the planets prove the uniqueness of Mercury with un-
mistakable clarity. The Sun and the Moon are paired and separated
from the rest of the planets by each being given a single, pure sign
denoting its quality:

Sun: ○   Moon: ☽

The Jupiter-Saturn and Mars-Venus pairs are likewise inescapable, based on their symbolism. All four of these planets are double-
compound, partaking of the pure solar or lunar qualities blended with
the earthly—Earth being represented by the cross:

Jupiter: ♃   Saturn: ♄
Mars: ♂   Venus: ♀

Unique and apart, Mercury is made up of the symbols of the three
primary forces—Sun, Moon, and Earth. It is the only planet that combines the solar and lunar symbols. These are held in harmonious
balance by the symbol of Earth:

Mercury: ☿

This relationship is presented clearly and concisely in the
diagram on p. xiii.

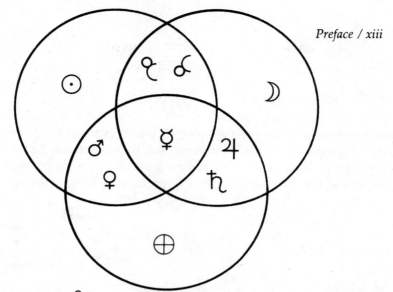

The symbols ☊ and ☋ represent the nodes of the Moon, Caput Draconis and Cauda Draconis, and do not enter into this discussion of the planetary pattern.

A second proof of the Mercury-central ordering of the planets is to be found in alchemy. Knowledgeable occultists would agree that the alchemists of the Rosicrucian era were profound searchers into mystical and philosophical truths. They wrote in riddles and placed the most abstruse of their knowledge in the form of emblems. Many of these clearly show the arrangement of the planets presented here, with Mercury of paramount importance in the center forming a triad with the opposed Sun and Moon, and the remaining planets in pairs on either side of Mercury.

In the *Thrésor des Thrésors des Alchimistes* by Paracelsus, a phoenix stands with wings spread on the black Earth. The Sun is under its right wing, the Moon under its left, and above its head Mercury is framed in a blazing stellar brilliance. Above the Sun is the mated pair of solar opposites Mars-Venus, and above the Moon the mated lunar opposites Saturn-Jupiter. (See p. xiv.)

The second illustration on p. xiv is from the work *Azote des philosophes* by Basil Valentine. It shows a hermaphrodite, symbolic of Mercury and the Magus, standing triumphant atop the chaotic dragon, which is supported by the Earth. Above the head of the hermaphrodite is Mercury framed in a star. Notice the rays that emanate from Mercury and distinguish it from the other planets. Over the right shoulder of the figure is the Sun, and over the left shoulder is the Moon. Below the Sun is Mars-Venus. Below the Moon is Jupiter-Saturn.

In the third illustration, also from *Azote,* which shows the process of putrefaction, a dying man lies inside an alchemical vessel above which are on the right side the Sun and on the left the Moon. Again, the solar pair Mars-Venus is under the Sun and the lunar pair Jupiter-Saturn is under the Moon. Crowning the woodcut is Mercury. Saturn is shown black because Saturn rules putrefaction.

Examples might be further multiplied, but these are sufficient to show that a Mercury-central system of planets is not a new idea but was common among alchemists. Of course the Sun-central system is also often shown in alchemical illustration, but this only proves that alchemy is as traditional as any other magical art.*

The ultimate validation of the ordering and numeration of the planets as presented in this work is stated by the late Aleister Crowley

---

* The great John Dee was aware of the possibility of a Mercury-central system of magic and makes mention of it in his *Hieroglyphic Monad* (reprinted by Weiser, 1975). In Theorem XIII he writes concerning Mercury:
> In the progression we will notice this other Mercury will appear who is truly the twin brother of the first: for by the complete Lunar and Solar magic of the Elements, the Hieroglyph of this Messenger speaks to us very distinctly, and we should examine it carefully and listen to what it says. And (by the Will of God) it is the Mercury of the Philosophers, the greatly celebrated microcosm and ADAM. Therefore, some of the most expert were inclined to place him in a position of, and give him a rank equal to, the Sun himself.

Dee goes on to say that this exchange cannot be made in the "present" epoch without great peril. As throughout the *Monad,* he is deliberately obscure on this matter, but it is worth noting that he was aware of the possibility of replacing the Sun with Mercury.

in his book *Magick In Theory and Practice*. In the chapter on equilibrium he writes:

> Nothing must be lop-sided. If you have anything in the North (of the temple), you must put something equal and opposite to it in the South. The importance of this is so great, and the truth of it so obvious, that no one with the most mediocre capacity for magick can tolerate any unbalanced object for a moment. His instinct instantly revolts.

The instinct of any true Magus must be revolted with the traditional arrangement of the hexagram, which places the Sun in the center, thereby leaving the Moon without a counterweight, and also places androgenous and self-sufficient Mercury, symbol of the awakened center of the Magus, on the periphery. When Mercury is moved to the center and the Sun placed at the zenith opposite its mate, the Moon, at the nadir, then Saturn descends to the lower left point opposite Jupiter on the upper right point. The result is perfect balance.

The Sun takes the number three, which as the perfect trine is in harmony with its glory. Saturn takes the solidly material eight, which represents the cube just as the four of Jupiter suggests the square. Mercury assumes the central six, the number of God and of the enlightened Magus.

Extending the logic of a Mercury-central system to the chakras, Mercury must occupy the heart, which is the regulator of the emotions and activity, the mediator between the inner and outer worlds, between thought and feeling, between desire and action. The emanator of light, the Sun, naturally falls on the crown chakra, which is the resplendent thousand-petaled lotus, source of spiritual illumination. Saturn descends to the belly chakra to symbolize the process of breakdown and decay in the lower intestine.

On the Tree of Life Mercury accords well with the mediating and regulating nature of Tiphareth. The beauty of Tiphareth stems from its dynamic equipoise. This is its perfection. It does not create so much as balance. On the other hand, the Sun is a good extension of the radiant spiritual light descending down the Tree from the supernal triad. Located in Daath, the Sun represents the combined life-giving energies of Kether, Chokmah, and Binah. Saturn embodies the material preoccupation with form in the eighth Sephirah, Hod.

No doubt problems will arise when this new system comes into conflict with the old. For example, is the 3x3 magical square to be associated with the Sun or with Saturn? If the Sun, are the traditional spirits of Saturn, Agiel and Zazel, to be assigned to the Sun? It is impossible to simply shift the solar spirits Nachiel and Sorath to the number three because they are organically extracted from the 6x6 magical square. Yet if the Sun is to be placed in the upper point of the hexagram and given the number three, how can it also be given the 6x6 magical square?

Despite these awkwardnesses, when it was obvious that the traditional arrangement of the planets was illogical, unbalanced, inelegant, and, most importantly, unworkable by anyone who consciously recognized its weaknesses, it then became necessary to change it no matter what conflicts might be generated. If the central idea of a system is sound, details of its practical use have a way of working themselves out—and this new arrangement is magically sound.

It is suggested the Magus use the old system when dealing with old elements, such as traditional planetary spirits, and the new system when he creates his own personal hierarchy—as he must ultimately do once he has progressed beyond a certain formative stage. Also, the new system may be used generally when there is no contradiction. Neither system is absolute. Both are vehicles to help the mind approach certain magical realities.

This preface was written as a kind of offensive defense, to forestall some of the criticisms that will surely arise from those occultists married to traditional magic. One purpose of this book is to present a fresh outlook on matters that are very much taken for granted in the majority of modern magical texts. All that can be said to anyone who does not like the alterations made here is, feel free to ignore them. They are not dogma but are suggestive insights into a difficult and often self-contradictory subject.

Introduction

MAGIC HAS ALWAYS been a disreputable business. Until a few years ago, it could result in fines, imprisonment, torture, or execution, depending on how the lawmakers felt at a given period. In the Bible, Christians are cautioned not to suffer a Witch to live. "Witch" was an inclusive term for anyone who practiced magic, male or female, as well as those who sold poison, procured abortions and committed other crimes. The magician was classed with the dregs of humanity alongside the prostitute and the cutpurse.

Occasionally voices were raised in defense of magic. The Rosicrucian Michael Maier wrote in his *Themis Aurea* in 1618: "Magic (as some define it) is the highest, most absolute, and divinest knowledge of Natural Philosophy." However, he was not so bold as to defy the social odium in which magic was held:

> . . . yet this noble Science doth oftentimes degenerate, and from Natural becomes Diabolical, from true Philosophy turns to Negromancy . . . Hence it is that Magick lies under disgrace, and they who seek after it are vulgarly esteemed Sorcerers; wherefore the Brethren thought is not fit to style themselves Magicians; . . .

The Church derived much of its authority from supernatural events. These were always termed "miracles." When Moses cast down his rod before Pharaoh and turned it into a serpent, it was a miracle; but when the Egyptian priest also changed a staff to a snake it

1

was nothing but foul sorcery. A monk to whom these miracles frequently happened was sure to be called a saint. A layman who produced the exact same events would be burned at the stake. Hence a tongue-in-cheek definition of magic might be: "Miracles not sanctioned by the established church."

The objection of the Church was not against the result of magic, but its method. Miracles were gifts that God gave to the deserving. A good Christian did not ask for a miracle—he received one. The magician had the audacity to steal his miracles from behind God's back, so to speak. He produced miracles on demand, and made-to-order.

The implication was that the magician could not do this without the aid of the devil. It was diabolical to actively seek to upset the laws of nature. God might do so at his pleasure, but man had no right to ape him. Such effrontery must be punished. The magician must be cast down for his sin.

Satan was thrown from heaven for seeking to become like God. Adam and Eve were turned out of the Garden for essentially the same reason. Prometheus was bound to the rock when he defied Zeus and brought fire down from heaven. Christ was crucified for proclaiming himself the Son of God. The Magus is a direct descendant of this august company. He seeks to be the master of his fate and the captain of his soul. Yet he does not defy God, as the Church wrongly believed, but recognizes the godhead within himself.

It is significant that the persecution of magic increased in direct proportion to the secular power of the Church. In the beginning all Christians were magicians. They followed Christ's dictum and sought God within themselves. They were outcasts and rebels against society, in much the same relative position as the magicians and Witches of the Middle Ages.

In the early centuries of the Christian Era, magic was tolerantly ignored, or at most punished with a judicial slap on the wrist. It was only when the Church sought to tighten its stranglehold on all aspects of European civilization that practicing magic became a significant crime against God. Science, which was just standing erect on its wobbly legs, suffered the same persecution as magic.

This suggests that the true objection to magic was not theological, but political. The church fathers reacted against magic, not because it was in defiance of God, but because it stood independent from their pervasive authority. The Magus was not subject to the ecclesiastical pressures that could be brought to bear on a Christian believer.

Excommunication meant nothing to him beyond the social abuses it carried. He thought and acted according to his own creed, and cared nothing for the censure of the bishops.

The Church of the Middle Ages recognized only one truth—the truth it proclaimed itself. Such an absurd situation could only be sustained with an absolute suppression of freedom. Even minor challenges to its dogma were ruthlessly punished with death. It is not necessary to reach back into history for the effects of such a reign of terror. In Marxist societies the identical suppression of freedom in order to preserve self-proclaimed truths exists today.

With the rise of science came the decline of religion. The material was exalted over the spiritual. Magic was temporarily released from persecution in the climate of free speech that resulted from the centuries-long battle against the Church. However, it was not embraced by the new ruling hierarchy. Magic remained an outcast, and soon a different form of persecution arose. The rack and thumbscrew were replaced by ridicule and ostracism.

The ostensible objection of science to magic is opposite that of the Church. The Church hated magic because it worked. It saw magic as an instrument for releasing diabolical forces into the world. Science hates magic because it does not work. It sees magic as a pathetic delusion that lures plastic minds into worthless and mad pursuits, diverting human potential away from material works that have real value.

The true objection of science to magic is identical to that of the Church. Science seeks to rule society by controlling the minds of individuals. Magic provides a mental framework in which the mind can work independent of scientific dogma. Science perceives magic as a threat. Since, from the scientific point of view, anything not scientific is bad, magic is bad and must be suppressed.

It is ironic that science and magic were thrown together during the Church's persecution of new ideas. Galileo suffered as much from the Inquisition as Agrippa. Now that science reigns supreme, religion and magic have been put in the same category. Both are considered airy-fairy subjects, not to be seriously pursued by intelligent people— archaic carryovers from a superstitious past.

Of course the ridicule of science toward religion is much more muted than that directed against magic. Religion is now almost entirely a social institution and is perceived to have a value in controlling the irrational passions of the ignorant masses. It is the opiate of the people and is tolerated so long as it toes the line. To their eternal dishonor, the clergy have participated in gutting from religion all supernatural elements. Priests and ministers are now no more than social workers.

Magic, which has no perceived social value, and which has blithely come down through the centuries unchanged, receives savage attacks in the press and media. Thaumaturges and pagans are accused of everything from eating feces to killing babies. For many years magicians have been excluded from positions of social authority—there is no quicker way to lose a government or scientific post than to admit to practicing magic. But recently a new offensive has been launched to degrade magic in the minds of the general population. The "debunking" of the supernatural has become a serious hobby for many reputable scientists.

The persecution of magic for opposite reasons can be explained by the nature of magic. It is neither science poorly understood nor a superstitious form of religion. Magic is a separate and unique tool for acquiring and using knowledge. It is characterized by balance. It stands midway between science and religion and so is mistaken by each for part of the other.

Knowledge is made up of two components that may be called wisdom and understanding. Wisdom is the inside of knowledge; understanding is the outside. Knowledge is not complete unless it possesses both parts in balance.

Mystics pursue wisdom apart from understanding. They grasp the meaning of life, but are completely unable to express or apply their intuition in any way. Scientists pursue understanding apart from wisdom. They can manipulate matter and symbols, but are increasingly unable to find a purpose for their activities.

The human enterprise that combines both wisdom and understanding is art. The artist manipulates forms and materials at the direction of his spiritual insights. Magic is an art—the Art of making change in the manifest through the Spirit.

Magic is not and can never be a social institution. It is a present and personal quality: it exists only while it is actually being worked and only in the heart of the individual who is working it. Since it cannot be assimilated, it is perceived as inimical by all social groups.

The Rosicrucians understood clearly the personal and present quality of magic. They made no attempt to found churches or lodges after the masonic model. Instead, they cherished their Art in secret and passed it on from master to apprentice in much the same way that magical knowledge is still conveyed in India and more primitive regions. One of the six laws of the Rosicrucians states that every Brother shall choose a fit person for his successor. Another stresses the need for secrecy.

The restriction of magical knowledge has been widely misunderstood, even by those who practice magic. It does not result from a desire to keep magic within a small circle of the elect for selfish reasons—rather, it is inevitable, because magic cannot be passed on in any other way than from individual to individual.

The conveyance of magical power has two parts. The first and outward consists of the words, symbols and materials used in ritual. The other inner part is a spiritual illumination. Magic is vitalized from the inside out. Unless a spiritual awakening can be achieved, the material elements of magic are useless. Illuminations of the Spirit cannot be produced by institutional methods. For this reason magical schools are ineffectual and usually fail when their founder dies.

Given the universal disrepute of magic and the difficulty of finding a competent teacher, the question arises as to why anyone should seek to learn the Art. The answer is that magic is the best way to satisfy a hunger for meaningfulness. That hunger is growing in society, and there are increasingly few ways to meet it.

The Church has sold its truth for material illusions. The truth of science is too narrow: science sees the world through a keyhole. Conventional art has lost its purpose. It no longer knows where it is going or why it ever wanted to get there. But magic has remained pure because it cannot be dissected. Where it is fixed into place it ceases to exist.

The average man is an empty vessel. He walks and talks with the animation of apparent life, yet he is not a human being but a kind of biological automaton. None of his thoughts originate within him. He has neither will nor desires of his own. He is a leaf blown this way and that on the winds of habit and fashion.

What has happened is that the center has gone out of Western culture. For centuries Europe was like a great wheel rolling majestically forward toward a certain and meaningful destination. Suddenly the hub was kicked out of the wheel. The wheel has continued forward on its momentum for the past several hundred years, but the spokes of the wheel are beginning to fly apart.

The hub of the wheel was Spirit. Spirit is what gives meaning to life. It makes true things true and good things good. It is the final measure of any action. Take it away, and there is no method for distinguishing right from wrong. When the center is removed from anything, it becomes destructive.

For a time a man without the light of Spirit inside him will continue to perform right actions out of habit. He has been taught to act a certain way by his parents. He imitates the behavior of his peers. The songs he listens to, the books he reads and the films he views all take for granted a certain ethical code. The mind is lazy. It requires effort to question the reason for an action. So the man acts as he has always acted, never doubting.

Eventually, however, the more energetic people will begin to question why they are doing certain things. Why they should get married, for example. Or why they should prolong the life of the terminally ill. And because the spiritual center is dead within them they will get no answers to their questions. Actions which they have continued out of habit will suddenly appear absurd.

Feminism is a fine illustration. For centuries men and women abided by an unexpressed code of behavior. Men wore pants, women wore dresses. Women wore makeup, men did not. Men worked, and women maintained the home. Suddenly a few people asked why. Since Spirit was cold inside them, they received no answer. They measured their behavior against the external template of science and found it meaningless. So they decided to stop what they were doing.

At first the inertia of society hindered them. But since there was no positive force opposing them, only habit, feminism grew. This should not surprise us. Any social behavior divorced from the touchstone of Spirit will appear meaningless, and any intelligent person will abandon meaningless behavior.

The trouble is, social customs and mores are not meaningless. They only appear absurd to those who have lost the ability to sense their meaning. As ever more customs are abandoned, society will gradually fall apart. This is quite apparent today. The institution of marriage has collapsed. Abortion is common. Euthanasia is becoming an accepted practice. Incest is on the rise. Criminal law no longer admits the notion of punishment, but speaks of rehabilitation. Homosexuality is acceptable. Examples could be multiplied indefinitely.

Magic provides a way for those lost in the confusion of the world to find themselves. It offers no dogma, but the means to awaken the center of Spirit that exists within each human being. The center binds the loose spokes of life together and gives cohesion and purpose, where before there was only a vacuum.

More than this, magic makes it possible to use the limitless potential of Spirit to shape the world in accordance with the desire. It goes beyond the conventional aspirations of religion, which is concerned with escaping from the torment of the world into the bliss of heaven. Yet it does not fall into the delusion of science, which tries to make a heaven out of concrete and steel.

In magic, heaven and earth are one all-pervading timeless unity. No one can flee the world because the world is a vision they have created within their own mind, and no one can run away from themselves. Heaven is not some distant state difficult to attain but is constantly present and enfolding all things. It is only necessary to look in the proper way to see it. Man creates his own hell on earth and cannot escape until he stops creating it.

Thus the reasons for seeking to learn magic are compelling. It awakens the spiritual center and gives direction to a purposeless and hopeless life. It enables its possessor to pursue the good and avoid evil. It provides the tools to solve human problems, both psychological and physical. Most importantly, the magical perception allows one to see things for what they are beneath the veils of illusion surrounding them.

Most people hold magic in contempt because they look at it with only their outer vision. They see magic from a worldly perspective, and from this viewpoint magic is indeed absurd. It is only when viewed with a measure of spiritual awareness that magic can be considered a reasonable and worthwhile pursuit. Since spiritual vision is such a rare commodity few people make a deliberate and conscious decision to study the Art. They are drawn to it by blind need and an innate natural propensity.

To be ripe to receive magic requires an inner revulsion against contemporary society. The future student must be thoroughly fed up with the world around him. He must no longer accept its condemnation or approval. He is in flight from the responsibilities that are expected of him. Often he will be desperate and will pursue several futile avenues before finding magic. He may be considered mentally unbalanced. He may be a rebel or an outcast. In any case he is a square peg in a world of round holes.

Before he can approach magic in a productive way, his nausea at the world must be inverted into something positive. Usually this occurs at the personal level. Seemingly by chance he encounters a human being who is spiritually awakened, and he recognizes intuitively the worth of that person. He idealizes his paragon and seeks to emulate him or her. In doing so, he makes the first blind call upon his own Spirit, which begins to awaken.

At this point he will be drawn, apparently by accident, into his first contacts with magic. A book will fall into his hands, or he will attend the lecture of a practicing occultist. Fueled by his burning need to find some way to perfect himself, his interest in magic will grow. At first his reaction to magic will be humor and reflexive aversion. But as he studies more deeply, the flame of his Spirit will strengthen, and he will begin to see the meanings that lie hidden in the absurd statements of magical texts.

It is not necessary that he encounter a magical adept, although this will certainly facilitate his advancement. The personal conveyance of the flame of Spirit can take place across the gulf of time and space by means of books. Also there are spiritual entities that watch over and mutely direct the progress of worthy seekers after magical truth. It is these beings—emanations of the godhead—who shaped his life for magical attainment long before he felt the least interest in the study of magic.

Magic may be profitably pursued by either sex at any age. Traditionally it was thought that a true understanding of magic required mental and physical maturity. The best age for studying magic was said to be from the mid-twenties to around the mid-forties. Younger people were held to have insufficient life experience. Those older were considered too set in their ways for original thinking. As with any general rule there are many exceptions.

There is a masculine and a feminine magic. The first is vigorous and usually rigidly structured, relying on symbols and words extensively—an intellectual magic. The second is less showy and more organic, relying on herbs and effigies, scents, colors and songs—an emotional magic. In more traditional terms masculine magic would be called wizardry, and feminine magic would be called Witchcraft. It need hardly be added that both sexes may practice both forms of magic, since everyone is innately androgynous (possessing masculine and feminine characteristics). Incidentally, the tendency toward androgyny is more evident in people naturally suited to magic.

Magus is an ancient Persian word meaning "wiseman," and may be applied to anyone who seeks magic through the Spirit. Magician is a better term for someone who pursues magic for material ends, for example, personal power or wealth. The Magus is firstly a spiritual being. Those divorced from Spirit cannot be called Magi whatever their apparent magical abilities. Bereft of Spirit such powers are always illusory, doomed ultimately to fail and betray their owner.

Many young people study magic because they hope to gain power of a physical, emotional, intellectual or social kind over others. Since their ultimate object is power, what they study is the materialistic illusion of magic, not true magic. Their efforts always end in disappointment or disaster. Fortunately they usually give up before they can do themselves any real harm. They are not motivated enough to withstand the rigorous discipline that even a false study of magic entails.

For those who seek the true magic through the Spirit, there are many obstacles to overcome. Social censure can exert a powerful and subtle force of repression on even the most liberated mind. The Magus is reviled as both a fool and a degenerate: a fool because he chases after an illusion, a degenerate because magic supposedly entails immoral and even illegal acts.

He is subject to ridicule. No one takes his statements seriously. He is laughed at or avoided. More materially, he finds that he cannot get a responsible job once his magical interests become known. He may be forced to choose between his spiritual convictions and his earning power. If he has a family or other dependents that choice will be difficult.

The usual defense against social censure has been secrecy. Serious students of magic are reluctant to proclaim themselves. Many will not allow their birth names to be linked with any aspect of the occult. When they write letters or submit articles to occult newsletters they use a pseudonym. Their occult contacts are made through an anonymous box number. If the subject of magic comes up in conversation, they remain silent.

Skepticism of magic and all other spiritual things will generally have been ingrained in the Magus from birth. The inner, unconscious conviction that a magical act is not possible is very difficult to root up. Even when the Magus thinks he believes in magic, he may inwardly disbelieve. Skepticism is utterly destructive. Magic lives in the mind.

The deep conviction that a thing is not real or true destroys it on the mental level. When magic is undermined in the unconscious, it cannot even begin to act in the world.

Skepticism in the minds of others can also work on the Magus to suppress magical events. The Magus should never tell uninitiated persons in advance that he intends to produce a specific magical effect; their disbelief will communicate itself to him and will undermine his faith, making magic impossible.

The best remedy for skepticism is experience. Once a successful act of magic has been accomplished, even a small one, the barriers to future magic are weakened. The new Magus will usually begin in the realm of the psychological, where science assures him he can have an effect, and only later with increased confidence, will he move into physical magic. It is not that one is easier than the other; but rather, the Magus expects mental magic to be easier than physical, and his expectation makes it so.

The greatest barrier to magic is the modern Zeitgeist. *Zeitgeist* is a word meaning "the spirit of an age, the way a people looks upon itself and the universe." For five hundred years the Zeitgeist of the Western world has been shaped by science. Science has gradually excluded all trace of spiritual things from the world view. If the Magus accepts this viewpoint he can never work magic. Magic has no place in the universe of science. When the Magus thinks and acts in terms of the popular perception, he automatically renders magic an absurd anomaly.

The first step toward freedom is the realization that the world is a creation of the mind. This is difficult to achieve. People tend to believe that their view of the world is absolute and unchanging—that an Australian aborigine and they see exactly the same sky and mountains when they stand side by side looking at them. They also believe that they see the world in the same way their distant ancestors saw it—that if they were transported back to Elizabethan London, they would see the city as Shakespeare saw it. Both assumptions are wrong.

The mind does not passively accept the sensory information that enters it. It is creative, and continuously builds up the world out of the millions of bits of data it processes, in much the way a newspaper photograph is made of countless tiny dots. The sole knowledge a human being has of the world is the interpretation created by his own mind.

This is why Eastern mystics say the world is a dream. What is usually thought of as external and substantial is actually made of the same stuff as a dream image. It exists in the same place—the mind— and is mentally projected outside what are perceived to be the limits of the body. There is no difference between inside the body and out- side. Both exist within the mind. There is no root distinction between the mental and the physical; all is mind.

To say the world is an illusion is not to say that it does not exist. This is a common error of those who are too eager to embrace the transcendent view. The salient point is that human beings can never know anything about the absolute world with their everyday aware- ness. Everything experienced is an interpretation—a metaphor, if you will—of something else.

There is a useful experiment for grasping the way in which the mind creates the universe. Close your eyes. Now mentally remove yourself from the universe and try to imagine what is left. Remember, if you have an image in your mind, that means you are still present in the universe and have violated the rules of the game. In fact, if you hear, smell, taste, feel or sense anything, you are still in the universe.

By trying this experiment you will quickly realize that without a perceiver, nothing can be perceived. If anything remains, it cannot be known apart from the mind. Space does not exist without the percep- tion of distance. Time does not exist without the experience of change.

Only in this century has science begun to creep up on the magical perspective by means of higher mathematics. Einstein demonstrated the relative nature of time and space. Relativity is the notion that the nature of things depends on how they are perceived, and is not intrin- sic in them.

Magic can exist in a transcendent view of the world. When the physical and mental are perceived as one and when the inside and outside are not seen to be divided, the idea that spiritual force can be projected across space by the desire and can affect material objects is no longer an absurdity. Magic is understood not to violate the laws of nature but to overleap them, in the same way that multiplication is not a violation of the laws of addition but a transcendence of them.

Every individual creates his own universe in his mind. These per- sonal universes are not the same, although they are similar when formed by members of the same time and culture. They are joined to each other by the common spiritual ground—or underground—that underlies them all. Magic can pass through this unground, enabling the mind of one universe to affect the universe of another mind. The underground is timeless and spaceless and therefore does not exist. Another name for it is the Unmanifest. It is the highest concept of God.

All magic, great or small, is a direct communication with the Unmanifest. This communication takes place by means of the mathematical point, which is omnipresent. The opening of the point is communication with the godhead. The point is opened by the creation of a vortex. The vortex is created by egoless desire.

Magic operates outside the boundaries of physical laws. The idea that science can examine, or even comment on, magical phenomena is absurd. The effects of magic are neither proportional to their causes nor predictable. An effect may not correspond in a logical way with the cause, and the same cause may yield wildly different effects on separate occasions.

Magic chooses its own means to an end. The action of magic is in defiance of the laws of chance. Each magical act is a miracle, even those that appear mundane. Magic often will use physical coincidence, or luck, to accomplish its end. Just as water chooses the easiest course to the sea, so will magic disturb the balance of probability as little as it may. If natural means fail to serve, it will call upon the supernatural, but only after all natural solutions are frustrated.

All scientific laws are founded on the naive assumption that the cosmic scale of probability never tips. Magic is built on the opposite conviction that the pivot of the scale is not fixed and can be acted upon by human will effectively directed. The balance of chance is delicately hung; when it is upset the results can be startling.

A stone released falls to earth. There is nothing to prevent it. The molecules of air around the stone strike it on all sides with uniform frequency. But if the air molecules struck the stone on the bottom more often, the stone would rise. Such an event is not impossible, just unlikely. Magic makes the improbable happen.

There is a tendency to look upon the action of magic in a muddleheaded way, as a force that acts within the boundary of the physical world and bends the laws of nature with sheer brute energy supplied by the Will. Needless to say, this is absurd. No force of wishing a thing will alone make it happen. If this were so, sports such as basketball would be impossible. The fans in the stands would be wishing the ball all over the court.

Magic does not depend on a great force of Will but on the effective direction of the Will to the source of all power, the Unmanifest. This is physically very easy. There is no need to grunt or strain. Indeed, there is no need for elaborate rituals or grandiose incantations. Traditional instruments and forms are at best aids in creating the proper climate of mind and at worst obstructions.

The modern mind, educated within the limited framework of the physical laws, revolts against some of the manifest absurdities of traditional magic. For example, few people would take literally the assertion that there are little men living and burrowing in the ground like mealworms, amassing large hoards of gold. A rational individual living within the Zeitgeist of Western culture who tried to force his mind to such a literal belief would be erecting a barrier in the way of his progress. Yet five centuries ago many sought magic specifically for gaining power over gnomes.

The classic texts of magic, which are called *grimoires*, were penned by medieval Europeans. It is necessary to understand their ignorance of physical facts now taken for granted. Vast stretches of ocean were uncharted. The very shape of the world was in doubt. When sailors came back with wild tales of a great armor-plated beast with a single horn on its nose or of a race of black men with their faces located in their stomachs, the listener had no way of knowing that one tale was true and the other false.

The notion of gnomes would not have seemed improbable to the writers of the grimoires. They had no reason to dispute the many reports of their sightings by miners all over Europe. The idea that the mountains were once beneath the sea or that there were great petrified bones of giant lizards to be found under the earth would have seemed vastly less likely—yet these last two things are known to be true today. A contemporary reader of the grimoires, having no reason to doubt many of their statements, would accept them on faith.

It may once have been possible for the apprentice in magic to set aside his brain and absorb the eternal truths of the Art through the soles of his feet, as it were. It may still be possible today in some Eastern societies. Zen Buddhists in Japan use *koans*—short paradoxes or riddles—to buffet the rational mind until spiritual insight dawns. But such methods are poorly suited for the modern Westerner, who is highly dependent on his rational faculties and more reverent of them than the Easterner.

Reason cannot be suppressed or circumvented; it must be

accommodated. Centuries ago it was possible to accept traditional magic literally. It is no longer possible, anymore than it is possible to believe that the world was created in six terrestrial days. The Bible is in much the same position as the ancient magical texts. Faced with obvious incongruities, the intelligent reader must either deny them or interpret them in a new way.

The most common response is an attempt to alter the terms of magic to suit the modern Zeitgeist. Increasingly, magical texts are written with buzz words derived from science. A buzz word is a word used so vaguely that it has lost its specific meaning and retains only an emotional connotation. "Vibration" is a favorite of modern occult writers, along with "energy" and "electricity" and "magnetism." The use of material terms to describe spiritual events is often unavoidable, but there is little attempt made by these writers to distinguish a term as used in magic from the same term used in science.

Magic is presented as a subtle branch of science that relies on material forces and works within the parameters of physical laws; the implication is that when science develops delicate and sophisticated-enough machines, it will be able to measure and predict magical effects. Modern writers on the occult tend to shy away from any mention of God or references to Spirit. This is in sharp contrast to the grimoires where prayers to God are effusive.

The results of scientific magic are not promising. Magic cannot be materialized. It exists only within the living spiritual heart of the individual. When it is dissected it ceases to exist. A rational mind cannot accept magic into a material framework no matter how hard it tries. Sooner or later it recognizes the incongruities.

A better approach is to elevate and expand the perceptions so that the mind is no longer shackled by the modern Zeitgeist. Instead of materializing magic, the Magus must spiritualize his thinking and transcend formal logic. The grimoires can then be studied fruitfully, and traditional magic practiced without the rising obstruction of unbelief.

It must be emphasized that transcendent thinking does not negate or defy reason. Reason is perfectly valid within its own sphere. The awakened Spirit embraces reason in complete harmony. With magical perception it becomes possible—indeed inevitable—to see the same statement as absurd and true simultaneously.

Using spiritual truth as a touchstone, the Magus can examine traditional magic critically and extract those methods and elements best suited to his nature. He becomes able to separate the gold from the dross, the effective symbols from the meaningless scribbles. More than this, once he perceives the root of magic he can use the specific techniques in the grimoires as models for his own unique rituals and methods.

The grimoires started out as the records of the magical experiments of individuals who were schooled in the traditional magic of their day. They were never intended as holy texts that must be copied and imitated down to the last letter. Yet over the centuries this is exactly what they have turned into, until it became commonplace to believe that the very form and wording of the procedures had its own power and that any departure from it would destroy the magic.

This misunderstanding can only be entertained by those who look at the outside of the Art and are blind to its center. It is equivalent to judging a man by the clothing he wears. The imitative approach to magic is futile. Even if a would-be sorcerer succeeded in following to the letter the quaint instructions of the grimoires, his magic would fail because he lacked access to his center of being, from which all magical vitality flows.

The converse is that magic can be worked effectively by someone without the least knowledge of traditional methods. Intuitive magic relies entirely on the subverbal urgings and directives of the Spirit. Self-inspired magicians usually will pick up an entire collage of disparate bits and pieces of lore and superstition that nonetheless works for them because they are in touch with the Unmanifest.

The best approach is a balanced approach between traditional elements that have proven effective over time and inspired elements that resonate strongly in the personal psyche of the Magus. Magical learning usually begins from the outside in, although it is vitalized from the inside out—that is, beginners practice the mechanical part of magic without being able to infuse it with vitality, and only later do their gestures and words begin to acquire power.

Over time the magic of an adept becomes more individualized as inspired elements replace those drawn from tradition. Most workable magical systems use the grammar of traditional magic but possess their own unique vocabulary. However, it is important that the Magus, in the first flush of running to obey the instructions of his newly awakened inner voice, does not completely throw away traditional methods. Traditional magic has survived because it is grounded in spiritual reality. Even when a practice seems meaningless, there is usually a magical rationale at its base. One measure of attainment is the degree to which the Magus can make sense out of traditional or folk practices that on the surface seem utterly meaningless.

The purpose of this book is twofold: to assist in the awakening of a transcendent view of the universe and thereby liberate the reader from the prison of the materialistic Zeitgeist of modern society; and to rationalize as much as possible the traditional elements of magic and so remove the early barriers to learning that were erected by the revulsion of logic.

The book is structured as a progression from God to man. The first half traces the great symbols of the Art from the simplest to the more complex. The second half examines the composite techniques of magic in which those symbolic elements are used. The structure is organic, designed to unfold the understanding like a flower.

In 1801 the English occultist Francis Barrett published a book on the theory and practice of magic called *The Magus*. It was a monumental achievement. Barrett intended it to be the *summum bonum* of magical texts. In it he gathered and collated occult knowledge from all ages, illuminating it in the light of the learning of his time.

Over the past two hundred years the universe has changed. Natural understanding has grown, and spiritual wisdom has all but disappeared. The *New Magus* is an attempt to make magic accessible to the intelligent modern reader without asking him to compromise either his understanding or his reason.

However, the higher purpose of the *New Magus* could not be expressed more clearly than by the words Barrett used in the Introduction to his book to describe its purpose:

> . . . to free the name of Magic from any scandalous imputation; seeing it is a word originally significative not of any evil, but of every good and laudable science, such as a man might profit by, and become both wise and happy; and the practice so far from being offensive to God or man, that the very root or ground of all Magic takes it rise from the Holy Scriptures, viz.—"The fear of God is the beginning of all wisdom;"—and charity is the end; which fear of God is the beginning of Magic; for Magic is wisdom, and on this account the wise men were called *Magi*.

Part One

MACROCOSM

UNMANIFEST

The All is divisible into two fundamentally different parts. On one side of the dividing plane is the universe of forms called the Cosmos, realm of motion and light. It comprises not only the everyday world of the five senses but also the infinite number of polarities that spring from manifest being—hot and cold, day and night, good and evil. Whenever a thing is perceived as independent or unique it falls onto the side of the division that is the manifest universe. Cosmos is larger than the scientific universe of galactic clusters because, in addition to time and space, it contains noncorporeal forms such as dreams and gods.

On the other side of the dividing plane is what cannot be known or perceived in any way. This is the universe of the uncreated, or Chaos. The ancients usually pictured it as a seething gray mist in which undefined monsters dwelt. This is artistic license since the Unmanifest lacks all qualities, including mistiness and grayness, and its inhabitants (if it could be said to have any) are without form or duration. By its very nature the Unmanifest is inconceivable. Any picture or model a philosopher might form of it becomes at once invalid precisely because it has been formed, and therefore no longer represents the formless universe. Even featureless space has dimension and exists in time; it is a part of creation and cannot be used to represent the Unmanifest.

The dividing plane between the manifest and Unmanifest is not a thing in itself, but the place where the two universes press close to each other. It is an interface such as the one that separates the surface of water from air or the one called the present that separates past from future. The interface has no shape or dimension of its own and cannot be described graphically. It is called a plane merely for convenience.

This division of the All is relative, based on the human perspective. It may be compared with the purely human division of time. From an absolute vantage the All is unified and will always remain so. To see the unity would require that the observer step outside the universe: which is the same as saying it would require that he step into the mind of God. Such a vantage is not possible for imperfect mankind.

Before time began, the Unmanifest was alone, without size or shape, without duration. Time was not. Space was not. Form was not. Matter was not. Energy was not. Yet all things now existent were then in potential, as yet unconceived. The Unmanifest is absolute freedom, possibility without limit, sovereign Chaos. The Unmanifest is God.

> To see a world in a Grain of Sand
> And a Heaven in a Wild Flower,
> Hold Infinity in the palm of your hand
> And Eternity in an hour.[1]

So wrote the metaphysical poet William Blake, who understood the nature of God. For if a thing has no size, no weight, no time or place, then it is everywhere and nowhere simultaneously. At once it is immense and minuscule and both and neither of these conceived extremes.

The ancient Hebrews also grasped the great truth that God cannot be conceived. Any form the mind attempts to impose on the Unmanifest is inapt and at once becomes sacrilegious as it degrades the highest intuition of the nature of God. Other ancient races perceived this dimly, but they allowed the truth to slip away in their hunger for a deity they could understand in human terms. To yearn toward the All and not to give it a human face required a courage they did not possess.

It is a hard truth for people brought up in a traditional religious system. The reader (who will hereafter be called the Magus in hope and expectation) has set himself to become greater in understanding than the mass of humanity, and he must grasp the concept of the

Unmanifest, for the entire Art of magic depends upon this single truth. The Magus must understand the All if he is to understand himself and his work.

The Unmanifest created the universe of forms from a single point within itself by an act of divine Will. Within this point the diversity of the physical world—the ten thousand things of Chinese philosophy— grew by rational stages from desire to idea to form to materiality, in a way analogous to the growth of a living creature in the womb.

The ancients tried to express this idea by presenting the universe as a giant egg floating in the endless womb of God. Around the egg of creation is a shell that cannot be breached from either side without destroying the respective universe that is violated. Thus man cannot know God without destroying God (which is impossible), and God cannot enter the created universe that is made of his own outpourings without destroying creation. This is why it is said in the Bible that a man cannot look upon the face of God: to do so would bring about his instant annihilation.

The creation of the universe did not destroy, change, or diminish the Unmanifest. The Unmanifest and the manifest can never overlap, but every created thing is composed of both aspects of the All. Since the Unmanifest is without dimension, it has truly been observed that God dwells within all human beings. But the magical meaning of this is that the totality of God is present in each blade of grass, every speck of dirt—in every form whether beautiful or ugly. Indeed, the entirety of the Unmanifest is present in each mathematical point in the universe. God is everywhere. An Arab proverb states: "To the pure all things are pure." It might equally be said that to the godly all things are God.

If God is thought of as an endless mirrorlike sea and the act of creation as the splashing of a hand on the waters of that sea, then the manifest universe may be conceived as the ripples that expand from the impact. The ripples have no separate substance in themselves, being formed of the waters of the sea, yet they are distinct from the flat surface. And when the ripples have reached the extent of their travel and returned to their starting point, the sea will be as it was before.

The interface between the Unmanifest and the manifest, which is usually pictured as a shell around the egg of the universe, will hereafter be called the Veil of Unknowing because, throughout history, men have tried to peer behind it, always without success. The act of attempting to understand the All from the viewpoint of the material world is absurd and doomed to failure—thus the ultimate futility of science.

However, the barrier between the universes can be passed and is passed regularly by the simple changing of state from manifest to Unmanifest, and back again from Unmanifest to manifest. The All enters its creation and acts upon the world through its many emanations. Its potencies cross the Veil and are transformed into manifest things. These include the burning bush, the voices of Joan of Arc, and others more subtle. Man merges into the All through death—by "crossing the Veil"—at which point his need to understand distinctions, which is an aspect of the manifest, ceases. After death all individuals become God—not parts of God, for the All has no parts but is whole. Any part of the Unmanifest is all of the Unmanifest. The All is indivisible.

The Veil is crossed by the totality of being at birth and at death. When a human is conceived physically in the womb, the finer elements of divine conception join, and the personal human essence comes into being. At death the human identity, or soul, disperses and the physical body returns to the earth, but the divine essence that was the foundation of the life escapes across the Veil back into the bosom of the Unmanifest.

This passage across the Veil is true of all created things, not only human beings—poems, beasts, rocks, even a summer sunrise. Each comes into discrete being out of the Unmanifest, and to the Unmanifest each ultimately returns.

The divine act of creation did not happen once at the beginning of the universe nor once at the beginning of life. It is happening constantly everywhere. In a single second every human being is re-created an infinite number of times. This is why Blake said: "If the Sun & Moon should doubt, /They'd immediately Go out."[2] It is useful in this matter to meditate on the flame of a candle, which is a metaphor of the physical universe. It exists, has shape and endures, yet is made of nothingness that rises from nowhere, momentarily forms the flame-body, and then vanishes upwards into the nothingness from whence it came. It is also useful to meditate on the wave.

Just as both universes are in every man, so does living man occupy a portion of both universes. He is formed both of the clay and of the Light. Old alchemical woodcuts show Adam (archetypal man) standing with his feet on the Earth and his head through the heavens, signifying symbolically the two universes, the Veil, and the intermediary place occupied by the human race. It is incorrect to say that man is half in the world of forms and half in heaven. In truth only the smallest fraction of what humanity perceives itself to be is touching God, the merest tip of the finger, as the artist Michelangelo portrayed so well in his painting of the Creation on the Sistine Chapel ceiling.

The Unmanifest must never be thought of as another place. This was the mistake made so often by the less enlightened of the ancient philosophers and mystics, and it is nonsense. The Unmanifest is without dimension or change. It should be thought of as around and within, permeating every atom of the universe but not a part of the material world. It is equally sound to think of it as enfolding all things or as completely present in every point of every separate thing.

Part of the problem in understanding may have been the ancient model of the universe as an egg floating on a sea of gray mist. This suggests that there is an outside of the universe—a contradiction in terms—where the nebulous being called God lives. Using such a model uncritically, no one could gain a workable conception of the All.

A better understanding for the modern age can be attained by picturing the universe as a great doughnut with a very tiny hole in its center. The skin of the doughnut is continuously flowing out through the top of the hole and around the hub, and then returning back to the hole by flowing inward on the underside, as the arrows show:

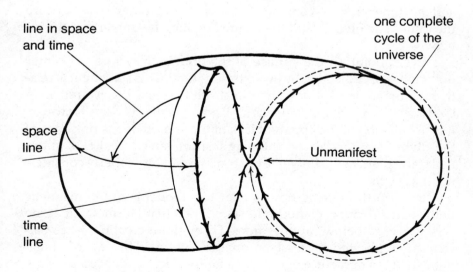

Cutaway Model of the Universe

The doughnut is Cosmos, also called the universe and the manifest. The dimensionless hole at its center is Chaos, also called the Unmanifest and God. Although the picture suggests space around the doughnut and a volume within it, the Magus should realize that this is a two-dimensional representation of a mental model, and exclude everything except the flowing skin of the doughnut and the point at its center.

A line drawn over the skin of the doughnut radially through the center represents a line of time. A line drawn around the hub represents a line of space. Both kinds of lines may be multiplied infinitely. Both are circles. Both end where they begin.

It will be observed that any point on the model except the center must exist in time and space. The time it takes a point to flow out of the center, around the hub, and back into the center is one cycle of the universe. To a man riding this point, the universe will seem to expand and contract, but from an absolute, or godly, view the universe is unchanging and eternal.

All travel is in both space and time. If someone could travel through space without traveling through time, he would exist everywhere at once. Conversely, if someone could travel through time without traveling through space, he would be forever nowhere. A diagonal line on the surface of the doughnut represents travel in time and space. There are an infinite number of such lines.

The model demonstrates that the farthest reaches of the universe and the dimensionless center from which the cosmic egg was born are the same. The outside and the inside are one; the universe is the in-between.

Every point on the surface of the doughnut can be the center point if it is occupied by the awareness of God. This statement is relative to human perceptions since, in absolute terms, the awareness of God is constant and simultaneous in all points of the universe. However, it is the illusion of the apparent lack of the simultaneous presence of the divine Eye that allows the manifest universe to exist. Man can make any point in the universe the center point by properly considering it as such.

It is worth noticing how similar this model is to the magnetic fields that surround planets and stars. The great Hermetic doctrine "As above, so below" applies here. Throughout creation, large patterns are replicated endlessly in smaller patterns. The flow of a magnetic field is a miniature version in an imperfect material guise of the unfolding of the universe.

In the same way, each person is a miniature replica of the universe, a microcosm. Within the human mind at the point of the absolute, or true, Self is a portal through the Veil of Unknowing. In the average person it is closed and locked. Only the crack under the door emits the blinding white brilliance that is the first emanation of the Unmanifest, the primal expression of the Will of God. The Magus when awakened and made wholly aware has the power to reach through the Veil and draw out from the sea of limitless possibility various potencies that can then be manifested in the world of forms.

For this reason the Magus is granted rule over all spirits, even those of the inner circles of creation who possess great powers, such as the archangels. None but God is set over man. None but God can overthrow man—but often man is made to overthrow himself through the deceit and guile of evil spirits. There are only two forces that can thwart the desire of the Magus—the Will of God, and his own ignorance.

Magically, the Unmanifest is the source of all power. It is neither good nor evil, but raw potential. Into the blood of the All the Magus dips his hand when he meditates, and from this reservoir of limitless possibility, he draws his words and signs of command. The whole of the art of magic is in learning to reach across the Veil and bring the gold of the Unmanifest into perceived existence.

It is common in magic to speak of angels, demons, ghosts, elementals, and so on. Opinions as to the nature of these various spirits differ, but generally they are regarded as possessing considerable powers of their own, which they occasionally choose to exhibit for the terror or delight of mankind. They are usually described as intelligent but lacking the spark of Divinity in man that enables him to ape the part of Creator.

Many superstitious adepts firmly believe that their magical power stems from the good will of these spirits. For example, the fakirs of India, when asked how they perform their magic, will confide that they do nothing themselves but merely call upon the spirits to work their bidding. They believe the whole potency of their magic lies in their ability to cajole the spirits with sacrifices, adorations, and promises of service.

This view betrays an ignorance both of human potential and of cosmic law. Even if such a childish concept were correct (that spirits were independent beings who could be wooed), their power would still stem from the Will of the Unmanifest, as exemplified in the primary emanation of Divine Light. The spirits could do nothing unless the Light at the center of the true Self of the fakir first granted them permission. The spirits delude the fakir into thinking he is dependent on them. In fact, the truth is just the opposite: spirits are wholly dependent on the unconscious power of man when they wish to exercise their purposes in the material world.

The Buddhists of Tibet have a somewhat clearer understanding of spirits than the Hindu fakirs of India. They admit the existence of such things as angels and demons, but maintain that they are illusions composed by the mind of man, even as man is a dream in the mind of God. They do not dismiss spirits as unreal, for they understand full well that mental realities are no less potent than physical realities. Both are founded ultimately in God.

The Western Hermetic view is similar to the Buddhist. The Magus does not believe spirits are wholly independent beings with a status equal to his own, but neither does he make the mistake of dismissing them as complete fabrications of his own fancy. When a Magus evokes a spirit, he is aware that it is given its shape and personality by his mind, yet not by the part of his mind that is his personal identity, but by the unknowable part that is God. Once created, a spirit has as much reality as its creator, since both are created by the All.

The spirits are devices employed by the Magus, either consciously or unconsciously, to manipulate the powers of the Unmanifest, in the same way a blacksmith will use a clay vessel to carry molten metals intended for casting. When the Magus calls upon a spirit to perform a task, he is really opening a door into the Unmanifest through the point of his true Self, and it is his own higher potential that transforms his desire into reality. Yet even though the form of a spirit is an illusion, it still has the power to kill should the Magus be foolish enough to grant it the right to do so.

The question of reincarnation is a vexing one to Eastern minds. Since the concept is not a part of the Western psyche, it seldom troubles practitioners of the Hermetic art unless they have steeped themselves in Buddhist or Hindu philosophy. However, it is useful to place reincarnation in the context of the Unmanifest.

There are two views of reincarnation. The first supposes the soul, the personal identity, endures through a series of births and deaths in order to gather a store of life experience, and that through the soul any man or woman may recall the events of past lives. This is a vulgar superstition that no educated Buddhist would tolerate for an instant, yet it is held by the vast majority of people.

The more enlightened opinion is that the soul is mortal and perishes with the body, but the Spirit that lives in all beings survives death and is successively reincarnated with its stock of life experience in order to evolve to a higher state. According to this view, the individual identity does not survive but the foundation upon which that identity was based does. An educated Buddhist would maintain that the Spirit does not cross the Veil at each death but moves from person to person until its wheel of births and deaths has been fulfilled.

The fault in this thinking is that it supposes the Spirit of God can be divided and that one portion can gain more experience than another. A Western adept would say that since the spark of Divinity at the center of each human being is one with the All, it has no need to cross the Veil after death: it is the Unmanifest in its entirety, and the veil that barred it from the bosom of God was the veil of human flesh surrounding it during life. Therefore, each birth and death is a complete round of incarnation that returns the acquired measure of life experience back to the Unmanifest.

Man is like a worm that burrows and lives in the wooden handle of the carpenter's plane that the Master Builder uses to shape his Great Work. Human identity is the worm. Human function is the fulfillment of Divine purpose. The body is the plane. When the plane breaks or wears out, the Builder does not fashion another lovingly around the worm. Only the incredible conceit of the worm could imagine such a thing.

No, the Builder casts the broken plane—and the silly vain worm—into his fire and makes a new plane, shaping it to suit the purpose of the Work and using it as an extension of his Will to achieve his end. And another silly worm takes up residence in the handle and fancies itself Lord of the Manor!

The All cares with infinite compassion for the least of its manifestations, which it creates out of love and desire. Not without reason did Christ say that God is aware of the fall of the least sparrow. But what is important to mankind is not always important to God. The Magus remains humble and soft-spoken, no matter how extensive his earthly power, since he can never be certain that the insect he steps on is not more useful in the scheme of things than himself.

CREATION

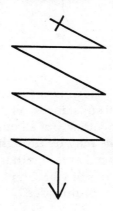

000: ALL/NOTHING

In the beginning the Unmanifest was All. God lay asleep in a timeless slumber without dreams. This nothingness that is the highest state of the All can best be likened to the state of the human mind during dreamless sleep—it is without duration or quality.

00: ALL IS ALL

Then desire stirred within the depths of the Unmanifest. Some mystics believe the movement was brought about by a crisis within the All that necessitated change; others say it was a voluntary act of love. For reasons of his own, God chose to consider himself. He awoke throughout his substance and became aware of its All-potential without yet analyzing its quality or extent. In a way utterly alien to mankind, the Unmanifest experienced itself with that which it was experiencing.

This is nothing like the "I think, therefore I am" of Descartes. The first act of God cannot in any way be grasped directly from the perspective of the manifest universe. God perceived his own vastness without the benefit of measurement or point of view. He understood his greatness, not as mankind understands great size or number, but as an infinitude of potential. This is not understanding in the sense "I am" but rather in the sense "All is All"—that there was nothing beyond him, for he was everything that might be.

0: ALL IS LIGHT

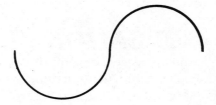

With an awareness of his Allness, God grew aware of his texture or substance, which was all substances, all qualities, not one after the other, not even blended together, but all qualities in potential before they become qualities. This may be thought of as an endless sea of white light that is experienced as Self rather than considered by Self, containing all colors, all levels of vibration that could be. White noise is a material approximation of this idea.

Within this sea of white light, desire ranged endlessly seeking some limited quality upon which it could fix itself and rest. But as yet there was nothing. The absolute freedom embodying the Will to real-ize all potential was as yet unrealized. The frustrated desire of God recoiled upon itself, falling inward ever closer together, becoming ever more dense, metaphorically assuming a circular and then a spiral direction of travel.

This questing inward after fulfillment is known as the "primal swirlings" and may be pictured as flecks of light dancing in a whirl-pool.

1: I AM ALL

•

The tightening spiral coalesced into the first glimmering of a sense of Self—a mathematical point without dimension or substance. This point gave the perception of the All a vantage from which to consider itself. From this point God could regard the measureless light extending away endlessly in all directions.

2: I AM I

————————

The eye (or I) that considers must consider something. A second point of necessity at once was born even as the first point came into being. The second point may be thought of as a reflection of the first, like it in all respects but discrete from it. The separation of these points did not at this stage have measure. The salient understanding is that they are separate.

The awareness of God could take up residence in one point and view the other, considering it as a thing apart from himself even though it was still within his own substance. At the same time, the omniscient awareness of God was resident in the second point, looking back at the first. There is no way to distinguish one point from the other, to call one point the Self of God and the other point its reflection.

This act of considering an object became a resonating pulse from point to point, a pulse without a period of duration—in other words, a line, the first dimension.

3: DISTINCTION

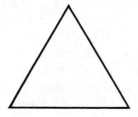

Again God considered himself in his new aspect, which neces-sitated the precipitation of a third point of view. From this third point God looked back at the line, his initial awareness of a discrete Self reflected in and reflecting that Self. The second dimension was born, the plane surface, as yet outside of time and space. This is symbolized by the triangle.

Were the third point to precipitate in line with the other two, it would not yield a higher vantage of awareness, since it would per-ceive the other points as points.

4: DIMENSION

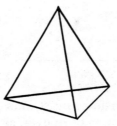

The awareness of God shifted out beyond the plane in order to conceive it as a separate reality, forming a fourth point and defining the third dimension of space, symbolized by the four-sided pyramid. As yet space did not exist, since space has distance (one point is farther from another than a third), and the concept of distance involves time, which had not yet been born.

5: FORM

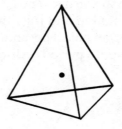

The fifth point, from which the eye of God considered the first four that formed the pyramid, could manifest either inside or outside the four enclosing planes of the pyramid. These two possibilities were distinctly different and gave rise to a conception of form with its enveloping skin, or interface, yielding the embryonic idea of motion—movement through the barrier between inside and outside—with its associate notion of time, the fourth dimension.

6: CHOICE

The sixth point, which in the series of drawings is seen outside the pyramid, gave birth to the earliest of the moral dimensions—those above the level of space-time. It showed the possibility of choice. God might look at the pyramid from the outside or the inside, which are very different points of view, and must choose one or the other alternative.

A necessary evolution of the basic concept of choice was the varieties of possibility inherent in any decision. Every question can yield three possible answers: Yes; No; and Yes/No. This triplicity is expressed in all the holy trinities of gods the world has known. In Christianity it is Father, Holy Ghost, and Son. In Hinduism it is Brahma, Shiva, and Vishnu. In the faith of the ancient Egyptians it was Osiris, Isis, and Horus. Symbolically it is embodied in the triskelion, a design of three appendages radiating from a center point, which occurs in such diverse cultures as the Celtic, Greek, and American Indian.

7: AFFIRMATION

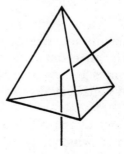

The seventh point is the essential Yes, a rushing forth with purpose, an assertion that may be called male in character, although each sex embodies all three choices.

8: NEGATION

The eighth point springs into being immediately as a reaction to the initial Yes. When a body moves toward one thing, it moves away from something else. When water is poured from one vase to another, the first becomes empty as the second becomes full.

The eighth point is rejection, a pulling away, the basic No. It can be called female in the same way the seventh point was termed male; however, the female sex can both affirm or deny in its own way.

9: RECONCILIATION

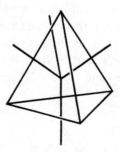

The ninth point forms immediately as the tension between Yes and No manifests itself. It is the reconcilement of opposites, the center on the line between extremes. In moral terms it is the understanding that transcends good and evil. Sexually, it is androgynous.

To mankind the notions of Yes, No, and Yes/No seem very distinct. However, the pyramid, which may be turned every which way without disturbing the meaning it conveys (since each facet and line are interchangeable with every other facet and line), reveals that the distinction between polarities of choice is only apparent, not absolute.

This does not mean that good is the same as evil. Polarities are real to the perception of humanity. No one can disregard love-hate, hot-cold, or up-down with impunity. But the model suggests that from outside the realm of forms (a perspective only available to the Unmanifest) one choice can replace another.

Consider Yes and No as opposite ends of a piece of string. Yes/ No would be the middle point between the ends. One end looks very much like the other. The only distinction is that one end is on the left and the other end on the right. If you walk around to the other side of the string, the end that was on the right becomes the one on the left, and vice versa.

Now take the string and tie it in a circle so that the two ends meet and merge into one another. Who can tell the left, the right, and the middle? This is the way the Unmanifest views the world and its affairs.

10: SUBSTANCE

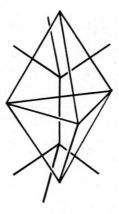

The tenth point of view taken by the eye of God is the perspective of materiality, where all the abstract relationships that came into manifestation are precipitated as rocks and trees and men. This tenth level of manifestation of awareness is where humanity perceives itself to live. It is best pictured as a point below the base plane of the pyramid, which forms a second pyramid that is the exact mirror image of the first. The second, reflected pyramid is the realization of the preceding nine points of view in matter and energy.

The upward-pointing pyramid of nine emanations is an illusion to human perception, whereas the second downward-pointing pyramid is crystallized, or precipitated into being, out of the nine higher viewpoints by the tenth point alone. From the perspective of the Unmanifest the inverted pyramid is the illusion, being only a reflection of the "real" ninefold emanation. The dreams of man are the realities of God; the dreams of God are the realities of man.

These are the ten stages followed by the unfolding desire of the All as it examined itself. They are the underlying process of the birth of the universe. All manifest things, from atoms to galaxies, are born out of the Unmanifest in this way by an act of divine Will.

LIGHT

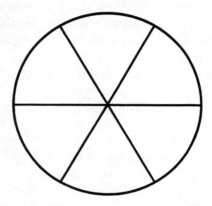

The Light is the purest expression of the Will of the Unmanifest in the material universe. It takes the form of a blindingly brilliant pearl or blue-white radiance, like the radiance of a star, but it is featureless and formless, suffusing the physical surroundings in which it is experienced. Accompanying the Light is a sense of awe, and often a fear so intense that the individual bathed in it may wish to hide himself, as Adam hid in the Garden of Eden.

This is the Light Saul experienced as he journeyed to Damascus: "And suddenly there shined round about him a light from heaven: And he fell to earth . . . trembling and astonished" (Acts 9:3-6). This is the Light Christ was said to radiate at times: "And his face did shine like the sun, and his raiment was white as the light" (Matthew 17:2).

All true prophets have experienced the Light, which is a universal phenomenon cutting across times and cultures. However, it should be understood that it is not a physical radiance in its essence, and no mere mortal could endure its unalloyed purity: "The light which no man can approach unto; whom no man hath seen, nor can see" (I Timothy 6:16). What is perceived as the Light is only a reflection in the physical realm of the vibration of divine Spirit. Physical white light is the highest metaphor the human mind can create to suggest the true desire and purpose of the Unmanifest.

A man or woman need not be a prophet to experience it. It can and has descended upon the most humble of individuals, and in all cases has transformed their lives. For the Light conveys, in deeper language than words, deeper than images, the great Truth of life. When a person has been "enlightened," he understands in his heart why he was born and what he must do with his time on Earth.

The Magus views the Light as a real phenomenon of the mental kind to be sought out as a source of transcendental wisdom. His most common and earnest magical act is to court the Light in the hope that it may manifest itself in all its brilliance. To attain this desire may change him in ways society would not deem favorable. When the Magus attains harmony with the All, the things of the world often lose their illusion of importance. The very reason the Magus thinks he desires the power and wisdom of the Light may become meaningless once the Light has transformed him.

Therefore, the petty dabbler in the Art had best think twice before he seeks the Light, lest he find himself changed beyond recognition. Although in truth he has little to fear; the Light only manifests to those who are worthy to receive it in the judgment of the All.

The magic of ancient China was based on introducing the circulation of the Light throughout all levels of the human being by means of traditional meditations on "the square inch field of the square foot house," the point between the eyebrows.[3] Carl Jung was of the opinion the Westerner should not court the Light in this way. He believed the Eastern and Western minds were fundamentally different and that what was beneficial in the East would be psychologically destructive in the West.

This fear is unfounded. The Light expresses itself to each according to his understanding and capabilities. The Western mind is active—in the West the Light will induce right actions. Joan of Arc is an instance of the Light acting on the Western mentality.

Blinding whiteness is the purest manifestation of the divine Spirit. The same potency can also show itself more subtlely as a voice, a form, a symbol, even an odor—the odor of sanctity sometimes spoken of in connection with certain saints. All these derivations of the Will of the All convey wisdom pertaining to the orderly unfolding of the universe.

In the same way the smallest material light instantly banishes darkness (which has no real existence but is merely the absence of light), so does the Light of Spirit have absolute power over the forces of Evil. The Magus should seek the Light in times of trial or when he is doubtful and afraid, any time he finds himself assailed by the Darkness. If he seeks with an open heart, it will come. As Christ rightly observed: "Ask, and it shall be given you" (Matthew 7:7). But if he plays the hypocrite, he will seek in vain, and devils will mock him.

The Magus should ask the Light to instruct him in the Art of magic. It will do so if his purposes are honest and if magic is a part of his personal destiny. He may ask for the names of spirits, the signs that will bind their Will, their true forms according to his understanding, and all other aspects of the Art.

Usually the Light will speak through intermediate spirit entities as it is too exalted to deal directly with the material illusions of magic, although sometimes this happens. The Magus will be granted the wisdom that accords with his stage of development. This will not be the information he requests, but as he progresses, he will discover that the Light knows his needs better than he himself. The Light is not antipathetic to magic, merely above it. The Light is the highest instrument of the All as the Art of magic is the highest instrument of man.

Unfortunately, since the Art is so often used for unworthy ends, the highest expressions of Spirit often shun it. The materially minded Magus will be able to summon powers enough, but these will be powers of Evil, whose underlying desire is not his evolution but his destruction. The basis of the Evil force will be the same as the Good, the Unmanifest, but its color will be black, its odor foul, its taste repugnant and bitter, its touch slimy, and its visual aspect loathsome.

It might be wondered how the source of Light can also be the source of Darkness. The answer is that the Unmanifest is the source of all things. The Light is the Will of the Unmanifest to change and experience itself through its emanations. The Dark is the inertia that resists this Will.

Within each man and woman is an innate sense of the Good. By doing acts and thinking thoughts that harmonize with this inner sense, the Light can be courted. There are rituals of the Art that are designed to focus this desire to draw down the Light, but these are only empty gestures without the desire itself. In those habituated to good acts and thoughts, the sense of right will be strong. They will be able to talk about truth and justice almost as though they were physically present in the world. This is the Light speaking in them.

In those much out of harmony with divine purpose, the sense of the Good will have atrophied and will be hard to grasp, like the whispered words of a sickly child. These persons the Light will not enter.

To court the Light, they must first cleanse themselves inwardly and begin to strengthen their sense of the Good by right thoughts and actions. When they have attained a degree of harmony with divine Will, the Light will begin to reveal itself in small ways, leading ultimately to the illumination of the white radiance.

It might be well to emphasize that the cloying, saccharine notion of goodness that exists in the minds of the pillars of respectable society often has little in common with the innate sense of the Good that lives in the heart of the individual and speaks with a quiet but clear voice in times of need. It is this inner sense of Good that will precipitate the Light. Society's "good" is an empty shell for worms, where the face of the true God upon which it was modeled can be but dimly traced.

SERPENTINE

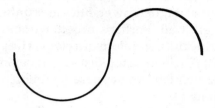

At the dawn of creation when the great Unmanifest began to stir itself—but before it attained the first point of Self-awareness—there came into being a kind of motion. This was not motion as mankind understands it, for manifest motion exists in three-dimensional time-space. This primary motion was more akin to desire.

On the great shoreless sea of nothingness came a pulse that was like waves on water, which move across the surface but do not move the body of the water. It was like the vibration of the string of a musical instrument or the undulation of the body of a serpent.

This primal pulse of desire gave a quality to the infinite nothingness, which may be called Light, or Spirit. Physical light is only a pale reflection of this Light. Nothingness came alive with pulsations that were as yet undirected and uniformly balanced.

Consider the serpent. Undulations flow along its ribs, but the position of its ribs is not altered. When a snake is held up by its tail, the hand holding it can feel the power of the undulations that run down its sides, yet the snake is not moved. Conversely, when a snake is watched as it flows through the grass, it does not appear to move at all because the curves of its body stay in the same place; but actually it is moving through those curves and quickly vanishes from sight, with an apparent speed that is much greater than its actual rate of progress.

In petroglyphs and primitive art all around the world, one of the

most common symbols is the undulating line, which is taken to represent the body of a serpent and serpentine motion generally. People
who live close to the land have the leisure to watch the simple manifestations of nature, and in the serpent, they recognized a great mystery.
How can there be motion in something that does not move? When the
waters of a lake rise and fall and yet stay in their place, how is it that
waves travel across the surface? What is the wave itself?

Energy, a scientist might answer. But this is only a word for a mystery and no answer at all. Perhaps a better understanding can be
gained by considering the pendulum of a clock. The pendulum swings
to the right. When it reaches the top of its arc, it begins to descend and
swings to the left. It maintains this apparent motion back and forth, yet
never moves from its place.

The Magus should ask what happens at the infinitely small fraction of time when the motion to the left becomes motion to the right.
The pendulum slows and slows, and for a timeless moment only, it
stops; and then it begins to accelerate in the opposite direction. The
motion to the right is counterclockwise (for the arc of the swing
defines a section of a larger circle). When reversed, the motion is
clockwise.

At the instant the pendulum stops at the apex of its arc, its motion
effectively ceases to exist in our universe. It becomes, to use a word of
physics, "potential," and this is an apt word, for the motion travels
across the Veil of Unknowing, which divides the universe from the
Unmanifest, and literally ceases to be for an infinitely brief instant.
When it emerges across the Veil, it is inverted, the mirror image of its
former self. It is the same in appearance, but all its energy has been
flipped from right to left. The measureless instant the pendulum is
stopped is a single point in time. The point is the door between the
two universes.

It may be observed that when viewed from the side—that is, from
the second dimension of space—an object traveling in a circle appears
to imitate the motion of the pendulum. It goes to the right, slows, then
begins to accelerate to the left and repeats the cycle.

Recently biologists made an interesting discovery regarding certain small flagellate microorganisms (tiny creatures who move by
means of a whiplike tail that they beat rapidly). It had been thought
that the tail moved back and forth like the tail of a fish, until close
observation revealed that it was in reality a spiral, which the tiny creature
produced by rotating his tail on a biological swivel joint. The tail had

only appeared to beat back and forth due to the limited perspective of the biologists. In fact, it corkscrewed like a propeller.

The motion of a wave is only mysterious because it transcends the limits of human perception, traveling beyond the artificial boundaries of awareness in a way that is cyclically apparent. All other things also transcend time and space, but in ways that are not so readily observable. It is because the human mind fails to acknowledge the existence of other dimensions that this travel is not obvious.

The waves of serpentine motion never do quite form a point, but they begin to define it. This is a difficult concept. The point around which the wave moves can be abstracted from the wave, but the wave never actually forms it. Serpentine motion is motion searching for a point without reaching it.

The Unmanifest rides the crests of its numberless undulations of desire, yearning for a vantage from which to achieve an awareness of Self. But it is everywhere frustrated. In the primal sea of Light, crest and trough cannot be distinguished, and such concepts as right and left have no meaning, for distinctions merge into one another smoothly without a break.

Wave motion does not cease when concrete form appears but continues to manifest underneath matter. The human body gives evidence of the wave, which is one of the foundation blocks of matter. The clay of which all men and women are formed is animated for a time by the wave of life and given ephemeral form; then when that wave passes, it is permitted to crumble back to the earth from which it arose.

The thing called the present has no real existence, but is the crest of a wave called time; and the waters yet to be lifted are called the future, and the waters once again quiescent are called the past—yet all belong to the same vast sea, independent of the wave, which passes but does not create or destroy any vital essence.

Time is an illusion. All things exist at one and the same moment, or rather, outside that moment. This is why magic works as freely in the past and future as in the present. This is the base reality that makes precognition possible. As Einstein is reputed to have joked: Time is what keeps everything from happening at once. Time is a convenient fiction created by the life awareness on the material level. One man's time is not another's. The time of a horse is not that of a man.

Serpentine motion suggests how force is projected in magic. Everything in the world happens in pulses. Effort is balanced by rest.

Action gives way to reaction. The master in one thing becomes the servant in another. Anger is replaced by regret. If it were possible to exert an even effort continuously—and it is not—such an effort would be absolutely futile and incapable of accomplishing even the smallest effect.

Knowing that life is a complex web of pulsations, the Magus is enabled to direct his Will in short bursts where it will do the most good. For example, in society there are many pulses, one of which is patriotism-pacifism. If the Magus believes his nation is lacking in martial readiness and wishes to do something about it, he will not exert himself when the pulse of pacifism is rising; rather, he will bid his time until it has reached its crest, then add his force to the swing in the direction of patriotic fervor.

This simple principle applies in personal affairs. When you wish to convert someone to your way of thinking, do not meet their opposition head on. First allow them to spend their arguments and protestations; then, when they have fallen silent, send a powerful pulse of your Will to swing their mind in the opposite direction. Of course, there will be eventually be a reaction against your manipulation. This can be anticipated and lessened in intensity, and the next period of receptivity can be made use of with even greater effect, so that the sum total is to move the person in the direction of your desires.

This phenomenon of action-reaction goes beyond what are considered magical means. It applies on all levels of being. However, the methods of the Art can be used with great effect to augment or lessen a cyclic tendency as required.

In this matter the coolest calculation is needed. It is not satisfying to allow the opposition of another person to spend itself without reacting. The heart wishes to oppose the crest of emotion with a similar but opposing crest, but the result of this is deadlock. Counter forces cancel each other out. The Magus must rise above his animal instincts and control his reactions if he wishes to bring his desires to fruition. He must sacrifice a momentary, futile satisfaction for a real, sustained advantage.

As with all magical techniques, reading the pulses of life and gaining control over them can be used for both good and evil purposes. It is not wrong to gain an advantage over another person—life largely consists of a contest for supremacy—it is only to be condemned if the Magus uses his power in unlawful or contemptible ways.

CIRCLE

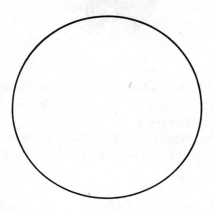

The primal pulse of desire that stirred in the boundless Light of the Unmanifest could reach no end, could find no fulfillment by extending itself. Retreating from the limitless All, it turned inward even as a serpent will curl up for comfort in the cold, and the pulse became a circle, which is a wave turning upon itself. This idea is represented by the ancient symbol of the serpent pierced by a sword that pins it to the earth:

It is also implied in the oriental symbol of the yin and yang, which shows a wave enclosed by a circle. The fixing of a wave causes it to exhibit a circular motion. (See diagram on p. 46.)

A circle marks the boundary between outward and inward going. It is the balance of these two opposite tendencies. As such it has no thickness but merely divides, in the same way the present divides the past from the future. When the pulse of desire begins to rotate, a circle is created. This is the serpent with its tail held in its mouth:

The circular tendency that arose before the formation of the first point is not a circle as the human mind normally understands it. A circle drawn on paper presupposes three-dimensional space. The primal circular desire took place before space-time, when there was no form, no point of Self-awareness, only pure desire acting in a void. It did not act toward anything because there was nothing else. Rather, it fled from unending nothingness. Having gone out in all directions, so to speak, and discovered no thing, it turned away and in upon itself.

The symbol of a circle is often used to represent totality. This is only accurate with regard to the manifest universe. The Great Circle is the one that surrounds creation. By nature, circles divide the known from the unknown. The Unmanifest must be thought of as outside all circles.

For an individual the largest conceivable circle represents the personal universe—that part of the absolute manifest universe that he perceives through his senses, his memories, his thoughts and dreams. The individual's personal universe is always a smaller circle than the circle of the manifest universe, simply because no one can know everything. Within the personal universe are lesser circles representing levels of personal control. These nestle one inside the other, wheels within wheels. The outermost circle is that least affected by the personal will; the innermost circle is that most affected, and is what the individual usually thinks of as "self."

The perceived self is never the true Self. The true Self cannot be perceived, since it is the ultimate vantage of perception. Only God can know himself totally, perceiving Self with Self. In symbolic terms the true Self is the point at the center of the circle, infinitely small and thus nonexistent in the universe. Therefore, it is not really a part of the circle. The perceived self is the smallest circle of which the human ego can gain any hint. In a sense, as man draws closer to his real Self all his senses begin to go out of focus and his perceptions become blurred, until he reaches a circle where he is able to define nothing.

A circle is characterized by the separation of inside from outside. Inside is order; outside is anarchy. In magic a circle is used as a wall of protection to divide the greater hostile world from the zone of law. The most obvious magic circle is the human body. Men look upon the inside of their skins as their own property to do with as they see fit. Mystics extend the personal sphere to the aura, a supposed invisible field of energy that is shaped like an egg around the body and that protects the perceived self from hostile psychic "vibrations," just as the body insulates it from extreme heat and cold. Animals have their territorial limit, another kind of magic circle. The border of a country is a magic circle established by a society.

Just as the human mind will limit an idea into a single symbol—its name—so that it can be manipulated, the Magus uses the magic circle to limit his power in order to concentrate it and render it more effective. The circle defines and focuses the domain of Will. However, when something is gained something else is lost. By taking supreme command of the area defined by the ritual circle, the Magus voluntarily gives up his measure of control over the forces of the greater part of his personal universe.

This explains the many dire warnings against breaking the circle during a ritual working. Having for a time abdicated his power outside the ring, the Magus is defenseless against the many forces of evil that gather there, attracted by his ritual display as moths are drawn to light.

Since only the Magus and his helpers, if any, have symbolically renounced their authority outside the ring, only they are in danger. A person in the next room, unaware that a ritual was taking place, would be under no threat at all since he would be guarded, as always, by his personal circle of perceived self. In drawing the magic circle the Magus has deliberately abolished his personal circle of protection— or rather, expanded it to accomodate his magical purpose—and must rely for protection on the larger circle of the Art.

The sole purpose of the magic circle is to create a miniature world in which the Magus is the ruling god. The forces of Chaos, the frost giants and other titans, are excluded. Little wonder they gather outside the border of the ring and wait their chance to make mischief. Within the circle the Magus temporarily upsets the natural balance of things. The circle becomes his magic Sky House, and he the Sun King around which everything revolves.

In separating an area of space for a ritual working, the Magus must exclude the potencies that are inimical to him. The interior of the circle is accordingly purified, or emptied, and made into a blank slate the Magus can write his Will upon. Techniques for purifying the circle will be presented later in this book.

After the uncongenial forces are driven out, the Magus must invite the favorable forces directly involved in the working to come in. This is done by making a magical aperture at the center point of the circle, through which the benign energies can enter. This technique will also be given later.

Magic circles may be permanently marked by physical boundaries. This was done by neolithic peoples such as the creators of Stonehenge. Witches traditionally are pictured as drawing their circles in the earth around their feet with an Athame, or on the floor of a chamber with chalk. The sorcerer of literary romance is usually pictured inside an inscribed geometric figure.

It should be understood that the physical circle is only a model upon which the Magus may fix the real circle of the Art, which is inscribed in the imagination. Of itself a physical circle has almost no power. It must be charged by the Magus by overlaying it with a mental circle that is always drawn from inside at the center point around himself and anyone who may be assisting in the ritual working. The Magus need not stand at the center, but his awareness must reside at the center point as he draws the magic circle.

The most effective magic circles are of human dimension. If

they are drawn around a single individual, the radius should be the reach of the arm or the arm coupled with the staff or wand. In Wiccan covens a rod is driven into the earth and a sash from a robe is fixed to it, then the circle is inscribed at the extremity of the sash. This is large enough to accommodate the thirteen of the coven.

It need hardly be said that if the ritual involves five hundred, the circle must be large enough to hold them. In rituals involving large numbers of people, it is often convenient to form the circle from the living bodies of the participants, who link hands and make a ring. Since the participants are part of the circle itself, they can never be outside it and are in no danger from destructive energies unless they break the ring. Their bodies and their personal identities merge into a social unit that shields the leader of the ritual from the hostile outer forces.

Once the inherent nature of a circle is understood, many previously puzzling questions become clear. This is why so many dances involve the linking of hands; why mediums join hands around a table; why children play Ring Around the Rosie—all intuitively sense the power of a circle. On a more elemental level this is why electricity runs in a ring, and why the Earth is round.

In alchemical drawings the creation of the universe is pictured as a white dove (divine Spirit) flying in a circle, trailing after it Light, and enclosing a section of primordial Chaos. The linking of this circle marks the birth of the world. This visual image presents the essential understanding of a circle.

The Magus draws his circle clockwise in imitation of the course of the Sun, Moon, and stars across the heavens, establishing his rule of order under the Light. He imagines the circle forming of white flickering fire and floating in the air at the level of his heart, which is his customary physical center. Always he takes extreme care to link the beginning of the circle with its end.

If the circle is not completed, it will admit the forces of Darkness. These forces are always dangerous to the Magus when the circle is empowered. Their menace is a necessary condition of the effectiveness of the circle. In forming the circle the Magus voluntarily gives up his power outside it for the term of its existence. There will never be a time in his development when he can step with impunity through a formed circle. No matter how powerful or knowledgeable he becomes, once he forms the circle around himself he is defenseless while outside it. Indeed, the greater his power within the circle, the greater his degree of vulnerability without.

The beginner may be tempted to test the dangers outside the circle by deliberately stepping through its boundary. Most often nothing will happen. The very fact that he can casually break the circle indicates that it was never a living reality in his mind. Any fool can draw a ring around himself, but it takes the Will of a Magus to empower it—to bring it alive. Only when he sees the flaming ring with his open eyes, when he feels the heat from it and hears the flutter of its burning, when he experiences pain on touching it, will he destroy himself by breaking it.

The traditional story of the practitioner of the black arts who is discovered in the cold light of morning stretched half across his chalk circle, with his eyes open in a fixed gaze of horror and claw marks on his throat, is only a slight embellishment of the truth. More often than not such unfortunates are pronounced dead of heart failure or stroke or seizure. Or they may be found in a coma or catatonic state. One can only try to imagine the horror, called up from the darkest depths of the subconscious, that causes such conditions.

Magic cannot be half real and half illusion. If power is to be gained inside the circle, it must be given up outside. If the angels of Light are to be rendered tangible to the eyes of the Magus, then he will also, perforce, see the demons of the Pit in all their loathsome detail. If the Magus wants to extract the good out of the Art, he must also learn how to deal with the evil. In short, if the circle works at all, it works on both sides.

All too often the talented beginner will succeed in pumping some measure of energy into his circle and then, through stupidity or pigheadedness, will violate its boundary. The least he can expect is a shock that will leave his flesh numb and burning for hours, perhaps days. The worst is probably the birth of a madness that will be difficult to shake off. Complete nervous breakdowns are not uncommon.

Although the circle is two-dimensional, drawn in a plane parallel to what is perceived as the flat surface of the Earth, it is symbolically a representation of a complete envelope that encloses its maker from top to toe. There is no danger that devils will slip under or over it. Often the envelope is imagined as a cylinder extending endlessly up and down; but it seems more accurate to conceive it as a sphere, the circumference of which is traced by the flaming ring.

In some modern practice this sphere of protection is delineated by three circles set perpendicularly to one another, each circle being drawn in one spatial dimension. This is a needless refinement. However, the three interlocking rings are useful for locating the point of Self, as will be explained further on.

A variation on the magic circle is to limit its scope to the boundaries of the aura. Then when the Magus moves about, his magic circle moves with him, thereby eliminating the danger of stepping outside it. This requires great powers of visualization and should not be attempted by a beginner.

A trick used by the ancients to facilitate the forming of a portable magic circle was to link it with a magic ring. The ring became the physical locus of the circle. The sliding of the finger into the ring symbolized the entry of the Magus into its envelope of protection. So long as he wore the ring he was guarded. He projected his Will along the axis of the circle, usually through the right index finger. The rotation of the ring on the finger represented the mental tracing of the circle that empowered it; a counter-rotation stood for the circle's withdrawal and dissolution.

The circle should never be used frivously or taken for granted if the Magus wishes to avoid diminishing its potency. Its formation must be a complete and separate act of Will, considered beforehand, solemnly made and, when its purpose is over, as solemnly unmade. One of the final acts of any ritual is to erase the circle and return the personal universe to its natural balance of forces—that blending of the benevolent and the malevolent which is perceived by the individual as the norm, neither hostile nor helpful, neither lucky nor unlucky.

The circle is unmade by absorbing its psychic flame into the extended index finger of the left hand, or into the ritual instrument held in the left hand, while turning in a counterclockwise direction. Generally speaking, the right side of the body is for projecting, the left side for absorbing. Clockwise motion focuses and precipitates; counterclockwise motion disperses—at least in the Northern Hemisphere. This is because the right side and righthand motion follow the path of the Sun and other lights, whereas the left side and lefthand motion seek the darkness.

Most who claim an understanding of magic simply leave the circle hanging in the air when the ritual is over and step heedlessly through it. This is very bad practice. It shows that they have not yet understood what the circle is. That they get any results at all is due to the fact that when they turn their minds away from the circle, they unconsciously unmake it. However, some practitioners of magic foolishly attempt to make the magic circle a permanent fixture in their ritual chambers, which they step through and break again and again in their comings and goings. This is both stupid and dangerous.

In magic, what is made must be unmade. What is done must be undone. What is achieved must be counterweighted with an equally significant act. Everything is balance. The Magus dares to shift the scales in one direction. He must then move them an equal amount in the opposite direction lest his temerity be punished. Whenever he gains what is not his by right, he must lose something equally precious.

SPIRAL

The spiral is perhaps the most common of primitive symbols. It finds expression in the art of such diverse cultures as the American Indian, the pre-Buddhist Tibetan, the African tribal, and pagan Norse. Usually it is assumed to represent the emanating power of the Sun. This is true in a limited sense, but it should be understood that the Sun is only a material expression of manifesting energy and that the spiral refers the mind back to the original principle, even as does the physical Sun. Both spiral and Sun are symbols of the underlying reality.

Sometimes the spiral is drawn with a wavy line, showing that the primitive artists intuitively recognized the close connection between serpentine and spiral motion—that one was a natural consequence of the other. In nature both are exhibited in the movement of the serpent, which progresses by means of the wave and, to conserve its inner heat, turns itself in a spiral through the circle of its body.

The galaxy is a model of spiral motion, as is the path of certain subatomic particles. All movement around a point is made up of the inward spiral of concentration and the outward spiral of dispersion acting in some degree of balance. When the balance is perfect, a circular motion results; however, there is nothing perfect in matter. The paths of the planets around the Sun, once thought of as circular and then as elliptical, are really spiral as the planets slow minutely year by year due to natural forces.

In the manifest universe spiral motion often takes the three-dimensional shape of the cone, where the rotating force focuses on a single point along an axis. The spiral force moves toward the point of focus when it is passing from the universe to the Unmanifest, and away from the point when it is manifesting in the universe.

In the boundless Light of the Unmanifest before the creation, the analogy to the cone was the Will to achieve the desire for Self-awareness. What began as a fleeing from the limitless outer reaches of the All became a turning circle, then an inward spiral as the eye of God crossed the boundary of balanced forces and sought to find itself by manifesting a point. Thus the spiral began as a negative motion of withdrawal and wrapping inward for protection, then became a positive and active striving to realize the center of Self.

Referring this to the serpent, at the start the undulating serpent draws itself inward for protection from the cold. Then it seeks to devour itself to appease its hunger. Whereas at the circular stage of motion it held its tail in its mouth, in the spiral stage it begins to swallow its tail. This very common symbol of the dragon devouring its tail is always the search of Chaos to manifest itself through the point, and the corresponding search of manifest being to reunite with the boundless All.

To perceive this truth, project ahead mentally the natural consequence of a serpent eating its tail, were it possible to carry this process through to its conclusion. Eventually it must vanish from the world. Where can it go? There is only one door out of the universe—the mathematical point, which is without dimension and thus unbounded by time and space. Black holes are serpents swallowing their tails.

The spiral in action becomes the vortex—sometimes called the tourbillion in magic—about which so much nonsense has been written. Occult writers like to speak in whispers of the dread power of the tourbillion, but they never get around to telling their reader precisely how it works or what it is. The skeptical reader should be forgiven if he wonders whether such writers know what they are talking about.

The vortex is the spiral acting with intent along a ray toward a point. It can be observed in the hurricane, the cyclone, the whirlpool, the dust devil, and the lowly screwnail. It is power focusing for a purpose. The ultimate expression of that purpose is either destruction or creation: that is, the passage of a thing from the manifest to the Unmanifest, or from the Unmanifest to the manifest.

On the material level this creation or destruction is implied rather than overt. When a car is caught in a cyclone it may be battered beyond recognition, and in this sense, its identity as a car may pass from creation, but the physical glass and metal does not disappear.

The nature of the vortex explains why ancient Hebrew and Babylonian writings said that God manifested out of a whirlwind. All creative acts of God must pass through the point by means of spiral motion. It is the only way to get from there to here. It is why the dervishes of Turkey spin themselves into delirium and call their god the Axis of the World.

Symbols of the spiral acting along the ray abound. The cone is the traditional headgear of the wizard. Cave paintings in France depict men dancing in cone-shaped hats. Merlin, the magician of the court of King Arthur, is commonly pictured in a tall sky blue cone hat with stars and planets painted on it.

In the popular press, Witches are always shown wearing black cone hats—the black color intended to suggest both evil and the unknown. Although practicing members of Wiccan covens laugh at these pictures, they are not so far off the mark as real Witches might think. Such images are the result of the collective will of society acting unconsciously. No single person decided to show Witches in pointed hats and then forced all artists to follow his decision. Witches are shown this way because this is the way they are perceived below the level of rational thought.

It is always unwise to scorn the symbols of the collective unconscious. In the Middle Ages, heretics who broke from the Catholic Church were thought of as a species of devil, literally as minions of Satan. During the Auto de Fey, the ritual festivals of the torturing and burning of heretics, they were forced to wear conical hats and costumes with diabolical symbols written upon them. The cone has always been linked with magic.

One of the most delightful objects to a child is the black hat of the stage magician. It is a hat that has no bottom. Things disappear into it without a trace, then miraculously reappear somewhere else across the stage. This hat is usually a topper. It need hardly be said that its natural shape should be a cone.

In a kind of pantomime drama with a cosmic significance, the objects of the stage magician disappear into the single point at the apex of the hat, where they are lost in the spaceless and timeless reaches of the Unmanifest. When the magician reaches into the hat, he draws the objects back into the physical world through the Veil via the aperture of the point. The objects seem the same, but if the child looks closely, there is a magical sparkle to them. They have been metamorphosed by their death and rebirth.

The pyramid is a kind of cone. This is why it is universally felt to be a source of power by those who have no knowledge of occult things—the human mind subconsciously recognizes meaning in the underlying forms of nature.

The triangle is a two-dimensional representation of the cone, and this is one of its most important symbolic aspects. For example, in ritual evocation the evil spirit is made to come into perceptual existence inside a triangle. The triangle acts as a prison for the spirit, but just as importantly is the lens whereby the spirit is enabled to manifest itself through the point.

A triangle widens from its apex down to its base, thereby emerging into manifest existence. Implied in ritual evocation is a similar but mirror-opposite triangle on the far side of the Veil of Unknowing. Of course this second hidden triangle, like the spirit it holds, is potential, not actual, since no manifest thing exists in the Unmanifest.

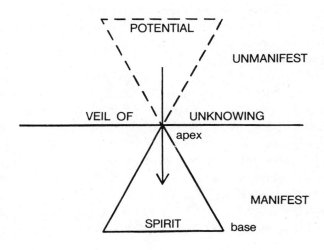

The ancient charm of Abracadabra, so often ridiculed, when written in its true form illustrates perfectly the manifestation of power through the point by means of spiral motion. Here the spiral motion is represented by diverging sides of the triangle:

```
          A                 ABRACADABRA
         AB                 ABRACADABR
        ABR                 ABRACADAB
       ABRA                 ABRACADA
      ABRAC                 ABRACAD
     ABRACA                 ABRACA
    ABRACAD                 ABRAC
   ABRACADA                 ABRA
  ABRACADAB                 ABR
 ABRACADABR                 AB
ABRACADABRA                 A
```

If the letters are made to diminish rather than grow, the force represented by the word is made to flow in the opposite direction across the Veil. This second form was often used to cure sickness. As the letters grew fewer, the sickness became less until the twelfth day, when the patient was cured.

Since magical energy is not projected through the physical universe, it cannot be measured materially. It is sent through the dimensionless Unmanifest by means of the point doorway opened by spiral motion. When returned to manifestation through a second point at the object of desire, it affects the human awareness first as psychic reality, and then by reaction manifests on the physical level.

It is the common error of science to attempt to measure magic as a very subtle material force. This is doomed to failure. The end result of a magical action may manifest itself in the material circle of being, but the mechanism of magical projection is beyond time and space—it does not exist in the universe of scientific instruments. Therefore the scientist is both correct and incorrect when he asserts that magic is unreal.

The Unmanifest touches all points in the manifest universe. When a force is sent across the Veil, it is immediately in contact with every point in creation. It does not have to travel to a given place: it is already there and here and everywhere. To reach its target the magical potency need only recross the infinitely thin barrier that is the interface between the two universes, the Veil of Unknowing. Since the Unmanifest is outside of time, an object or force entering and leaving it would appear to an observer to bounce off or be reflected from the Veil.

This is the secret meaning behind the black hat of the stage magician. This is how magical force can travel from place to place unaffected by distance and unaffected by time, capable even of reaching into the past and future, for the Unmanifest touches all that was and is and ever will be. This is the rationale of the warp space drive of science fiction writers, which can only be achieved by magical means.

There are four kinds of spiral motion. Each is named according to the direction of the movement of awareness along it. This movement is always two-fold; it can be inward or outward, and at the same time, it can be clockwise or counterclockwise. By reflecting the spiral and reflecting it again, these forms result:

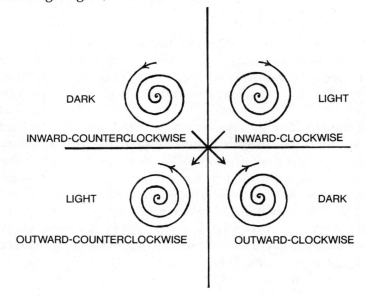

The vertical arm of the cross divides clockwise from counter-clockwise motion, and the horizontal arm divides inward from outward motion.

Spirals diagonally opposite are doubly inverted in both radial and rotary motion. However, the track of the two spirals is the same, and one can be laid over the other without discrepancies. The spirals that are vertically or horizontally opposed are mirror reflections of each other. In the vertically opposed pairs the radial motion inverts and the rotary motion remains the same. In the horizontally opposed pairs the rotary motion inverts and the radial motion remains the same.

An inward spiral in either direction indicates a focusing and projecting of intent. Followed to its conclusion, it is an opening of a door into the Unmanifest for a specific purpose, that is, interest expressed to God. True prayer involves the inward spiral. The inward spiral is the instrument of the Magus.

An outward spiral in either direction indicates realization and coming into being. It is the opposite of the inward spiral of intent and may be described as intention realized. This is the pouring forth of potential from the Unmanifest, or God's answer. For this reason the outward spiral is the instrument of God.

Clockwise motion is in harmony with the Light. It follows and imitates the progress of the Sun. It is a turning of the back on Darkness. It means construction, evolution, and law and order.

Counterclockwise motion is against the Light. It frustrates and opposes the motion of the Sun. It is a turning to embrace Darkness. It indicates evil, destruction, and confusion.

The reflective quality of the Veil causes it to invert the rotation of a vortex passing through it. An inward spiral sent by the Magus is always answered by an outward spiral from the Unmanifest. When the Magus makes an inward-clockwise spiral, it is answered by an outward-counterclockwise spiral; if the Magus should make an inward-counterclockwise spiral, it will be answered by an outward-clockwise spiral.

This relationship can be seen in the preceding diagram. The Unmanifest is represented by the point where the arms of the cross intersect. Movement of Will across the Veil is diagonal. The upper half of the cross represents the dark and light of the Magus. The lower half is the dark and light of the emanation of the Unmanifest, which is inverted by reflection.

An inward-clockwise vortex initiated by the Magus is in harmony with the Light. Its answer is an outward-counterclockwise vortex sent to balance it from the Unmanifest. This is why the two pans of cosmic balance are sometimes represented by opposite connected spirals:

In rituals of white magic the Magus initiates an inward swirl clockwise to transmit the purpose of the ritual to the Unmanifest. At the close of the ritual, he then initiates an outward-counterclockwise spiral to stimulate on the physical level the answering pulse from the Light.

This second vortex is commonly thought to erase and cancel the first. Nothing could be farther from the truth. The outward-counterclockwise vortex is a necessary consequence of the inward-clockwise vortex. It balances the first and fulfills it, completing the cycle of manifest-Unmanifest. It does not in the least oppose or negate the first vortex.

The four spirals form two pairs, one of which is of the Light and the other of the Darkness:

1) *Inward-Clockwise.* This is a lawful and constructive desire projected into the Unmanifest through the doorway of Light.

2) *Outward-Counterclockwise.* The orderly and lawful unfolding of purpose and realization of desire under the Light.

3) *Inward-Counterclockwise.* This is the focusing of unlawful desire and its projection through the doorway of Shadow. It may be described as a prayer offered to Satan, who is the inertia of matter.

4) *Outward-Clockwise.* The answering vortex from the Unmanifest cast in the form of shadow and delusion. The fulfillment of chaotic and evil intent.

Gandhi sent an inward-clockwise spiral to the Unmanifest when he preached nonviolence. The answer was the outward-counterclockwise spiral of peaceful revolution.

Hitler sent an inward-counterclockwise spiral to the Unmanifest

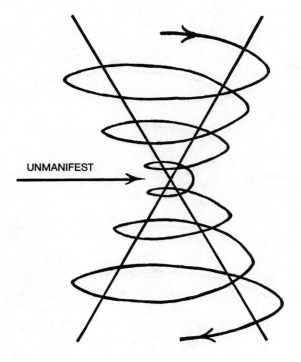

UNMANIFEST

INWARD-CLOCKWISE

VEIL OF UNKNOWING

OUTWARD-COUNTERCLOCKWISE

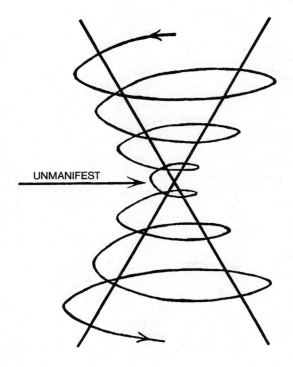

UNMANIFEST

INWARD-COUNTERCLOCKWISE

VEIL OF UNKNOWING

OUTWARD-CLOCKWISE

when he preached the enslavement and extermination of the "lower" races. The answer was the destruction of the Nazi empire, an outward-clockwise spiral.

It should be pointed out that evil intention cannot be cast in the form of a clockwise spiral to deceive the All and lessen its retribution. No one can deceive God. Evil intentions always form a counterclockwise spiral, regardless of what mask may be put over them. The Magus may turn clockwise in his magic circle until he falls down, but if his intentions are contrary to the Light, his inner motion will be perceived by God as away from the Sun.

To create a magical vortex, the Magus must first be in accord with its true nature. The vortex is begun outwardly with the body as the Magus starts walking in a spiral path around his magic circle. Gradually he moves in to the center until he is rotating on his own axis; then he transfers the rotation to the mental circle of his being, drawing it ever tighter in toward his point of Self. When a crisis is reached, the intention of the Magus will have been sent into the Unmanifest.

The physical rotation is only an aid to the mental and spiritual rotation. Simply spinning like a top will itself produce nothing. Conversely, all acts create vortices. The spiral path the Magus dances or walks around his circle is only the outward model of the vortex created by his heart and mind. The real vortex is brought into being by the intention of the Magus.

All vortices act through the center point of the Self. There is no other door. However, the point may be projected outside the perceived self of the Magus for convenience, for example, into the triangle that is to contain an evoked spirit. But the Magus should know that all the points he can possibly consider are really only one point, that of his true Self, which is the center of the universe. The Magus can experience nothing beyond what he is, but he is All.

POINT

.

The point corresponds to the perspective adopted by the observing intelligence and is thus a symbol for the Self. True Self is at the absolute center of the universe. The center of the universe is not a fixed point in time and space but is wherever the eye of God pauses to make its observations. Any point can be the center of the universe, for all points are one, engendered within a single point in the Unmanifest. The true Self of a man is the observing eye of God and so at the center of the universe.

The personal universe of an individual is that part of manifestation which he contacts through the avenues of his senses, thoughts, or dreams. Everyone has a unique personal universe that corresponds with more or less accuracy to the universe of manifestation.

Each personal universe begins with the conception of its perceiver. From its point of Self the new being looks out upon the universe of manifestation at the emanations from God, seeing them directly without their veil of forms. Its reaction is terror and frustration, both emotions stemming from its inability to command these powers. At once it begins to confine the manifestations of the All into envelopes, thereby demonstrating that it is capable of manipulating mentally and, by extension, physically. The process begins in the womb but is accelerated sharply by the shock of birth.

This is the fall of man. Adam sinned when he drew a circle of flesh around himself to cover his nakedness, his lack of a barrier between outside and inside. In the Garden he was united with God and knew everything without conceptualizing; but when he accepted the apple, he created his own ignorance by dividing wisdom into circles of knowledge, which separated him from the heart of being. Every infant completes its own fall from grace the moment it utters its first cry.

In the creation of his personal universe, the child is aided by those who have gone before him. He uses the symbolic tools and molds made by society—his forebears, his peers, his relations—to gain a measure of control over the vast and unmanageable world of emanations. In vulgar terms he forces the lights of God into bottles and caps them, then stores them away where they can do as little violence to his feelings as possible. This is one meaning of the myth of Solomon, who bound the demons of the world by the power of his ring and commanded them to enter a vessel of brass.

When something is gained, something is lost. In exchange for sanity and peace the child gives up its perceptions of much of the subtler emanations of the All. His personal universe is always smaller than the real universe. He can only see as far as the crest of the surrounding hills of his world, for he has chained his point of view, his Self, in a cage of flesh and peers out through the locked windows that are his eyes.

Inevitably his view of the world becomes unbalanced and distorted. Some aspects of being he sees well; others he cannot bear and shuts them out from his perceptions. In this manner he shifts his own sense of what he is away from the center of the universe.

The point has much in common with the circle. The circle is an expanded point, a point with an inside. The point represents another universe, which is utterly separate from the manifest world. The circle also separates utterly the inside from the outside. When an object is looked at by someone it takes its identity from the circle around it, which defines its extent both physically and figuratively.

A flower, for example, is utterly separate from the rest of the world. To the observer, who draws the circle unconsciously, there is "flower" and there is "everything else." The flower is as separated from the rest of creation as the Unmanifest is separated from manifestation.

The Magus is not satisfied with his personal universe, which his own fears and the customs of society have made for him. He senses that the real world is a larger and more wondrous place than he has been led to believe. He knows that there is danger in relinquishing the common view, which was born of the necessity for survival, but like the philosopher of olden times, he yearns to put his head through the sky and look upon the mechanism that drives the stars.

To do this, he must make his own point of view accord with the center point of the universe. What he normally thinks of as self is not his true Self but an illusion he has created; in the same way, the tables and chairs he looks at through the windows of his eyes are forms he has made. Only when he locates his center can he view the larger universe of emanation from its true vantage and see it undistorted by the lens of his ego.

It is in the interest of the Magus to see the universe truly. When he perceives it as it is, he can manipulate it. That he has the power to manipulate the universe is without question. He manipulated it when he created his own personal world of forms. But to shape it in a way apart from the dictates of society, to change it in a magical way, he must see again with the eyes of a newborn child and not cry out.

A phrase often used by popular occultists is "to raise one's level of awareness." Like most cliches it has meaning hidden beneath its surface. The Magus must lift his viewpoint out of the hole he has dug for himself and elevate it into the sky so that he may look upon the wide world. The beginning of this is to realize that he alone has created with his Will his inside and outside, and that there is no real distinction between them. The sensations that begin within his flesh and those that originate through his eyes are one: both report on forms other than his true Self.

He must realize that his body is not his Self, because he can regard it as he can a tree or rock. He can feel the pumping of his heart, see his fingers move, and hear his own voice.

Then he must realize that his feelings are not his Self, for the identical reason: he can observe their operation as things apart. When he stumbles and falls he becomes annoyed. His face flushes and his heartbeat speeds up. He curses his clumsiness. He perceives the world around him as a hostile place. Yet he is not the emotion anger.

Next he must understand that his thoughts, which he has been taught to cherish as the most personal and private expression of his being, are not his Self. His spring of consciousness is only the echo of something else and arises as a sympathetic resonance only after some deeper process has taken place. All thoughts are born below the level of words. The mind takes the essence of the thought and translates it into language, which then plays across the conscious awareness.

The products of experiences—memories and personality—also are not the essential Self of the Magus. They may be taken out and looked at by the true Self just like faded photographs of days gone by. Neither his face, his name, his clothing, his friends, his social standing nor any other observable thing is part of his essential Self. These are aspects of his personal universe, looked upon by him but not taking part in the act of observation.

Only by shearing his true Self of all the forms and illusions he has clothed it in throughout his life can the Magus begin to see the universe of manifestation from its center. This process of stripping away the veils of illusion will align his center point with the center point of the single underlying reality of things.

Then he will understand that all points can become the center because all are contained in the first created point, which is Kether, the Smooth Point, the White Head; and this first point is without dimension. He will see that his creation of his personal universe is analogous to the creation of the manifest universe by the All and that his true Self is in unity with the Unmanifest—he and the All are one—and he will realize it was only his willful foolishness that blinded him to this simple truth.

RAY

It is the ray that joins the desirer to the object of desire. The ray is Will in action. Merely to look at anything is to send forth a ray of intent, for an understanding of even the simplest matter is the result of a creative mental effort to size up, to put into perspective, to touch, to taste, or to recall a mental image. The personal universe is a creation of the Will acting along numerous rays through the avenues of the senses. The Magus can never look upon anything that is not a creation of the Self and thus joined to him. For this reason all that he perceives can be affected by his Will.

A reciprocating ray occurs when the Magus sends forth his point of perspective along a ray, then looks back from that new viewpoint at the place he has left. This initiates a returning pulse of Will that oscillates back and forth with infinite quickness, so that the awareness of the Magus seems to occupy two points at once. In reality it is shifting from one point to the other so rapidly they seem to merge.

The ray is most often symbolized by a line, or a beam of light extending from the eye (the primary sense organ in modern man) to the object of desire. The ancients believed, quite naturally, that this was the mechanism by which the sense of sight operated—that through the eye was put forth a power that touched the object looked upon. Only when science began to analyze the nature of light was this idea displaced and ridiculed. The eye was then seen as a passive receptacle, a kind of window through which light entered.

The poet and mystic William Blake wrote:

> This Life's dim Windows of the Soul
> Distorts the Heavens from Pole to Pole
> And leads you to Believe a Lie
> When you see with, not thro', the Eye[4]

Blake knew that passive seeing is a pernicious delusion; and that if a man believes himself detached from the things he looks upon, he must also believe many other fictions destructive of the truth.

The view of science is most useful in scientific matters. But in magic the old view is of more practical value. In magic the eye is an organ of immense power. Through it men can control and be controlled by other men. It is through the eye that rays of Will are most often projected into the circles of the personal universe that lie beyond the sphere of the perceived self.

Such eye magic is very common among simple peoples of the world. In north Africa and India, in the rural regions of Italy and Spain, and even in the more developed countries of Europe, the Evil Eye is accepted as a reality that must either be avoided or countered with a magical act.

The Evil Eye is no more than the projection of malignancy through the eye along a ray to the object of hatred. It is considered most effective when it enters the eye of the intended victim. Common folk will swear they can feel such attacks on the surface of their skin, which begins to prickle, and will maintain that to meet the gaze of the Evil Eye is fatal, for then one is caught like a bird under the gaze of a serpent and bereft of the powers of speech and movement.

The ray is a kind of geometric metaphor for the temporary shifting of the point of Self from one place in the personal universe to another. In reality the Self does not and cannot move; it is the fixed center of the universe. But its perspective on the personal universe changes, giving the appearance of the shifting of awareness. It would be better to say that the personal universe moves in relation to the Self.

Momentarily the person giving the Evil Eye becomes his enemy; and that which is within the enemy's natural circle of protection, his mind and body, falls under the direct and easy control of the attacker. This can occur unconsciously when a strong-willed person sends forth a glare of envy or spite and wishes ill on the head of his neighbor—especially if this is done in a somewhat cold-blooded and detached way. Or it can be deliberately brought about through magical means.

In seemingly projecting his point of Self along the ray, the attacker gains access to his foe's subconscious, if only for an instant when the other is surprised, and he leaves within the personal sphere of his foe a seed of hatred, which is interpreted by the victim's subconscious mind as self-hatred. The hate matures like the chick of a cuckoo in its foreign nest, and eventually it succeeds in killing the fondest hopes and plans that are the psychic children of its foster parent. The victim's powers are turned against him. All his attempts to succeed fall to ashes. He hurts himself and those he loves over and over in an unconscious effort to fulfill the self-hatred that has been placed within him.

Most attacks of the Evil Eye are unconscious and are easily frustrated. The Evil Eye can be avoided by turning the back, looking aside, or walking in the opposite direction. The attack can be emotionally turned aside by giving in to the wishes of the person who unknowingly casts the ray, thereby placating him. This was the method suggested by Jesus Christ. In these ways the victim of an attack can avoid becoming an unwilling participant in his own downfall.

The Evil Eye can be thwarted in more active ways. In Morocco it was the custom to bare the backside at the attacker. This is a form of mockery that has the effect of making the person giving the Evil Eye angry, causing him to turn the power of the Eye on himself. Scornful laughter is the modern equivalent of this practice. Sullen, spiteful people often draw mocking laughter for little apparent reason. Such laughter is an unconscious attempt to turn aside their malice.

Sharp objects such as nails and needles may be used as charms against the Evil Eye. The popular explanation of their effectiveness is that they prick the Eye and blind it. This is symbolically true. The evil is returned along an opposing ray to its source. The opposing ray is given a physical focus by the needle or other pointed object.

Bright colors, shiny things, coins and bells that jingle, shells, bits of amber—all are used to attract the first malignant glance, which is thought to be the most hurtful. Mirrors are used for this reason, as well as for reflecting the glance back to its source.

The most common defense is the symbol of the open hand, which is represented in a wide variety of patterns. The examples on p. 72 as well as all the following figures, are from north Africa.

Other charms against the Evil Eye are themselves shaped like eyes on the assumption that if an eye sends the evil, another eye can return it:

Effective charms can be made combining the stylized forms of the hand and the eye:

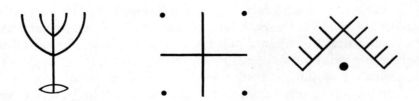

The power of these signs stems from their underlying symbolic meaning, which directs the forces of the victim's mind effectively for defense in the same way a circuit will channel electricity for a particular purpose. Since the symbols operate below the conscious level they need not be intellectualized, merely considered and absorbed.

These signs are most useful against unintentional malicious projection of the Self. They remove doubt and help generate self-confidence. All the power for defense comes from the mind of the defender. The signs will, however, offer little protection against a willful attack from an accomplished adept. Conscious attack requires conscious defense.

Happily, the ability to project the point of Self along a ray is difficult to master. It is seldom taught because it is so dangerous, both to the user and the person used. At one time in Tibet priests learned how to invade the body of another and usurp it so that they might continue to occupy the Earth after their physical death. The technique is similar to the casting of the Evil Eye except that when the Self of the priest occupied the body of another, it expelled the rightful owner and remained in unlawful possession. Outwardly such a theft is marked by a sudden and complete change in the personality and habits of the dispossessed individual.

There is a danger in projecting the Self for any length of time as it leaves the physical body without a center, therefore without a protective circle and prey to the incursions of astral forces who might wish to employ it for purposes of evil. When the Self is shifted along the ray, the body becomes an object on the periphery of the personal universe, no more or less significant than any other object. The Self is aware of it as it is aware of the sky. Having lost its center, the body is defenseless.

Astral travelers who lose their link with their physical bodies—which is symbolized by the so-called "ectoplasmic umbilical"—have great trouble finding their way home, and they may find that their body has been invaded by some opportunistic entity who has long waited for just such a chance. Then a battle of Wills ensues, and the entity, drawing the strength of conviction from its stolen physical limbs, usually wins.

All pointed objects symbolize the ray. The sword is a channel of force that focuses and culminates at the point of its tip, where its edges converge. The same may be said of the spear, pin, dart, needle, dagger, and even the gun. Perhaps the best symbol of the ray is the arrow, which flies freely through the air, directed by an act of will to pierce its target. The arrows of Cupid are rays of Will. The sword of Justice is a ray. On a more mundane level the pointing hand in old-fashioned printed notices is a ray.

Indeed, the gesture of pointing a finger is a powerful metaphor for extending the Will and is often used by the Magus in ritual and in everyday situations where the exercise of magical force becomes necessary. It need not be a grand and theatrical motion. In a public place a firm and unequivocal pointing at the object of desire is enough. Such a gesture is mainly for the benefit of the Magus as an aid in focusing his attention, although a stronger link is established between the Magus and his object if the ray travels from eye to eye.

Just as the active eye of the Magus is an excellent instrument for sending the ray, the passive receiving eye is highly susceptible to its effect. The Magus who wishes to influence another person will make his intention known to that person by using the gross avenues of the physical senses to communicate his purpose. Magic, like water, always seeks the easiest and quickest course.

The ray implies cause and effect. Desire, residing at the point of Self, is extended by the Will to unite with its object. Using the ray like a psychic knife to pierce through the hole opened in the point by the vortex, the Magus bridges the Veil between the Unmanifest and creation. When the first word of God, in the form of a lightning stroke, split the primordial sea, it was the ray in action.

All magic involves the ray projected either inwardly or outwardly; though in truth this distinction is without meaning. To project magical intent over a distance, the Magus must transmit desire through the point of Self. Magical force never travels through space: it enters the Unmanifest and at once reemerges at the object of desire, having been seemingly reflected from the mirror surface of the Veil.

To realize any desire is an act of creation. The Magus focuses his Will on a symbol (some form his mind can manipulate) that acts as a talisman of power and drives the forces in the material world to actualize his intent. This same process takes place when a carpenter makes a chair. First he creates a mental image of the chair that is so clear to his interior eyes he can almost see it before him; then the image drives him to bring his mental creation into physical being.

The carpenter makes the chair with his hands. The Magus knows that his hands and the world around him are one and the same. By harmonizing his personal universe with the single universe of divine emanation, he makes the forces of nature into the muscles and bones and sinews of his microcosm—for the real microcosm is not the body of man, but the entire personal universe he creates around his Self.

To project magical force, the Magus must psychically create a pulse and wrap it around itself clockwise to give it a spinning motion, which draws it in upon itself. This shrinking vortex concentrates the force of the pulse to a point. Finally it is threaded into a ray of Will, like a bead of light onto a string, and directed to the object of desire. It should be understood that these images are only models for the essential forces involved, which can never be grasped by the conscious mind but only apprehended indirectly.

The Will picks up the means of accomplishing its end from the limitless possibilities of the Unmanifest, and when it emerges through the Veil into the world at the object of desire, this potential effect is precipitated into manifestation through an expanding counterclockwise vortex. The Will does not actually travel through the Unmanifest. It would be more accurate to think of it as creating a wave or charge on the surface of the Unmanifest that is instantly compensated for and neutralized, the result being the expulsion through the Veil of the desired magical effect.

It also should be emphasized that the vortices need not be tangible or visible to the naked eye. The expanding vortex is merely symbolic of the realization of the desired end. It can, if necessary, be made to manifest physically as a whirlwind, but this is an excessive display of force that does nothing to further the purpose of the magic. Such displays are like the sparks that fly off from a whirling electrical generator—they are so much energy wasted.

CROSS

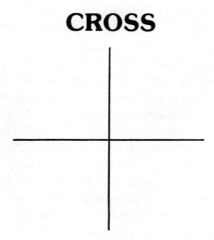

The cross is a ray interrupted in its natural course by an opposing ray of Will that exactly cancels its effect. At the same time, the second ray is frustrated by the first. Because these two rays overlap at right angles, their force is spread out rather than focused in a single direction. The point where the arms meet embodies the blending of opposite potentials. It is where hot meets cold, wet meets dry, and love meets hate. Here all movement is negated and fixed. The perfect cross has arms of equal length that intersect at their center points.

The cross exhibits itself in the warp and woof of all woven fabrics. Each individual thread has its strength along its length, but no power to resist force applied against it to the side. But when two threads are crossed and locked into each other, their force vectors are balanced. The whole cloth will resist tearing not only at right angles but from all directions.

Just as Christ is the third element in the divine Trinity and reconciles the other two, so is the juncture of the cross the balance point between the powers represented by the arms. This point is outside time and space. Raised upon the cross, Christ became immortal, no longer subject to change and decay. The cross is symbolically separate from the constantly shifting forms of being. Thus the host is blessed with the cross to lock in its purity—in a sense it is set outside the world of forms.

When a man is born he perceives the world as a sphere, which is symbolized in nature by the perfect circle of the sky. His first act is to send out a ray of awareness, creating polarity and dividing that perfection into two. Similarly, the limitless horizon is divided by the arc of the Sun into the north and south hemispheres. The polarity created by the first ray seeks its balance. So it happens that a balancing arc is mentally cast across the path of the Sun, further dividing the world into hemispheres of east and west. This is how the four points of the compass originally came into being. Mankind could not conceive of the division into east and west until it had perceived the polarity of north and south.

The cross is much older than Christianity, indeed as old as time, for it is a universal symbol that conveys an unchanging meaning to all peoples whatever the outward interpretation that may be forced upon it. The pattern the god Prometheus took when bound to the pillar by Zeus was a cross. The Norse god Wotan crucified himself on the eternal ash Yggdrasil in order to peer into the mysteries of the timeless realm where magic is born.

In other cultures the same mystical message is conveyed in slightly different forms. The Sioux Indians used to suspend their braves by their pectoral muscles so that they might receive illumination through suffering. In the mythology of the Maya, the severed head of the sacrificed divine being Hun-Hunahpu, when placed in a tree, caused the tree to flower.

One prominent Western interpretation of the cross is endurance—to stand against time and change with a fixed purpose, unbroken and unbreakable. The Norse rune Nyd, which means roughly "the will to endure," takes its form from an irregular cross: $\uparrow$.

The Christian cross is not regular, but has a vertical arm that is considerably longer than the horizontal. This signifies that the masculine, active principle is exalted in Christ over the passive, feminine side. The vertical ray is akin to the primal lightning and is always the male principle. The horizontal ray suggests the surface of the primal sea and is always female. Also, the intersection point of the Christian cross is near the top, indicating a movement toward the Light. For these reasons it emphasizes triumph and victory.

The pagan and Christian views of the cross find an interesting union in this lyric of Cynwulf, an Anglo-Saxon poet who lived around A.D. 750. This description is taken from the *Dream of the Rood:*

Methought on a sudden I saw a cross
Upreared in the sky, and radiant with light.
Brightest of trees, that beauteous beacon
Was dipped in gold, and bedight with jewels:
Four at the base, and five on the beam
Glistened on high; 'twas no gallows tree,
Emblem of shame, but the souls of the blest
Were gazing upon it, God's bright angels,
The glorious creation, all kindreds of men.
'Twas a tree of triumph; but troubled was I
Stained with sin, as I stood and gazed
On the cross of glory, aglow with light.
Layers of gold, and glittering jewels
Covered its bark, and buried the wood.
Still through the gold that garnished its side,
I was 'ware of wounds where once it had bled,
Scars of a battle old. I was bowed with sorrow;
But the vision filled me with fear when I saw
That it changed its hue—now chased with gold,
Now stained with blood and streaming wet!

Here the pagan notion of the cross of trial is blended with the Christian emphasis on the cross of glory, and this is very much the understanding that has come down to the modern West.

The cross was often linked with the circle in ancient times. This form of glyph occurs in Neolithic carvings such as the Hallristingnor (⊕) and is a letter of the Phoenician and older Greek alphabets (⊗). The best known circle-cross is the cross of the Celts:

This is not merely an architectural device for surmounting the structural weakness of stone, but is a complex philosophical statement.

The circle divides the inner from the outer and fixes a limit to the limitless. It represents the world of change and form. The cross reconciles the opposites of manifestation and thus symbolizes changeless and formless eternity. Therefore the circle is a symbol of material life, and the cross a symbol of death, or eternal life. Together they embody the revolving wheel of creation.

The cross can easily be derived from the circle by considering the circle edge on. The revolving pulse of the circle, viewed from the edge, becomes either the back-and-forth or up-and-down pulse of reciprocating rays:

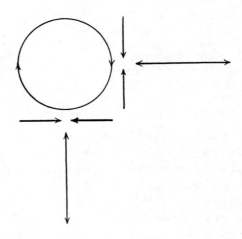

Thus any cross may be graphically thought of as two interlocking circles:

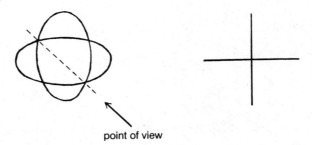

point of view

The circle-cross similarly represents three interlocking circles:

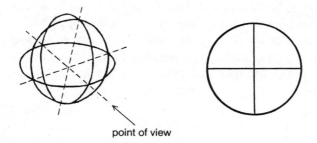

point of view

The circle-cross is often used to locate a point in space, for example, in gun and bomb sights. In magic the circle-cross locates the Self in the center of the personal universe, which is usually represented physically by the heart, where no movement is and where all things move around. This is done by visualizing three axes passing through the Self, each perpendicular to the others, and extending to the spherical inner surface of the aura.

Because of its inherent nature the cross is always used for defense, never for attack. It will absorb and distribute force but has no ability to emanate it. The Magus crosses his own body to protect himself from hurtful change. He projects the cross onto exterior objects to preserve them or to lock in potencies he has infused into them.

The cross is not a symbol of good but is a symbol of protection. It negates force. In melodrama where the fearless vampire hunter crosses his mallet and wooden stake to ward off the approach of the blood-sucking fiend, he is not so much evoking Christ as he is blocking the ray of desire emanating from the vampire.

Magically the cross is projected in the same way as the circle of protection. It is visualized in the imagination as a stream of glowing fire that emits from the index finger of the right hand or from the magical instrument and is painted in the air or on the object to be guarded. To empower the cross, the Magus must consider each arm in a separate act of Will, then balance the two against each other to realize the peace that resides at the point of intersection.

It should be drawn first from top to bottom, then from left to right on the object to which it is applied. These are the natural lines of descending force. When the cross is made over a charm or other object, the beam of the cross is drawn from right to left. But when the cross is made by the Magus over his own body, the beam is inverted and drawn from the left to the right shoulder. The key to remembering is always to draw the beam from the left side to the right side considered from the perspective of the thing to which it is applied.*

In magic the cross may be used singly, in groups of three to accord with the trinity of first principles, or in groups of four to stand for the powers of the material world:

If it is necessary, the Magus can destroy the cross by tracing it in reverse order to the way it was formed, first mentally absorbing the horizontal ray from the right to the left of the thing crossed, then the vertical ray from the bottom to the top. Potencies are always absorbed into the left side of the body.

Black magic sometimes employs the inverted Christian cross in its rituals as a mockery of Christ. When the Christian cross, which has a man shape with a head and a foot, is inverted, it becomes a symbol of futility and waste. A similar suspension from the course of world events is seen in the Tarot trump The Hanged Man, who depends from a cord tied around one ankle, his legs crossed and his head near the earth. In the case of the Hanged Man, the suspension is meant to suggest futility rather than evil. However, the two are basically one.

The essential cross in its purest form is a figure in perfect balance with arms of equal length. It cannot be inverted or turned from left to right. For this reason its meaning is eternal and can never be debased by the instruments of Evil. Like the radiant Light of Spirit, it is always itself.

---

* The cross is drawn in the *Golden Dawn* and related texts from right to left on the body of the Magus. This procedure results from a basic error in viewing the Tree of Life. Many people think the Tree is illustrated as seen from the front, when actually it is shown from the *back*. Therefore the part of the G.D. prayer of the cross "ve-Geburah, ve-Gedulah" is left to right on the human body.

TRIANGLE

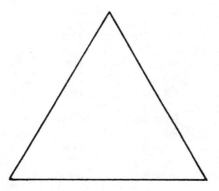

The triangle is the strongest unit of architectural construction because it will not rack or deform under stress. Its material qualities express its absolute nature. It is fixed and eternal—it cannot be altered in part without destroying the whole. Formed of three points joined each to the others by two reciprocating rays, it defines the second dimension of space.

The number three is used to symbolize completion on the level of Spirit. The triangle is a glyph for the perfection of the Unmanifest as revealed through its highest trinity of emanation. It is the force that goes out, the force that takes in, and the force that reconciles opposites. Since this trinity is most apparent in the sexual polarity of the material world, the triangle is bound up with imagery of father, mother, and child.

The upward-pointing triangle is often said to stand for the phallus, and the downward-pointing triangle for the delta of Venus when these figures appear in primitive art and religion. This view betrays a limited understanding of symbolism. It would be just as true to say that the upward-pointing triangle symbolized fire, and the downward-pointing triangle, water. Both the phallus and the elementary principle of Fire are themselves only symbols for the active emanation of the first trinity. Fire is no closer to the Absolute because it has physical substance, whereas the triangle is an abstract geometric—if anything,

TABLE OF TRIANGLE

	1	2	3
Babylonian	Anu	Ea	Enlil
Egyptian	Osiris	Isis	Horus
Hindu	Brahma	Siva	Vishnu
Greek	Chaos	Gaea	Eros
Roman	Jupiter	Juno	Minerva
Teutonic	Wotan	Frija	Donar
Christian	Father	Holy Ghost	Son
Motions	Linear	Rotary	Vibratory
Colors	Red	Blue	Yellow
Elements	Fire	Water	Air
Heavens	Sun	Moon	Star
Earth	Lightning	Rain	Wind
Speech	Subject	Verb	Object
Space	Up-Down	Left-Right	Front-Back

its physical nature sets fire farther away from its root essence.

A triangle may be rotated so that any side acts as the base and any point as the apex. The opposite principles are in this way shown to be composed of the same stuff acting in reverse polarity. If the triangle is rotated rapidly, its three points trace the line of a circle, which has no top or bottom, illustrating that from a change of perspective any point of the triangle can be made to replace any other. All spring from the unity of the first point, Kether, the White Head.

The child is formed from the equal participation of the male and female, just as any point of the triangle gains its identity by virtue of its relationship with the other two points. When the child matures, it becomes either a man or a woman and in turn gives rise to its own androgynous offspring.

Sexuality should not be seen solely as material in nature, but as the lowest aspect of a cosmic principle that acts on all levels of manifestation. When the ancients made their trinities of gods male, female, and child—or hermaphroditic—they were not lowering the dignity of the All, but were elevating human understanding of sexuality.

It is no more narrow-minded to think of God as a male than as a female, or for that matter as an it. The Unmanifest embodies all three in its primary emanation, the Light of Spirit. Since human understanding can never hope to grasp the Unmanifest whole, in its representations of God it must do the best it can not to distort or obscure the clearest conception attainable.

Mankind must divide the All to consider it, and the smallest number of this division is three. The male principle must be considered first because it is the principle of ignition that goes out from the unity of Light. However, the female aspect of God is not second in a temporal sense, because it springs into being with the becoming of the male, and both occur before the beginning of time. Likewise, the child, or neutral, principle is not third in time but is only third in logical exposition. Even as the male and female separate, they reunite and create a product on a level lower than the primary unity.

Errors in understanding God arise when a culture emphasizes one point of the triangle above the other two. All error is imbalance. A distorted notion of the Creator must result, and the qualities of the gods of a culture always correspond to the point of the triangle in ascendancy.

In Islam God is male and is expressed in all his maleness through the prophet Mohammed, man of warfare, of conquest, of command.

In Islamic culture men dominate, not only where it is their natural right, but also in many areas more commonly controlled by women. Women are, in a real sense, appendages of their male counterparts, forbidden to do anything useful that might give them authority. The veil they wear is symbolic of their forcible removal from worldly affairs.

Instances where God is viewed as female are less common—not, as is widely believed, because societies are controlled by men, but because the usefulness of the male principle is more obvious to a people who want rain to fall and crops to grow. Being the active element of the trinity, the male face of God is the one that makes things happen. However, cults of female gods, existing away from the center of societies, can be observed. The modern Wicca movement worships the Earth Mother in her many guises. Cultures devoted to the Goddess tend to be inward-looking, inclined to the gentle arts and fond of illusion and secrecy. They build no empires, which perhaps helps explain their lack of prominence.

As for the worship of God as a child, Christianity is the most obvious example. In the Middle Ages Christ was often depicted as a babe in arms with a wise adult head or as a slender effeminate figure with a narrow waist and broad hips. Child-god cultures are characterized by an ambivalence between the active and passive impulses. No question is more puzzling to Christians than when, and if, they should turn the other cheek. The Western world suffers the incongruity of warrior popes and saintly Caesars because neither knows in his heart which pose he should adopt at a given moment. Christ shared this uncertainty. At times he lashed out at his tormentors, as when he drove the moneylenders from the temple. At times he doubted his passive role, as when he questioned his fate on the cross.

In the modern West there is a continuing attempt to exalt the male principle over the female. Ironically, this movement is served by women who have not yet realized what they are doing. By exalting the male role through their attempts to usurp it, they deify the male principle. At the same time, they hold the female role in contempt and derision, thereby turning their backs on the Earth Mother, who is the essence of their sexual being. This is an extremely unhealthy situation that cannot long continue without courting disaster.

Cultures that keep their trinity balanced are more stable in the long term than those that exalt one point over the other two. Hinduism is a religion in which no single aspect of the trinity is allowed to dominate heavily. Buddhism is another, with the added virtue that the Buddhist clearly recognizes all aspects of the trinity as illusions. A culture with many gods, like Hinduism with its thousands of deities, may be more rational, if it expresses a balanced trinity of principles, than a monotheistic culture where one face of the godhead has eaten the other two.

The drawback of a completely balanced trinity of forces is that it tends to make a culture inert. A society out of balance is at least on the move, even if it is moving to its annihilation. Where there is no movement there is no life, and virtue cannot express itself. Perhaps the best state of affairs is a slight bias toward the child principle, which creates tension and flux.

In magic the triangle forms the basis of practical working. Whenever the Magus acts, he tilts the finely hung balance of cosmic law, which is the natural order of things in creation. The nature of the balance can be understood by using the lever, one of the simplest machines, as a mental model. The lever in action can be considered in three parts. There is the force applied to one end, the transmitting medium, and the work accomplished at the opposite end. These three elements will be termed the mover, the moving, and the moved. They correspond to the desire of the Magus, his Will acting through the medium of the Art, and the end accomplished.

If one end of the lever is pulled down, the other end goes up. If one end is moved left, the other end goes right—always around the infinitely small point of the fulcrum. The fulcrum represents the aperture through the Veil and the Unmanifest. Work is put in and emerges inverted left to right and top to bottom out the other side, as though projected through a lens. The fulcrum may be shifted to vary the work produced. This will not generate more work—magically speaking, nothing is gained without its corresponding price—however, moving the fulcrum may produce more effective work.

Archimedes is reputed to have boasted that given a long enough lever he could move the world. He meant that for the greatest of earthly tasks, the necessary force does not have to be large if it is sufficiently focused. Much of magic is merely learning to focus power. The example of Napoleon is apt. The little Corsican had no more intelligence or vitality than many other men, but he discovered how to apply his strengths to his task, the conquest of the civilized world. He was only frustrated by the collective will of the English people.

The Magus always seeks to place himself in the role of the mover.

It is the mover of events who determines what is to be done and how. It is the position of control from which intention can be exercised. The Magus seldom enjoys the role of the moved, as it is not in his nature to be passive and accept direction from others; were it so, he would become a mystic. Most odious of all for him is to play the part of the moving instrument and cause the realization of an action initiated by the Will of another. This is to be at best an obedient servant, at worst, a slave.

A reality in life is that all men and women, even the greatest of adepts, variously occupy each of the three points of the triangle. It is an honor to serve as an instrument of the Light. The greatest in history—Schweitzer, Jesus, Mother Teresa—are those who have subordinated their will and passively given themselves as levers to God. Even on the human level it is often no disgrace to follow a great leader or perform his work.

The Magus must reconcile the desire to control his own destiny with the realization that all good ultimately depends on living in harmony with evolution, which is the unfolding purpose of the Light in creation. He must recognize that submission is as much a voluntary act as defiance. Or, as the poet Milton put it: "They also serve who only stand and wait."

The threefold aspect of God has been expressed through many different metaphors, each true in part but incomplete. One is grammatical—the subject, verb, and object. Another is geometric—the elements of point, radius, and circle. Eastern philosophy conceives the trinity as three kinds of essential motion—the Rajasic, Tamasic, and Sattvic. These have found a parallel expression in astrology as the Cardinal, Fixed, and Mutable signs of the Zodiac.

Briefly, this notion states that everything in creation is made of motion, which can be linear, rotary, or vibratory in nature. These motions are never pure but always mixed. The Rajasic, or Cardinal, is the male principle; the Tamasic, or Fixed, is the female principle; and the Sattvic, or Mutable, is the neutral principle. To some extent these motions correspond to the spiral, the circle, and the wave. The value of this view of the trinity is its denial that a thing need be material to be real.

As a ritual symbol the triangle is used sparingly, but might be employed more often with a little ingenuity. Its common function is the enclosing of evoked spirits outside the circle that protects the Magus. The Magus stands within the circle and calls up the hostile spirit inside the triangle located two feet away from the circle's outer edge.

The practical difference between the circle and the triangle in enclosing an aspect of manifestation is that the circle must be drawn from the center point, mentally if not physically, whereas the triangle can be formed from outside its boundaries and still enclose something apart from the personal protective sphere of the Magus.

The magic circle is an extension of the perceived self. It would be extremely dangerous to allow a hostile spirit to enter. Forces of evil must be kept strictly apart, not only outside the circle but imprisoned so that they cannot roam the greater world, where they might find the opportunity to work some deceit on the Magus.

The magic triangle is drawn with its base toward the circle. Traditionally it is equilateral and three feet long on each side. A focus for the spirit (which is an object made of materials that accord with the nature of the spirit and inscribed with the magical character of the spirit) is placed inside the triangle. The triangle is materially drawn on the ground or floor, but mentally traced in the air in a vertical position. The spirit is evoked at the apex, and as the sides of the triangle expand toward the base, it is drawn into manifestation. To banish, the Magus drives the spirit up and through the apex into Nothingness.

It would be an error to link the triangle with evil. It is a magical tool with qualities that can be used for good or bad purposes. Its primary meaning is the manifestation of force. The eye of God is represented shining forth from inside a triangle. Here the center is the first point from which all else emanates, and the three corners are the primary trinity. If the triangle is collapsed, this radiation of first principles can be shown graphically:

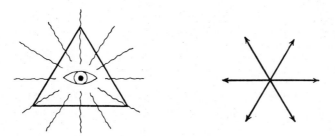

Each of the sides, which are the north-south, east-west, and up-down axes of space, has a common center in the pupil of God's eye.

The Chinese game of rock, paper, and scissors reveals a deep understanding of the trinity. Most children have played it. In the Orient it is taken more seriously than it is in the West. The two players shake hands twice in rhythm and then separate them to simultaneously form either the shape of a rock (fist), a sheet of paper (flat hand), or a pair of scissors (extended index and middle fingers). If the shape of both players is the same, they try again. Paper triumphs over rock by enveloping it; scissors command paper by cutting it; rock overcomes scissors by breaking them.

When these symbols are arranged in a circle, there is a definite rotation from point to point. Each object destroys another in the exercise of its function. It is the nature of scissors to cut; in cutting they destroy the ability of paper to fulfill its reason for being, which is to enclose.

The physical objects can be replaced by the elemental principles of Fire, Water, and Air. Water puts out Fire by smothering it; Air triumphs over Water by evaporating it; and Fire consumes Air to feed itself. A model of this circular motion can be observed in the lower seventh, eighth, and ninth Sephiroth of the Kabbalistic Tree of Life, where the motion proceeds in a clockwise direction:

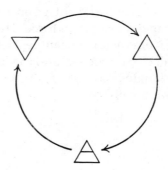

Each of the three principles triumphs over another, yet no principle is exalted over all. The element that defeats another is itself overcome by the element defeated by the vanquished. This should be considered in relation to the three faces of God. The child born of sexual union grows up to become either man or woman. If a man, he slays his father and weds his mother to produce a new generation. If a woman, she merges with her mother and renews her to remarry with the father.

The Chinese game can be inverted by substituting the more meaningful symbols of egg, bird, and serpent for rock, paper, and scissors. The hand signs used are the same: the fist is the egg; the flat of the hand forms the wings of the bird; and the two extended fingers become the forked tongue of the serpent. In this reversal of the game, the egg imprisons the bird, the serpent eats the egg, and the bird devours the serpent. The force now flows in the opposite direction. This form of the game has an ancient air about it that suggests its rightful place is in an age long past and forgotten.

TABLE OF SQUARE

	1	2	3	4
Elements	Fire	Water	Air	Earth
Names of God	IHVI Tzabaoth	Elohim Tzabaoth	Shaddai El Chai	Adonai haAretz
Letters of IHVH	Yod	He	Vau	He
Archangels	Michael	Gabriel	Raphael	Auriel
Apostles	Mark	Matthew	John	Luke
Beasts	Lion	Eagle	Angel	Bull
Quarters	South	West	North	East
Seasons	Summer	Fall	Winter	Spring
Motions	Linear	Rotary	Vibratory	Mixed
Worlds	Atziluth	Briah	Yetzirah	Assiah
Elementals	Salamanders	Undines	Sylphs	Gnomes
Winds	Notus	Zephyrus	Boreas	Eurus
Rivers	Pison	Gihon	Hiddikel	Phrath
Growth	Stalk	Fruit	Seed	Root
Colors	Red	Blue	Yellow	Black
Instruments	Rod	Cup	Sword	Shield

SQUARE

The square represents the perfect trinity of forces made manifest. Traditionally it stands for the physical world, but its meaning may be extended to cover all forms of being from the concrete to the spiritual. The Kabbalists recognize this broader significance when they make the fourth emanation of God, called Chesed, the seat of formation where all things exist in the bud, not yet unfolded. Even something as insubstantial as an idea has its coming into being, where it passes from possibility to reality.

The square is associated with the four winds, the four corners of the Earth, the four elements, the four rivers, the four beasts, the four archangels, the four apostles, the four seasons, the four magical instruments, and the four letters of the Tetragrammaton—the unspeakable name of God.

In the triangle each point has direct communication with the other two. The triangle is a perfect unity. However, in the square each point touches only two other points through reciprocating rays, and is isolated from the third point. To gain any apprehension of the third point, it must rely on the mediation of the other two, which color and distort the nature of the third point even as they transmit some secondhand concept of it.

So it is in the world, which is a part of the Unmanifest yet paradoxically isolated from its highest expression. The Absolute can only be viewed indirectly by the effect it has on other created things. The myth of Adam and Eve represents the transition from triangle to square. Adam's sin was to draw a circle around himself and make a separate personal universe apart from the living universe that was God. The clothing he put on was a suit of flesh and ego. In the Garden Adam had no circle around him, but was an aspect of the unity of the All.

The four elements are a philosophical division of form into its essential qualities based on its kinds of motion. They are not physical elements as science understands them but the locus upon which the physical elements are based. Elemental Fire is not the fire that springs from a match—it is the prevalent inner quality of that fire. All material things are mixtures of the four elemental principles, with one being dominant.

 Fire is the male element. Its motion is linear and it originates action.

 Water is the female element. Its motion is circular; it receives and transforms the impulse of Fire.

 Air partakes of the mingled qualities of Fire and Water, being both volatile and cool, and is the product of their union. Its motion is vibratory.

 Earth is the crystallization of the three preceding elemental principles in the sphere of matter. Although it has no pure essence, its compound nature is perceived by the human mind as separate and unique. It is a reflection of the first three elements.

The supreme symbol of the divine trinity in action is the Tetragrammaton, made up of the Hebrew letters Yod-He-Vau-He, which are transcribed into English as *IHVH*. It is the nature of religions, with their inherent mystical bent, to overlook the fourth emanation of the Unmanifest. Considered as three, God is an ideal without concrete existence in the mundane world. But considered as four God becomes a practical reality. Little wonder that the fourfold division of the All is the single most important magical tool.

The Yod is the primordial lightning. It is the sword from the mouth. It is the Word.

The first He is the primordial ocean into which the lightning strikes. It is all potency waiting to become.

The Vau is the boiling that issues from the waters.

The second He is the solid rock that rises up from the storms of Chaos and the crawling things upon it.

The Magus will readily see that the first chapter of Genesis is not a fairy tale, not an abstraction, but is the actual way life came into being out of the oceans at the dawn of time. Yet the origin of life is not the truth hidden in the words, but is only a reflection of the Truth.

It is interesting to consider why the fourth letter of the Tetragrammaton is a second He, and not a different letter as one might expect. This is because as each level of the trinity actualizes itself, it reverses its polarity in order to maintain an overall balance. This is analogous to what happens when electrical charges reverse themselves. The negative becomes the positive and the positive becomes the negative.

Yod is the impulse to action. Vau is the realization of that action. The first He is the medium through which the desire of the Yod is transmitted. The second He is the returning reactionary pulse from the Vau that completes the cycle. There could be no order without this returning pulse since if it were absent, every motion would proceed endlessly in single directions. What grew hotter would continue getting hotter indefinitely, and so on. The second He restores the balance.

Consider the seasons of the year. Two are opposite (summer and winter), and the other two are essentially the same (temperate), except that the direction of motion is reversed from one to the other. That is, in spring the temperature goes from cool to warm, and in autumn it goes from warm to cool. The changing of the seasons is often thought of as circular motion. If it were circular it would look like this:

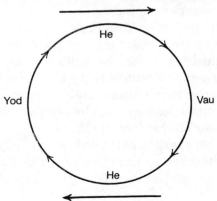

However, the actual motion of the seasons and all other cycles is spiral since each element is separated by time from the one it replaces. The summer of one year appears the same as the summer of the previous year, but it is completely new, and built on the summer that preceded it.

The four letters of the Tetragrammaton can be represented by a standing wave, which is exactly balanced by a second wave. The trough of one wave and the opposite crest of the other wave form a cycle with the four letters in the name of God:

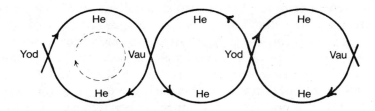

The wave model is two-dimensional. In three dimensions the cycle of becoming would be shown by the double helix, which is two spirals progressing in opposite directions of rotation along a cylinder, one clockwise and the other counterclockwise. When one observes it from the side, the double helix looks exactly like the standing waves. The intersection points of the spirals mark the Yod and the Vau; the opposite peaks and valleys place the first He and second He, which alternate along the waves or spirals.

The meaning of the balanced and opposite spirals is the mystery of the Caduceus of Hermes; it is the mechanism by which manifest things maintain themselves. When the oscillations are disrupted there is loss of being. The manifest returns to the Unmanifest. These spirals are the two serpents that twine around the life centers of the body, one ascending and the other descending. They can also be applied fruitfully to the ten apples on the Tree of Life.

Perhaps an understanding of the four elements in a cycle can be gained through another metaphor. Think of Yod as the heat in the rays of the rising Sun. These strike the surface of the water, the first He, and produce vapor, the Vau. The water is the means by which the energy in the sunlight becomes the energy, or movement, in the vapor. The vapor rises into the air, then at dusk descends and touches the chill earth, the second He, where it is transformed into dew. As it returns to its original form it warms the earth.

Within the perceived self of the individual the four elements of the cycle are at constant war with each other, each striving for ascendancy so that it may manifest itself unhindered. It is one of the primary tasks of the Magus to balance these elements, which when inside the mental body are called humors—the sanguine (blood, or Fire); the phlegmatic (phlegm, or Water); the choloric (bile, or Air); and the melancholic (black bile, or Earth). The struggle to reconcile these elements is never completely successful, and continues throughout life.

In the training of past magical schools, initiates faced trials by Fire, Water, Air, and Earth. Only by physically confronting the most terrifying material forms of the elements was the initiate deemed suitable to proceed to higher matters. An initiate might be forced to walk through a wall of flame with no assurance of escape on the other side; to swim a raging river; to climb a difficult rock face; or to crawl through the bowels of the earth alone and in utter darkness.

These tests have fallen out of common use. There are few who have the blind faith to undertake them today, and their value is questionable. Rather than demonstrating an understanding and command of the four elements, they only prove a brute animal courage. A fool who rushes in is of no great value, even to himself.

When the elements really have been inwardly understood and mastered to a degree, they can be manipulated to yield powerful mental and even physical effects. They are the workhorses of magic. Ninety percent of the purposes of the Art can be achieved through the four elements. Symbols and forms of magic lose their effectiveness as they grow complex and stray farther from the roots of the Art. The elements are dependable. Their natures are relatively easy to grasp and they convey the same meaning to all peoples at all times.

In ancient times the elemental principles were represented by the emblems of four beasts whose natures embody the underlying essences of the elemental forces: 1) Lion (Fire); 2) Eagle (Water); 3) Angel (Air); 4) Bull (Earth). It would be difficult to trace the origin of these figures; they go back to ancient Babylon, in whose ruins archaeologists have found their effigies, and doubtless their genesis is even earlier.

They may have arisen not long after the human race began to favor agriculture over the nomadic lifestyle.

On first look it appears that the Eagle would be a more appropriate emblem for the element Air than the Angel, but upon deeper consideration this is not so self-evident. Water is the medium of transmission, the element of formation, and the eagle has long been a symbol for the messenger or herald. Air is the element of thought, the product of the impulse begun with Fire, and angels are beings of the higher intellect. Even with these considerations many occultists still maintain that at some time in the distant past a mistake was made and the Eagle and Angel were inverted from their rightful places in the Zodiac. There is no way to prove or disprove this claim, so it seems best to use the traditional interpretations.

In the heavens the four beasts are placed at the corners of the Zodiac, each representing one of the elemental triads: Lion—Leo, Eagle—Scorpio, Angel—Aquarius, and Bull—Taurus. This assignment has been changeless for thousands of years. The beasts are also placed at the corners of the Earth, and here some difficulty arises. There is considerable argument about the proper placement of the elements and their related symbols around the compass.

There is little point in going into the various ways the beasts have been placed on the corners of the Earth. All the methods have something to be said for them, and something to be said against. But the fault they share in common is that they are arbitrary, even capricious. What is needed is something to base the assignment on.

This can be found in the heavens. All that is required is to transfer the relationship of the four beasts in the Zodiac, which has been hallowed by tradition and besides has much to logically recommend it, to the surface of the Earth. This sounds obvious, but the reason it has not been done is because the signs in the heavens must be inverted before they can be applied to the Earth.

Imagine that you are looking at the Zodiac in the sky. If the Zodiac is rotated so that Leo, the Lion, emblem of Fire, falls to the bottom (equivalent to the South) and the beasts are applied to the compass, then the Eagle, emblem of Water, will touch the East. But this is clearly wrong: the West is accepted as the quarter assigned to elemental Water. However, if you imagine the Zodiac falling flat onto the Earth and yourself viewing it from the back, the Eagle touches the West while the Lion is in the South, a reasonable assignment when all else is considered. (See the diagram on p. 99.)

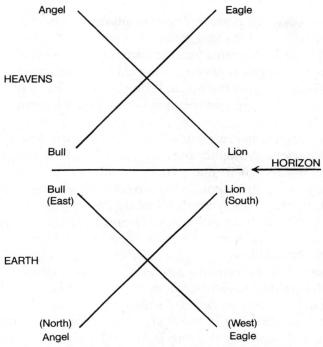

Fire is most appropriate to the South, region of blazing heat. Water is the traditional element of the West, where for the ancients the shoreless Atlantic lay. Earth can be assigned to the East, the direction of the unmeasured steppes that led to fabled China. North is the quarter of unbroken emptiness, appropriate to Air.

Cosmic man stands with the axis of the Earth along his spine, circled by the Moon and stars. On his brow is the Angel, elemental Air, symbol of his higher aspirations. The Lion, Fire, lies curled around his lower body, symbol of strength and generation. On his right hand sits the Eagle, symbol of life-giving Water, of mercy and love. At his left is the Bull and in his left hand, the dry, hard clay of Earth.

The beasts were considered too fierce and dangerous to be used as emblems of the elements. Over a period of time a sublimation took place and the beasts were replaced by the four angels drawn from the lore of the Kabbalah—Michael, Gabriel, Raphael, and Auriel. Later still, psychologically if not chronologically, the angels were replaced by the four apostles of Christ—Mark, Matthew, John, and Luke. All this was an attempt to reduce the forces of the elements to human dimensions so that they could be understood and manipulated.

Unfortunately, the forcing of the elements into human shapes circumscribed their powers. They became more controllable but less potent. The rule for the Magus is that when he is unsure of his ability, he should use the human or angelic forms of the elemental principles— the human when he is dealing with human things, the angelic when dealing with things of the Spirit. When he is confident of his magical ability and needs the maximum powers of the elements, he should employ the beasts.

The magical instruments—Rod, Cup, Sword, and Shield—are another ancient symbolic division of the All into four principles. These forms appear in many diverse cultures. The most common occurrence in modern times is the pips of ordinary playing cards. The hearts derive from the symbol of the Cup (Water); diamonds from the Shield (Earth); clubs from the Rod (Fire); and spades from the Sword (Air). The original forms are preserved in the Tarot, about which more will be said later.

These four instruments are used in ritual to channel the Will through a particular elemental principle and to project it to some point of desire. They work best on the outer circles of being, less well in the higher concerns of the Spirit, where concrete forms become redundant. As the Magus projects his Will through the instruments, they act like windows of stained glass, each of a single color that transmits its own wavelength of light. They are most effective when used in the imagination, called the astral world by occultists, especially when they are employed in some material concern.

It is sometimes claimed that through an act of Will the elemental forces can be used to directly affect the physical sphere—for example, to light a fire with elemental Fire alone. Such things are more often observed than attempted, and perhaps more often written about than observed. However, such claims should not be dimissed out of hand; in the infinite mind of God all things are possible.

The most accurate way to represent the elements is radially, grouping them in their natural order around a central point. This diagram best conveys the actual process of their emanation. The opposites of Fire-Water, male-female, and active-passive may be represented by interlocking triangles, which produce the six-pointed star that is the sign of the All-Father. The third element, Air, issue of the sexual union of the first two, is often designated by a circle, and this may be placed around the hexagram to show that Air is the reconciling power which makes division whole. Earth, the combination of the previous three elements and their reflection in the material world, is often represented by a square, which should surround the circle of Air.

The figure that results is a mandala, the Eastern term for a magic circle designed to precipitate a particular force into the material world. In a mandala the force is emitted from the center point, shaped by the symbols that surround the center, and then physically realized by means of the fourfold perimeter. This is why mandalas always have a center focus and are always surrounded by four, or a multiple of four. The figure below is designed to produce a true understanding of the elements:

TABLE OF PENTAGRAM

	1	2	3	4	5
Elements	Spirit	Fire	Water	Air	Earth
Magical Instruments	Lamp	Rod	Cup	Dagger	Pentacle
Colors	White	Red	Blue	Yellow	Black
Fingers	Middle	Ring	Index	Small	Thumb
Senses	Sight	Hearing	Taste	Smell	Touch
Life Forms	Man	Animal	Fish	Plant	Crystal
Emblems	Man	Lion	Eagle	Angel	Bull
Sephiroth	Tiphareth	Netzach	Hod	Yesod	Malkuth
Letters in Name of God	Shin	Yod	He (1)	Vau	He (2)
Names of God	IHVH, Eloah vaDaath	Jehovah Tzabaoth	Elohim Tzabaoth	Shaddai El Chai	Adonai haAretz
Archangels	Raphael	Haniel	Michael	Gabriel	Sandalphon
Orders of Angels	Malachim	Elohim	Beni Elohim	Kerubim	Ashim

PENTAGRAM

Five is the number of man. There are five fingers on the hand. The right hand is reflected in the left, which is its mirror opposite. A human being standing with arms and legs spread apart can with some difficulty form a perfect pentagram, the points of which touch the forehead, hands, and feet. This was accepted as profoundly significant by the Hermetic philosophers of the Middle Ages, as it served to confirm their intuited understanding that man and the pentagram are closely bound together.

The ordering of the points of the star is of some importance in practical working. It defines the structure of many rituals. The lower four points, which form a rough square, are given to the four elements and have been set in their order for thousands of years. They are emblematically depicted by the four beasts: 1) the Lion (Fire) on the lower right, 2) the Eagle (Water) on the upper right, 3) the Angel (Air) on the upper left, 4) the Bull (Earth) on the lower left. The fifth point of Spirit, or Light, emanates the four and is their origin.

Here is one way of drawing the five-pointed figure that shows the relationship of the elements. In three dimensions it is the pyramid of Egypt seen from the top. (See the diagram at the top of p. 104.)

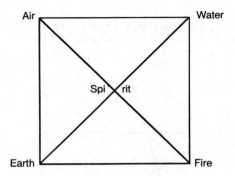

The point of Spirit is shifted from the center to the upper side of the square to signify its rule over the four elements and to emphasize that it is the point of God evident in all men and women. A figure like this is formed, which may be called the House of Man:

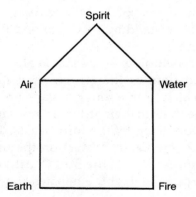

By equally spacing the points in a circle in preparation for the emanation of the sixth point from the center, the Magus achieves the pentagram. (See the diagram at the top of p. 105.)

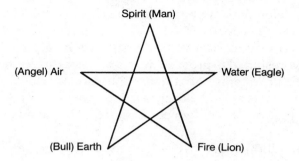

It should be pointed out that although the All manifests from the small numbers to the larger, and thus the small may be considered as closer to the Unmanifest, in magic the numbers are viewed from the perspective of the material world, and the higher numbers are assigned dominance over the lower.

The five elements in descending order of authority are Spirit, Fire, Air, Water, and Earth. This is the natural order they would assume were it possible to mix them and keep them from combining. It follows that the primary way of drawing the pentagram will adhere to this order. A single line is made from point to point and returned to its origin, forming a kind of involuted circle:

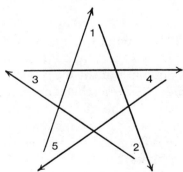

In the conventions of modern magic, the first line segment drawn toward a point of the pentagram invokes the elemental force of that point. A line drawn away from a point banishes its force. A pentagram drawn in the manner given above would be assumed by most adepts to invoke the powers of elemental Fire, since the first segment is drawn toward the point of Fire.

This results in a clumsy system, as anyone who has studied it will admit. Not all elements can be invoked from the point of Spirit. For example, Water must be invoked by drawing a line toward it from the point of Air. Yet why not start the line from the point of Earth? Because invocation is presumed to proceed in a downward direction? The line between Air and Water is horizontal, neither up nor down. The logic seems to be that it is at least closer to a downward-pointing segment than to one that points up, which is undeniable yet somehow unsatisfactory.

In this traditional system Spirit is invoked by beginning a pentagram at the Fire point and drawing the line first to the point of Air (called the active invoking pentagram of Spirit) and then by drawing a second pentagram beginning at the point of Earth and proceeding to the point of Water (called the passive invoking pentagram of Spirit). Neither of the initial segments points toward Spirit, therefore contradicting the rationale by which elements are invoked in this system. Drawing a line pointing toward Spirit is impossible since the segments from Fire to Spirit and Earth to Spirit are taken up in banishing the influences of Fire and Earth respectively.

This clumsy system is both illogical and unnecessary. Fortunately it may be readily dispensed with since it has no claim to ancient authority. Here follows an entirely new system for invoking and banishing the powers of the elements through drawing the pentagram.

1) Elemental force is to be invoked by drawing the pentagram in a clockwise direction. 2) Elemental force is banished by drawing the pentagram in a counterclockwise direction. 3) The line of the pentagram always begins and ends at the element under consideration.

These three simple rules are all that is necessary to rationalize the drawing of the pentagram. It is the circular motion of the line, mentally pictured and Willed, that calls up or banishes. It is the distinguishing of a particular point that isolates the elemental force under consideration. The new system achieves both ends elegantly and concisely. It is hoped that it will be found useful in ritual workings.

Since, as has been said before, it is naturally given to man to rule the four lower elements through his point of Spirit, the pentagram is one of the most potent universal symbols in all magic. No malefic force can penetrate its plane or its boundary when it is truly made. It can be drawn across a threshold as a barrier that few beings can break. It can be projected around the body as a protective armor against psychic or physical danger. If set in a whirling motion it becomes an offensive weapon that tears and burns.

Since the upward-pointing star exalts the Spirit, Satanists and others who use magic to subvert the natural unfolding of the universe for some imagined personal gain often invert the pentagram in their rituals. They assign the points of the inverted star to the five extremities on the head of a goat (symbol of the lower passions), which are the two horns, the two drooping ears, and the beard.

Knowing its significance, the Magus will turn in disgust from those who advocate the use of the inverted pentagram—not that it presents any danger to him, but simply because it is a deliberate attempt to befoul the Light.

Of course, not all black magicians announce their presence by the display of the inverted star. Many are hypocrites as well as perverters, and will use the signs and instruments usually associated with white magic for harmful and base purposes. The symbols of holiness are in themselves no defense against the powers of Darkness. Such symbols are mere vessels of Will and are sanctified only through use. A cup may as easily be filled with filth as with clear water.

Here is a speaking that was given to the author by an angel of Light in a dream. It is a true speaking, heard in the inner ear and recorded word for word:

"The symbols of Good when defiled and abused become the symbols of Evil."

Thus if an adept, whether through wickedness or stupidity, abused the pentagram of Spirit repeatedly, it would become useless in his hands, except to summon the powers of Darkness. Many workers of magic have been caught in this way, bound up by Evil while still thinking they dealt with the emissaries of Good.

The fifth point of the pentagram, last to emerge although it embodies the previous four, is the point that defines the nature of the figure. Without it the figure would not be a pentagram but would be something else. The point of Spirit is often represented by the flame of a lamp. In this guise it can be confused with elemental Fire. A better symbol is the spoked wheel, which suggests both the radiating and the wholeness of Spirit.

The wheel of Spirit is commonly drawn with eight spokes; but it is more accurate to represent it by a wheel with six spokes. (See the diagram at the top of p. 108.)

 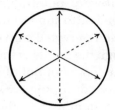

The three rays crossing at the center point of emanation represent the three primary elemental principles of Fire, Water, and Air and their opposite reactionary forces. The center is the Veil, in which the three rays are reflected and from which shines forth the radiance of Spirit. The combination of the three rays equals elemental Earth, represented by the darkness outside the circle. Thus, the wheel of Spirit suggests the radial emanation of the five elemental principles.

A three-dimensional verification of the six-spoked Spirit wheel is found in the diamond shape used to represent the tenth emanation from the All. As will be recalled, this is a pyramid of four facets with its reflection congruent to its base:

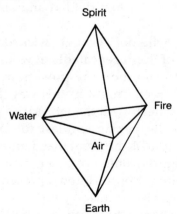

The top point is the element Spirit. From it descend the rays of Fire, Water, and Air, and these form the triangle of the base. The lower point, not directly connected to the point of Spirit, is elemental Earth. It is formed by the reunion of the reflected rays of the three primary elements. The diversifying action exhibited in the upper pyramid (unity into trinity) is inverted in the lower pyramid (trinity into unity). This is a visual metaphor for the inbreathing and outbreathing of Brahma.

When this Spirit wheel is set in the center of the mandala of the elements, a perfect expression of the unfolding of the first five emanations from the center is achieved:

The power of the pentagram may be contained and bound to a place or object by drawing a circle around it. This circle should always be drawn from the inside. The Magus must mentally unite himself with the symbol to be contained, form the circle around his transferred awareness, and then get himself out of it through the doorway that lies at its center, which is the only passage in or out of a closed circle. If this is done properly, the circle will have the power to contain.

In modern magic the pentagram is often drawn in the air through the floating line of the imagined ritual circle at the four quarters to bar the circle from any form of psychic attack. This is scarcely necessary. The circle is perfect and unbreakable. By linking it to the four pentagrams it is, if anything, weakened.

To clear a space instantly, the Magus may mentally send six pentagrams, expanding out from his center of Self, rushing along three spatial axes. This is an effective tool for banishing malefic influences. The pentagram can be cast like a flaming shield at a foe. It is inscribed on the surface of a material object to give the object a desired elemental charge. By standing with arms and legs spread the Magus can become the pentagram. Other uses of the figure will suggest themselves.

For those with advanced powers of visualization, the geometric duodecahedron (a solid formed of twelve interlocking pentagons) may be built around the Self. Magically this is an impregnable shell built upon five reflected (or ten) and six reflected (or twelve). These are two most powerful complex numbers upon which the Tarot, Kabbalah, Zodiac, and other systems are based. Pythagoras reputedly held the duodecahedron to be the most potent and perfect shape in the world.

The Tetragrammaton is expanded by the addition of the Hebrew letter Shin, which is in the shape of a lamp with three flames and magically signifies Spirit: ש.The two common forms of the Pentagrammaton are Yod-He-Shin-Vau-He (Yeheshuah) and Yod-He-Vau-Shin-He (Yehovashah). Magically the first name is given to the left hand of man and the second to the right hand. When the Magus pronounces them correctly with his hands upraised and his fingers spread to form pentagrams, the names are powerful instruments to invoke, rule, and banish spirits.

The first name suggests the point of Spirit in the center of the square of the elements. The pentagram is read counterclockwise following the order of the letters in the name:

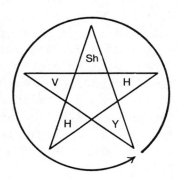

The second name is symbolic of the House of Man, where the Spirit, no longer hidden but exalted, has moved from the center to the top in preparation for the sixth emanation. Here the pentagram is read clockwise:

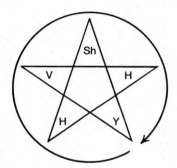

TABLE OF HEXAGRAM

	1	2	3	4	5	6
Planets	Sun	Mars	Venus	Jupiter	Saturn	Moon
Colors	Yellow	Red	Green	Orange	Blue	Purple
Motions	V Vibratory	— Linear	○ Circular	— Linear	○ Circular	V Vibratory
Elements	⊕ Spirit	△ Fire	▽ Water	△ Air	▽ Earth	● Inertia (Black Moon)
Directions	Up	South	West	North	East	Down
Senses	Sight	Hearing	Taste	Smell	Touch	Motion
Body	Head	Right Leg	Left Arm	Right Arm	Left Leg	Sexual Organs
Trees	Apple	Yew	Birch	Oak	Elm	Willow
Music	Trumpet	Drum	Guitar	Organ	Bass	Violin

HEXAGRAM

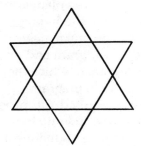 

The common hexagram is a six-pointed star formed by the intersection of two equilateral triangles, with one pointing up and the other down. The key to its understanding is balance. Opposites are expressed but do not dominate. Each extreme is held in abeyance by the other. In this sense it is similar to the cross, which also represents balanced force.

There is a second form of hexagram used in magic, called the unicursal because it can be traced with a single unbroken line. It is extracted from the common hexagram by drawing diagonal, rather than horizontal, lines between the pairs of points on the left and right sides. These diagonals intersect in the center.

The hexagram comes into being with the emanation of a sixth point from the center of the pentagram. The sixth point, which from the human perspective dominates the previous five, signifies the greater Spirit of the All, separate from man, whereas the fifth point is the Spirit given to the individual. The hexagram represents the Will of God realized and by association humanity acting in harmony with cosmic law. Of course the separation of the greater from the lesser Spirit is illusion. The eternal truth that all Spirit is one flowers forth, timeless and renewed, each time a messiah is born. But in the world of forms, the hexagram is traditionally thought of as the sign of God and the pentagram as the sign of man.

113

Kabbalistically the hexagram is the heart of Adam Kadmon, the *Microprosopos*, or Lesser Countenance. Hermetically it is the union of opposites, the mating of the Sun and Moon. In Christianity it is Jesus Christ. Magically it is linked to the seven planets of the ancients, which must not be confused with the planets of astronomy, for they are god-forms rather than material bodies.

It would be reasonable to assume that the seven planets would be most closely linked to the star of seven points, the heptagram. Traditionally this is not the case. It has been the custom in magic to assign six of the planets to the outer points of the hexagram and one to the emerging center point. Therefore, the hexagram to which the planets are assigned is on the verge of becoming the heptagram.

Under the symbol of the cross was described the process by which the perfect circle of the heavens was divided into two parts by the path of the Sun and then, to restore a balance, subdivided into four parts by the prime meridian. These divisions can be graphically presented by means of a simple grid like the one children use to play tick-tack-toe:

Quarter	Half	Quarter
Half	Whole	Half
Quarter	Half	Quarter

The whole is the fully enclosed space. The half is enclosed only on three sides. The quarter is not enclosed at all but bordered on two sides. If each pair of parallel lines in the grid were united, the result would be a cross, where the whole would be represented by the dimensionless point of intersection. The grid is a cross the center of which has been expanded to enclose a space.

It is vital that an understanding of the division of the whole into halves and quarters be attained because any grasp of the natures of the planets depends upon it. In astrology three essential figures are derived from the grid—the circle (whole), the crescent (halves), and the cross (quarters). Obtained by reason, these figures were assigned to the primary objects in the heavens most closely according with their meaning. Only two heavenly bodies have a diameter observable to the naked eye—the Sun and the Moon. All the others are merely points of light, with the exception of the Earth itself. It was inevitable that the Sun, Moon, and Earth should be given the three primary symbols.

The Sun is golden in color. Gold is the perfect metal, remaining bright and shining over centuries without decay. The orb of the Sun is a circle. Eternal and unchanging, the Sun is the giver of light, giver of warmth, giver of life. Self-sufficient, it requires nothing from outside itself. It is in all things perfect and complete, and for this reason was assigned the astrological symbol of the circle.

The Moon is silver in color. Silver is given to tarnishing quickly. When polished it is white, but when tarnished, black. The Moon is not perfect but increases and decreases, at times light on the right side, at times light on the left. Its full face is balanced by complete darkness. It gives no warmth and only so much light as it derives from the Sun. In fact, the Moon seems to require elements from outside itself since it pulls the waters of the oceans close and also draws the blood of young women. For these reasons it was given the sign of the crescent.

The Earth stands between the Moon and Sun, which seem to revolve around it. It is both fixed, in that it does not move, and changeable, as witnessed by the storms and seasons. The Earth can be warm like the Sun and also cool like the Moon. It was perceived as the meeting place where the rays from the other two bodies mingled and harmonized. For this reason the Earth was assigned the symbol of giving and taking, action and reaction, warmth and coolness—the cross.

Since man is the microcosm of the greater universe, the three primary symbols of the Sun, Moon, and Earth can be assigned to his body, resulting in this figure:

The circle of the head stands for the warmth and activity of the rational powers, which are volatile by nature. The crescent symbolizes the excretion of wastes, mainly a liquid process, and also the sensual and unthinking passions. The cross makes up the trunk of the figure, where reason and lust are joined. The vertical arm is the lightning stroke; the horizontal arm is the surface of the sea.

The remaining five heavenly bodies, which are uniformly dimensionless points of light and so form a distinct group, are understood through the combination of two or all of the three primary symbols. All meanings later assigned to them derive from this base.

Mars is the cross over the circle. In modern usage the cross has been changed to an arrow—symbol of Will that suggests the fiery aspect of the planet. It is the mixed essence of the malleable yet substantial Earth and the blazing Sun. Mars represents recklessness and force and is the symbol of conquest. Because it is an inversion of the natural order, the Earth over the Sun, it is generally malefic.

Venus is the natural opposite of Mars and is made up of the circle over the cross. The elements are the same but here the life-giving energies predominate, and Sun and Earth are in their right order. The Earth is the passive receiver of the rays of the solar orb that cause life to flourish. Venus is love in its numerous forms.

Jupiter is the crescent over the cross—again a natural order and therefore a positive symbol. But the love of Jupiter is not so selflessly given as the love of Venus, and Jupiter demands something in return. The acquisitiveness of the crescent evidences itself, making Jupiter the symbol of government and law.

Saturn is the worst aspects of the Jupiterian elements realized. The natural order is turned on its head, and the cross of Earth is exalted. Just as the cross over the circle was the driving energy of the Sun perverted for material ends, so is the chill mystique and secret power of the Moon advanced on the material level through the cross over the crescent. Saturn is the most barren and hurtful of the planets.

Mercury stands apart from the preceding four planets because it combines all three symbols of the Sun, Moon, and Earth. It is the most balanced and complete of the planets and the closest in character to man. This can be seen by comparing the sign of Mercury to the sign of the microcosm given earlier. Mercury is adaptable, at home in all circumstances, and not by accident is the symbol of magic and the Magus, as well as the magical gods Hermes and Thoth.

From these descriptions it will be readily apparent that four of the planets can be linked with the four elemental principles: Mars is the closest in nature to Fire; Venus is of the nature of Water; Jupiter has the mediating qualities of Air; and Saturn has the coldness and heaviness of Earth. Two of the planets represent the opposites of hot and cold, good and evil, etc.: the Sun is the extreme of Light; the Moon is the extreme of Shadow. The final planet, Mercury, is the balance of forces and best suited to occupy the center of the planetary hierarchy.

It is common practice in magic to assign the planets to the hexagram in this way:

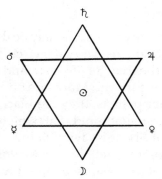

The most glaring error committed here is the placing of the Sun in the center. In magic the Sun is not the center of the solar system— the Self is the center around which all else revolves. The ancients had little problem with this idea. They automatically assumed that the Sun went around them and the Earth upon which they stood. Modern man, thanks to the indoctrination of science, may have to struggle hard to make this rather simple insight happen.

The planet nearest the Self both in distance and nature is the Earth. Since the Earth is not represented in the display of planets on the hexagram, it must be substituted for by the planet that most closely embodies its qualities. The best choice for the center is there-fore not the Sun but Mercury, symbol of balance, of magic, and of humanity.

To understand how the other planets may be logically assigned to the outer points, the Magus must see the hexagram presented in a more meaningful way:

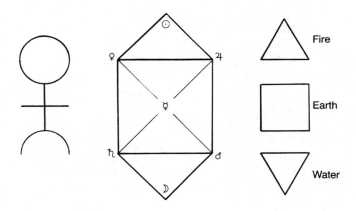

From the symbol of the microcosm may be derived a figure made up of a square and two triangles. The solar circle yields the triangle of Fire, the lunar crescent the triangle of Water, and the earthly cross the square of Earth. Since the Sun and Moon are opposites and stand as a pair apart from the other planets, they are placed at the top and the bottom. The Sun is the emanator of Light, which comes from above; the Moon is the ruler of Shadows lying below.

Mercury stands for the Self of the Magus, the center of his universe, and is placed at the balance point midway between the Sun and Moon where all forces converge and mingle. The remaining four planets are assigned to the elements at the corners of the square. Mars-Venus and Jupiter-Saturn are pairs of opposites and must be opposed to each other across the center. Mars and Jupiter are by nature masculine and should be placed on the right side of the square, as viewed from the back; Venus and Saturn are feminine and are to be placed on the left side.

This still does not solve the problem of the exact placement of the elemental planets. Should Mars, for example, be on the upper or lower right corner of the square? For the answer to this question the other form of the hexagram must be examined. The unicursal hexagram was developed in the early part of this century in an attempt to overcome the awkwardness of inscribing the common hexagram in the air during magical rituals. It can be traced continuously from start to finish in a way similar to the pentagram:

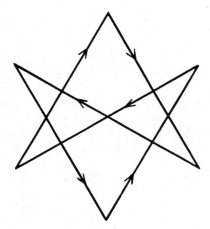

When the unicursal hexagram is analyzed, it is seen to be made up of two *Sigel* runes overlapped and joined at the top and bottom. Runes were the magical alphabet of the Teutonic peoples before the coming of Christianity. The Sigel—which means "sun"—was the rune used by the Nazi SS as their emblem: ϟϟ .

The Sigel is in the form of a lightning stroke and is a powerful symbol of creative force. It could be written right to left Ͷ as in the Old Norse alphabet or left to right Ͷ as in the Old English. If the two sides of the unicursal hexagram are separated, they will be seen as a Sigel rune and its mirror reflection. (See diagram on p. 120.)

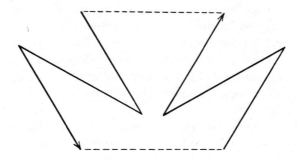

With this in mind the unicursal hexagram becomes understandable as a symbol of descending and reascending force—or in pictorial terms, the down strike of the lightning bolt and its reflection from the mirror surface of the water.

The figure of a square and two triangles given earlier is the two-dimensional version of the four-sided Egyptian pyramid reflected from its base. This may be called the three-dimensional hexagram. If the runes are thought of in three dimensions as well and rotated ninety degrees to each other, they trace with remarkable clarity the framework of the double four-sided pyramid.

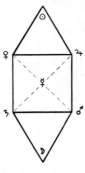

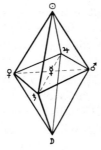

At last it becomes possible to rationally assign the four elemental planets to the points of the hexagram. The descending lightning bolt streaks from the Sun to the Moon and along its path are found the planets that contain its symbol, the circle. The reflected ascending bolt flies from the Moon back to the Sun, and on it are ordered the planets containing the Moon symbol of the crescent.

Mars, a masculine and fiery planet, will be located on the descending Sigel on the right side of the hexagram because the right is active.

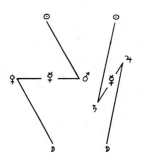

Venus, opposite of Mars, feminine and receptive in nature, will also be located on the Sun's descending Sigel, but on the left (feminine) side of the hexagram.

Jupiter belongs to the Moon's ascending Sigel because it contains the symbol of the crescent. However, it is masculine in nature and belongs on the right side of the hexagram.

Saturn is feminine and is placed on the left side of the hexagram along the ascending Sigel.

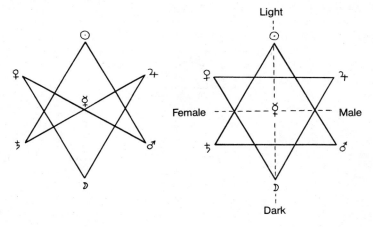

The arrangement of planets on the unicursal hexagram is the same as that on the common hexagram. The planets may be divided into a polarity of Light and Dark relating to the top and bottom of the hexagram and into a second polarity of male and female relating to the right and left sides.

The Magus will notice that this assignment of the planets to the points of the hexagram is not that which is used in modern magical practice. It must be left to his judgment whether he will blindly follow tradition or whether he will use his intelligence and intuition to study the matter for himself. The Magus should not accept the arrangement given here without question any more than he should toe the traditional line.

The numbering of the planets must be changed slightly to accord with their new positions. Traditionally the Sun, placed in the center of the hexagram, is given the number six. When the planet Mercury is moved to the center, it assumes the six. The Sun must then seek a new number. Saturn, assigned the number three under the old system, is traditionally placed at the top of the hexagram. Since the Sun is now at the apex, it is given the three, and Saturn must seek another number. The number that traditionally is given to Mercury is eight. This seems a rather heavy, square number for the winged god. However, it accords very well with the dark, cold character of Saturn. The other planets may be permitted to retain their traditional values.

In placing the numbers on the hexagram, it will be observed that the center is six, the number of the points, and that each pair of opposite numbers around the perimeter adds up to twelve, which makes an elegant and pleasing balance:

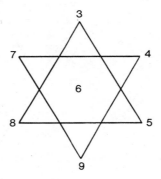

The use of the hexagram in ritual is similar to the pentagram, with the proviso that whereas the pentagram rules the elements—the natural servants of mankind—the hexagram rules the planets—god-forms of considerable potency. Although, as atheists boast, man did make the gods, he did not make them from nothing but patterned them on the invisible unformed essences that are the higher emanations of the All. Therefore, take care to use the hexagram only for noble and unselfish purposes.

Planetary forces are invoked by drawing a line of psychic fire from the planet's position on the hexagram in a clockwise direction. This line is to be repeated counterclockwise in the reflected triangle, beginning at the point directly opposite. For example, to invoke the powers of

Mars the upward-pointing triangle is drawn with the wand or index finger of the right hand in a fiery line in the air, beginning at the Mars-point and proceeding clockwise. When the first triangle has been closed, the second downward-pointing triangle is drawn, beginning with the Venus-point and proceeding counterclockwise back to its start.

The triangles are drawn in opposite directions because one is the mirror image of the other. When it is desired to summon the powers of Mars, the clockwise motion draws them forth from beyond the Veil. The following counterclockwise motion in the reflected triangle suppresses the powers of Venus, which would otherwise have a damping effect on the action of Mars.

When it is desired to banish or neutralize a planetary force, the inverse motions are used. The counterclockwise motion on the triangle of the planet in question suppresses the powers of that planet, while the clockwise motion on the reflected triangle encourages the powers in opposition to the banished planet.

The traditional method of invoking the center point of the hexagram involves drawing six separate figures. This is unacceptably cumbersome. Mercury is better invoked by drawing both the triangle of the Sun and that of the Moon clockwise, thereby calling forth their balanced forces. The invoked Sun and Moon in a single figure well represent the harmony of Mercury. Banishing is done by tracing the triangles of the Moon and then the Sun counterclockwise in the air.

The unicursal hexagram has neither a clockwise nor a counterclockwise direction of motion. When it is traced from start to finish, opposing swirls are created that cancel each other out. It can be begun or finished clockwise or counterclockwise, but its action is weak. Its use is not recommended for invoking or banishing. If a unicursal figure is needed, the heptagram should be employed.

TABLE OF HEPTAGRAM

	1	2	3	4	5	6	7
Planets	Sun	Mars	Venus	Mercury	Jupiter	Saturn	Moon
Numbers	3	5	7	6	4	8	9
Colors	Yellow	Red	Green	White	Orange	Blue	Purple
Metals	Gold	Iron	Copper	Platinum	Tin	Lead	Silver
Jewels	Topaz	Ruby	Emerald	Diamond	Jasper	Sapphire	Amethyst
Semi-precious	Ivory	Coral	Jade	Opal	Amber	Turquois	Pearl
Elements & Motions	—	◁	▷	V	◁	▽	○
Archangels	Tzaphqiel/ Ratziel	Khamael	Haniel	Raphael	Tzadqiel	Michael	Gabriel
Chakras	Crown	Brow	Throat	Heart	Solar Plexus	Bowel	Perineum
Trees	Apple	Yew	Birch	Hazel	Oak	Elm	Willow
Music	Trumpet	Drum	Guitar	Piano	Organ	Bass	Violin
Body	Head	Right Leg	Left Arm	Heart	Right Arm	Left Leg	Sexual Organs

HEPTAGRAM

 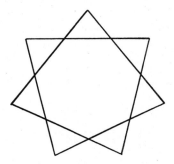

In magic that is in harmony with the Light the heptagram, or seven-pointed star, is always drawn with three points up and four down. It signifies the divine trinity exalted over the material quaternary. Whereas in the hexagram this rule is implied, in the heptagram it is expressed. In the hexagram a tension is created between the artificially separated point of the Spirit of man and the point of the Spirit of God—in the heptagram the tension is resolved, for the Spirits of man and God are reconciled and united in the higher trinity.

There are two unicursal forms of the heptagram. In the more common form the line is reflected from every third point. This results in a star with very sharp points. In the alternate form the line is reflected from every second point. The second form has blunter points and a more open center. The common heptagram is more often used in magic. The alternate form is sometimes used when space is needed in the center of the star for writing words or symbols. If the heptagram were drawn on the ground or floor to act as a ritual circle, the second form would be used.

As is true of all symbols, the heptagram can only be comprehended by regarding it from a higher level, which is the as yet unmanifested eighth point of its center. This point reveals the dynamic balance between the three of heaven and the four of Earth. The heptagram is not static but moving, a symbol of the conquest and victory of the flame of Spirit over the dull clay of the flesh. It is an apt symbol for the Crusades, and indeed it may be written as a triangle over a cross, action overcoming inertia, which can be stylized into a flaming sword:

When inverted, the heptagram becomes a most articulate symbol for the perversion of nature. Drawn as four points over three, it is the weight of fleshy needs and desires making a slave out of the divine Light, which should always be their master. Whereas the inverted pentagram signifies the perversion of man, the inverted heptagram is the perversion of God.

In magic the heptagram is used to link the powers of the planets to the Earth, or in other words, to the body of man. Man set at the center of the hexagram exalts himself when he takes the heavenly shape of Mercury and rises up among the stars. In the heptagram Mercury moves to the outer circle with the rest of the planets, and the center is occupied with the sign for the Earth, of which substance man is formed.

The ordering of the planets around the heptagram is determined in part by the order of the days of the week:

Wednesday (Mercurii dies) ....Mercury
Thursday (Jovis dies) ....Jupiter
Friday (Veneris dies) ....Venus
Saturday (Saturnus dies) ....Saturn
Sunday (Solis dies) ....Sun
Monday (Lunae dies) ....Moon
Tuesday (Martis dies) ....Mars

Some of the correspondences are obvious—Sun for Sunday, Moon for Monday, Saturn for Saturday—others are less apparent.This is because many of the old gods are no longer well known. Tuesday is named after the Teutonic war god Tiw, the nearest equivalent in the pagan hierarchy to Mars. Wednesday is named after Woden, the Germanic form of the Scandinavian god Odin, who is the northern divine magician, or Mercury. Thursday is named for Thor, who is associated with Jupiter, or Jove, because he hurls thunderbolts. Friday is named for Frija, a Teutonic mother goddess whose name means "beloved," and is linked with Venus.

The heptagram is drawn in one continuous line crossing from point to point. Mercury is placed at the uppermost point, and as the figure is drawn clockwise, the rest of the planets follow in the order of the days:

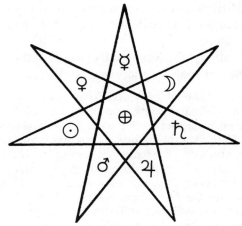

Notice that if a clockwise circle is drawn around the outside of the heptagram from point to point, the planets fall into their traditional order as determined by their apparent speed of motion: Saturn, Jupiter, Mars, Sun, Venus, Mercury, Moon. Also, beginning with androgynous Mercury the planets alternate polarity: lunar (♃), solar (♀), lunar (♄), solar (☉), lunar (☽), solar (♂).

Any planet may be invoked by drawing the heptagram clockwise, starting and ending at the point of the planet and banished by drawing the heptagram counterclockwise, also beginning and ending at the planet. The heptagram is more useful for physical magic than the hexagram because the heptagram is dynamic and active, whereas the hexagram is balanced and to some extent static.

Traditionally the magic under a particular planet was done in the hour and day of that planet—works of destruction were undertaken, if possible, on Tuesday; works of love, on Friday. This is an unnecessary restriction of the powers of the Magus. All planetary forces are equally effective at all times. If one *believes* the position of a planet (the physical representative of the planetary god-form) regulates its powers, that belief causes the planet's magic to be more potent when the planet is in a particular heavenly position. For example, a planet at the zenith of the heavens, or rising above the horizon, or in a particular sign of the Zodiac is considered more powerful than at other times.

The belief that the planets are allotted certain days of the week in which to act is a degeneration of the ancient belief that there was an astrological correspondence between the physical planets and the planetary gods. Both views are false. All power stems from the mind of the Magus, and this power is everywhere and always the same. This truth will not be acceptable to many people, but let the fools be foolish and the wise be wise.

The truth was always understood by adepts of the highest kind. It is stated in the ancient magical manuscript of *Abramelin the Mage*:

> Whenever ye shall see tables which do mark the days and their differences, the Celestial Signs, and other like matters, pay no attention thereto, because herein is a very great sin hidden, and a deceit of the Demon; it being one of his many methods of endeavouring to confound the True Wisdom of the Lord with evil matters. Because this True Wisdom of the Lord can operate and perform its effects every day, and at any moment and second. The Gates of His Grace are daily open, He wisheth, and it is pleasing unto Him to aid us, as well on this day as on the morrow; and in no way could it be true that He desireth to be subjected to the day and hour which men would wish to prescribe for Him; seeing that He is the Master to elect such days as He Himself wisheth, and also may they be sanctified![5]

In the human body, the microcosm, the planetary forces are represented by seven imaginary centers located along the axis of the spine. In the East these centers are called chakras. They are found at the crown of the head, on the brow between and slightly above the eyes, at the pit of the throat, in the center of the chest near the heart, at the solar plexus, in the pit of the stomach just below the navel, and at the perineum.

Depending on which of these centers the Magus chooses to consider as his point of Self, his personal universe will be colored and influenced by a certain bias of forces. None of the chakras is the true point of Self—or rather, all lie within the Self and exist at different circles of being. Through the intellectual trick of spreading the chakras along the spinal column, the Magus is able to experience each as a separate essence, rather than mingled together as is usually the case.

Since the perceived body is an illusion created by the Self—and the Self is All—once he has learned the method, the Magus may effortlessly shift his point of view anywhere within his body. This is just what modern man has done in believing his awareness resides in his head. The ancients believed the soul lay in the liver. In Tibet the unenlightened believe the point of awareness rests in the heart. All opinions are correct, all are incomplete. The Self exists throughout all perceived forms, for it can know nothing beyond what it is.

It may help to understand the chakras by relating them graphically to the Sephiroth of the Kabbalistic Tree of Life. The Tree is made up of ten Sephiroth, or emanations of the Unmanifest, arranged in three columns. If the columns are united, the right and left being drawn together to overlap in the center, the result is seven spheres of reality that correspond to the seven chakras along the spine:

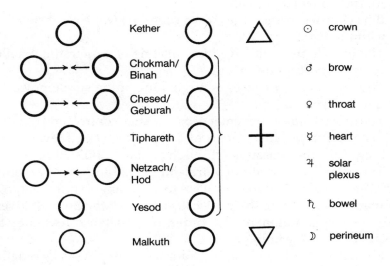

Provided they are legitimate, such relationships are useful because the knowledge gained through one system can supplement that gained by another and result in a strengthening of both.

It will be observed that the relationship of the planets to the Sephiroth differs from that given in the chapter on the decagram. The reason is that here the potentials of the planets are considered linearly, and under the decagram they are examined radially. Neither system is absolute. Both derive meaning from their context.

The planets are placed in order by their attraction to the polarities of male-female and Light-Shadow. The Sun is the extreme of the masculine and the radiant. It is set at the top. Closest under it is placed the masculine-active planet of the Sun, Mars. Next is placed the feminine-passive planet of the Sun, Venus. At the lower end of the axis the Moon represents the pole of the feminine and the dark. Closest to it is put the feminine-passive planet of the Moon, Saturn. Farther away is placed the masculine-active planet of the Moon, Jupiter. Mercury, the planet of balance, occupies the center.

By mentally entering any of the chakras, the Magus can experience the essence of the related planet with his senses from inside the planet. In effect, the white Light of his Spirit is refracted through a filter colored with the nature of the planetary being. Each chakra is a filter of a different color corresponding to the planet and the Sephiroth or Sephirah to which it relates.

If he chooses to enter the crown center he will feel himself to be one with the Light.

The brow center will give him a feeling of penetrating intellect and clarity of perception.

The throat center causes a burgeoning of the subtle powers of intuition and symbolism.

The heart chakra is the center of balance that controls and regulates the positive and negative forces of the perceived Self, even as the heart regulates the sensations through its rate of pulsation.

The solar plexus center controls the breathing of, and the nervous impulses within, the body. It is a focus for ingoing and outgoing information concerning the physical running of the body. It gives a sense of control, judgment, and order, physically expressed by the regularity of the breathing cycle.

From the bowel, or pit of the stomach, arises physical strength; a fact well known to all athletes, especially wrestlers and weight lifters. It is the furnace where matter is consumed for fuel. Its center yields a perception of dullness and heaviness, but also one of slow, inexorable strength that might be likened to the grinding of a great gear.

At the perineum reside the organs of sensual gratification and excretion. To enter this center is to experience the true meaning of lust, need, pain, and pleasure. It is dark and deep. The thought process is utterly alien to it.

To enter one of the seven chakras, mentally extend three rays from that center into the three dimensions of space. Each of these rays should be colored one of the three primaries—red, blue, and yellow. For example, if you are standing, the red ray should be extended from the chosen chakra up through the top of the head and down between the legs. The blue ray should be extended horizontally out the sides of the body from the chakra. The yellow ray should be extended horizontally through the front and back of the body. All three rays should intersect at right angles to each other.

Mentally enter the point where the rays intersect, which should be visualized as a small ball of white light. Visualize the world from the perspective of that point. Look back upon your brain as though observing it from the outside. Next, gradually let the white ball assume the color of the chakra's related planet while you imagine the entire universe slowly whirling around your new center of awareness.

This is a difficult exercise requiring great powers of visualization. The entry of the awareness into one of the seven chakras is something that must be learned—it cannot be taught, anymore than a person can be taught to ride a bicycle. Success will be heralded by a sense of vertigo and the impression that the stars revolve around the chakra that has been entered.

TABLE OF OCTAGRAM

	1	2	3	4	5	6	7	8
Planets	Sun	Mars	Venus	Mercury	Jupiter	Saturn	Moon	Earth
Colors	Yellow	Red	Green	White	Orange	Blue	Purple	Black
Nature	Flame	Explosion	Bubbles (Sea Foam)	Wind	Embers	Mud	Sea	Clay
Life Forms	Man	Carnivores	Herbivores	Birds	Reptiles	Amphibians	Fish	Insects
Music	Do	Ti	La	Sol	Fa	Mi	Re	Do

OCTAGRAM

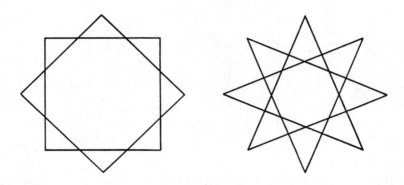

The common octagram is formed of two overlapping squares with a common center point, one square rotated forty-five degrees on the other. It is drawn with two separate lines, a distinction it shares with the common hexagram, and indeed the octagram has some similarities to the six-pointed star. The hexagram illustrates a duality of trines, the heavenly trinity balanced by its reflection. The octagram shows duality of fours, materiality reflecting materiality. The octagram is a symbol of the dense and solid.

There is a unicursal form of the octagram, shown above on the right. The two forms have the same base. A square is brought into being by opening the intersection point of a cross. This results in the grid of nine chambers mentioned in the discussion on the hexagram:

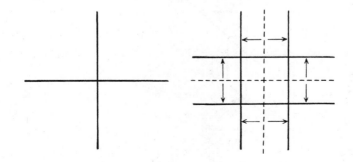

If a second grid is placed over the first and rotated forty-five degrees, the two forms of the octagram may easily be drawn from the resulting figure:

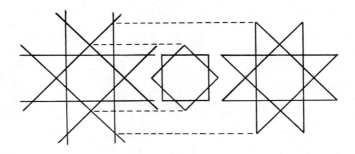

In three dimensions the balanced octagram is best represented by the cube, which has eight points of intersection and is in all dimensions regular. The cubic shape is used for the ritual altar upon which the four magical instruments are placed. The altar is the point in the center of the magic circle where force is focused and manifested. The cube is the ultimate symbol of matter, as the square is of form. With an intuitive understanding of this fact, occultists often place a piece of stone inside their altar or even form the altar itself entirely of stone, as was done in ancient times.

When the parallel sides of the cube are united, the three reciprocating rays that define the point of Self in relation to the universe emerge:

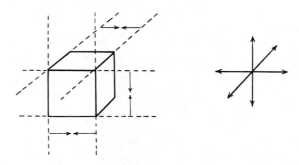

The essential duality in creation is action-reception. The two squares in the octagram are therefore the squares of active materiality and receptive materiality. When they are drawn of equal size, it signifies that the active and receptive aspects are balanced. The octagram is often drawn with two points uppermost to emphasize this balance.

In magical working it may, however, be useful to emphasize one side of the fourfold duality above the other. This can be done in different ways. One of the squares of the common octagram can be made large and the other small so that the large square encloses the smaller. The active side of matter can be indicated by a square with one corner uppermost so that it forms a diamond shape to suggest cutting and piercing. Passive materiality can be suggested by a square with vertical and horizontal sides.

These two forms can be found in Abyssinian amulets, Apache beadwork, Moroccan metalwork and embroidery, and in the art of many other cultures:

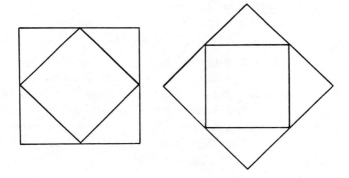

If the square encloses the diamond, it represents the hidden life force that lies sleeping in inanimate stone and metal. The diamond in the square is a symbol of the natural order. It is the spark of life in the embryo receiving its form within the nurturing walls of the womb. It is usually a female symbol—for example, it appears in the Cross of Uri, who is the Hawaiian female force of creation.

Inverted, with the square inside the diamond, the unbalanced octagram becomes a fearful symbol of animism, of walking trees and speaking winds. This is the symbol of Pandora's box opened and Solomon's brass bottle shattered. Most commonly regarded as a male symbol, it is used to represent the face of God.

In three dimensions one side of the octagram may be emphasized by the use of the truncated four-sided pyramid:

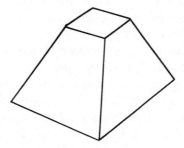

This elevates one of the squares to heaven, signifying that it is active. The sloping sides of the pyramid suggest the disposition of the currents of power that flow upward, due to the prayers of men, to the point in the air where the sides converge, then back down the center axis from the invisible gods.

The Aztecs used the truncated pyramid to perform their human sacrifices upon in the belief that the blood-force liberated there would reflux down to their cultural works. They did not understand that this force was of the Darkness, and it ultimately destroyed them; for when the Spanish conquistadors came, the Aztecs had no will to resist.

Since the dawn of history works of magic have been performed on high places. Altars and sacred groves can still be found on some hills in Europe, and churches were often constructed on the elevated sites of older temples. Mountains were revered as homes of the gods. Those seeking illumination climbed to the tops of peaks. The dead were buried under raised mounds.

All these diverse practices confirm an intuited grasp of the symbolic flow of forces along the sides of the truncated pyramid. Though its use has been forgotten, its power has not diminished. The truncated pyramid may still be used for magic today. It is an excellent place of meditation, prayer, and even ritual working. When the Magus cannot afford to travel to an existing pyramid (no doubt the common case), the pyramid can be created on the mental circle, and the floor of the ritual chamber imagined as the square apex. Alternately, any high place whose four sides converge can be used, even a modern architectural structure.

Another use for the octagram is in warding off the Evil Eye. Since it is based on two expanded crosses, it is an excellent symbol for deflecting psychic force. Moroccan artists sometimes emphasize the origin of the octagram by first painting two crosses and then painting over them the double square. In this way the crosses are physically embodied in the charm, although partially hidden under the second layer of paint.

The octagram has also been used as a devil trap to protect the home or other property against the hidden invasion of demonic forces. Upon looking at the octagram, the demons are believed to become transfixed and bound up in the eight-sided center of the symbol. For this purpose, however, a spiral such as that used by the ancient Babylonians is more effective.

TABLE OF NONAGRAM

	Family	Emotions	Occupations	People	Gods	Muses
1	CC	Devotion	Soldier	Gordon Liddy	Horus	Clio
2	CF	Exuberance	Athlete	John Glenn	Apollo	Terpsichore
3	FC	Spite	Bully	Richard Nixon	Thor	Thalia
4	FF	Confidence	Ruler	Franklin Delano Roosevelt	Jove	Calliope
5	FM	Contemplation	Priest	Henry David Thoreau	Hermes	Euterpe
6	MF	Arrogance	Feminist	Jane Fonda	Diana	Melpomene
7	MM	Caring	Nurse	Mother Theresa	Hathor	Polyhymnia
8	MC	Yearning	Whore	Marilyn Monroe	Venus	Erato
9	CM	Determination	Scholar	Albert Einstein	Thoth	Urania

NONAGRAM

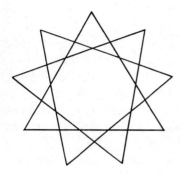 

Like the hexagram and octagram, the nonagram has two forms. The common nonagram is made up of three overlapping equilateral triangles rotated so that their nine points are equally spaced. A unicursal nonagram can be drawn with a single unbroken line reflecting from every fourth point.

Although it conveys a unique meaning all its own, the nonagram is also a composite symbol that extends the concept begun with the triangle and continued in the hexagram. The triangle is a symbol of the perfect trinity of emanations from the Unmanifest. In the hexagram this trinity is made polar, and a dynamic tension and interaction established. In the nonagram this conflict of opposite trines is resolved by the introduction of a third triplicity, and the tension changed into harmony.

By breaking each element of the first trinity into a lesser trinity, the idea of circles within circles and worlds within worlds is conveyed. In the occult, usually the ninefold division is as far as this understanding is carried. For example, Rosicrucians postulate a threefold division of man into body, mind, and spirit and then extend this triple division to each of the three levels. This results in nine aspects of man that are reflected in the macrocosm.

The Magus will perceive that when one sets out to divide the All, there is no reason to stop with a ninefold division. Kabbalists also divide creation into nine emanations that are materially embodied in the tenth. The tenth emanation then becomes the first on a lower plane of being. There are four of these planes, or worlds. But they further subdivide each of the emanations into ten and say there is no reason to stop with a division of 400 except the limitations of the human mind.

A great virtue of the Kabbalah is that it presents each emanation as possessed of its own unique nature and personality—as a living thing, not merely an abstraction or a multiplication of something else. Each book is only a collection of letters that have been repeated and rearranged, yet each has its own unique identity, which is by far the most important thing about it. So it is with compound symbols. When numbers are spoken of as multiples of lesser numbers, do not regard this as their essence but only as a tool to help reveal their inner natures.

Consider the trinity as a family. The Father-Father aspect would be wholly authoritarian. His element would be Fire of Fire, his instrument the Rod of Rods, and his action the ray of rays. On the earthly level he might be represented by Augustus Caesar.

The Father-Mother aspect would still be male in its ground quality, but its coloring would be female. Its element would be Water of Fire, and its instrument the Cup of Rods—the scepter drowned. It would be compassionate and nurturing and given to attempting to control through manipulating the emotions of the ones ruled "for their own good." This is the Pope-figure. Such men make well-meaning but bad kings. James I of England was one such.

The Father-Son aspect is revealed in the conqueror. His element would be Air of Fire—an explosive mixture—and his instrument the Sword of Rods—spear of war. This aspect combines the will to rule with the energy to conquer. Its weakness is an immaturity that may lead to rash acts. On the human level it is Alexander the Great.

The Sephiroth of the Kabbalistic Tree of Life illustrate graphically this three-times-three division and also show that the second and third trines are reflections of the first perfect trinity. Notice in the illustration on p. 141 that the trines are reflected vertically (top to bottom) and horizontally (left to right). This is confirmed by the numbering of the Sephiroth. On the outer pillars between the first and second trine, odd numbers remain odd and even remain even, but between the second and third trine, the odd and even numbers are reversed.

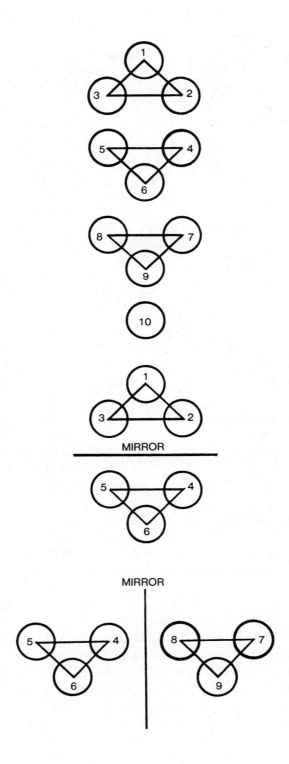

MIRROR

MIRROR

Another useful way of drawing the nonagram is in the form of three interlocking triangles descending in a chain:

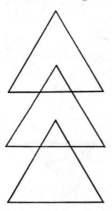

This figure is very common in magic. It is a way of saying that since the trinity is perfect, the next emanation following it must begin something entirely new at the center, which is the point of all origins.

The Greeks personalized this ninefold division of the universe into the Muses, who were nymphs assigned to the nine classes of letters—tragedy, comedy, epic poetry, lyric poetry, and so on. Originally there were only three Muses—Mneme, Melete, and Aoide. As Greek understanding developed it was found necessary to make a further threefold subdivision into nine, which retained the perfect wholeness of the trinity.

The Magus should find little difficulty in assigning powers to the points of the nonagram. Some possible correspondences are given in the table that accompanies this chapter. The powers are invoked by drawing the unicursal nonagram in the air with the right index finger or ritual instrument beginning at the appropriate point and proceeding in a clockwise direction. A symbol of the force invoked should then be drawn in the center of the nonagram.

In the central figure on p. 143 is given the nature of each of the nine points based on the trinity of Father-Mother-Child.

The direction of unfolding is clockwise. The unmixed qualities are placed 120 degrees from each other. They are joined by two rays to their mixed essences: for example, the Father-Father aspect is linked by rays (moving in a clockwise direction) to Father-Mother and

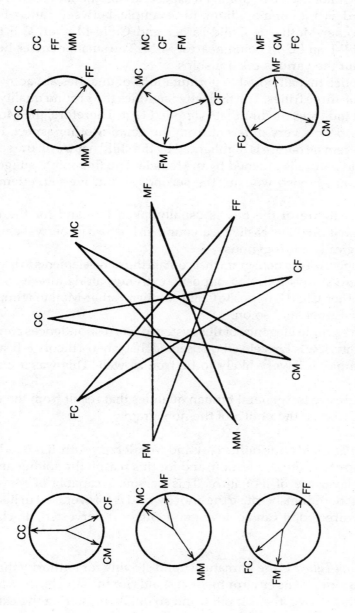

Father-Child. Each two unmixed aspects are blended together, using the third as a joining medium: for example, between Father-Father and Mother-Mother is Child-Father and Child-Mother, C-F being nearest F-F and C-M being nearest M-M. The smaller circles help to point out the various relationships.

Notice that all possible permutations of qualities are accounted for in the three trines. The first letter signifies the ground quality. The second indicates the tint that is applied to it. Therefore, the Mother-Child aspect is very different from the Child-Mother aspect. In the first the female nature is highlighted by the child nature; in the second the child nature is touched by the female. The first might suggest an impetuous, boyish woman; the second, an introverted, effeminate boy.

The figure of the boy is usually taken to stand for the child, although it might as easily be a young girl before puberty—children are magically androgynous.

Aspects of the nonagram that contain the same elements in inverted order are always found at opposite extremes along a reciprocating ray. Mother-Child is opposite Child-Mother; Father-Mother is opposite Mother-Father, and so on.

The simple elegance of this system of correspondences confirms its validity. It was Einstein who observed that when a theory is beautiful and simple, it is very likely to be true as well. This was a magical insight.

Here are the general human qualities that result from the meeting of forces at the points of the nonagram:

Child-Child is the perfect joy and wonder of youth. It is obedience to authority without question, and for this reason the soldier and the team player are of its nature. This person is capable of repetition without boredom, because the entire world is forever new in his eyes. If well directed, it can achieve good ends—if perverted, it achieves evil.

Child-Father is the immature mind striving for authority through the mastering of its environment. It stands for the athlete, the acrobat, the racing driver, the test pilot, and so on. By mastering the external world the internal world is also mastered.

Father-Child is the mature masculine mind perverted with the willfulness and selfishness of the child. There is great energy here, but it is expended in ill-considered ways. Dictators and boy-conquerors in all walks of life are of this nature. They can grasp but they cannot hold.

Father-Father is the perfect ruler. It is King Arthur of Camelot and Jove on Mount Olympus. Its personal qualities are eloquence, judgment, and keen insight into the hearts and minds of men.

Father-Mother is the priest and homosexual. Here the masculine and feminine conflict and create tension. The masculine is marginally dominant. This inner conflict often causes impotence. Nonetheless, this mixing of the strength and courage of the masculine with the sacrifice and caring of the feminine can be immensely powerful. This is the nature of saints and martyrs.

Mother-Father is the feminist or lesbian—the inwardly or outwardly masculine female. The tension between these two aspects creates anger and frustration that can turn into hatred. There is also much confusion. However, when the polarities are favorably balanced great individuals result, such as Joan of Arc, in whose breast the power to command combined with the love of her people and the willingness to sacrifice.

Mother-Mother is the perfect nurturer and protector. It is Florence Nightingale on the human level, the Earth Mother on the level of the gods. Its qualities are unselfishness, love, and sharing. It finds fulfillment in sacrifice for others.

Mother-Child is the mature feminine mind perverted by the willfulness and selfishness of the child. The feminine virtues of love and caring become lust and greed. There is no ability here to learn from mistakes, which makes pain and suffering inevitable.

Child-Mother is the immature mind striving for authority through mastering the inner world. It is the scholar, the scientist, the magician, and anyone who seeks power by shaping his own mind. In mastering the inner world the outer world is mastered also.

In practical working these general descriptions should be applied to known gods and goddesses, who can then be invoked through the points of the nonagram. They are also useful when creating unique god-forms with desirable qualities. Human beings can be separated into one of the catagories and magically acted upon through the appropriate point of the nonagram. Other uses will suggest themselves to the Magus.

DECAGRAM

The decagram can be drawn in two ways. The common decagram is made of two interlocking pentagrams, one pointing up and the other down. It accords with the structure of the Kabbalistic Tree of Life, which has an upper and lower division into five and five. It also has correspondence with the bilateral symmetry of the body, particularly the human hand and its reflection. The unicursal decagram is drawn with a single line and is used for invoking and banishing the powers represented by the points, as well as for forming the ritual circle.

It might be supposed that the number ten would have a deep significance for mankind in view of the makeup of the human body. This is indeed the case. Kabbalists look upon ten as the least possible number of emanations between the visible world and the unknowable All. They go farther than this and believe that only a tenfold division of the emanations is possible, saying "ten and not nine, ten and not eleven."[6]

This tenfold division is self-evident only from the perspective of the human mind. A starfish might very well perceive five emanations, and an octopus, eight. However, from the human standpoint only ten emanations are reasonable.

The Tree of Life of the Kabbalah, which has been mentioned many times previously, is a useful figure for separating the ten

TABLE OF DECAGRAM

	Sephiroth	Names of God	Archangels	Orders of Angels	Heaven	Color	Symbol	Beasts
1	Kether	Eheieh	Metatron	Chaioth haQadesh	North Star	Clear	Point	Phoenix
2	Chokmah	Jah	Ratziel	Auphanim	Zodiac	Tint	Line	Dragon
	Daath	IHVH			☉	Yellow	Swastika	Gryphon
3	Binah	Elohim	Tzaphkiel	Aralim	Houses	Shade	Triangle	Mare
4	Chesed	El	Tzadkiel	Chasmalim	♃	Orange	Square	Elephant
5	Geburah	Elohim Gebor	Khamael	Saraphim	♂	Red	Pentagram	Manticore
6	Tiphareth	Eloah vaDaath	Raphael	Malachim	☿	White	Hexagram	Sphinx
7	Netzach	IHVH Tzabaoth	Haniel	Elohim	♀	Green	Heptagram	Unicorn
8	Hod	Elohim Tzabaoth	Michael	Beni Elohim	♄	Blue	Octagram	Peacock
9	Yesod	Shaddai El Chai	Gabriel	Kerubim	☽	Purple	Nonagram	Kraken
10	Malkuth	Adonai haAretz	Sandalphon	Ashim	⊕	Black	Decagram	Aurochs

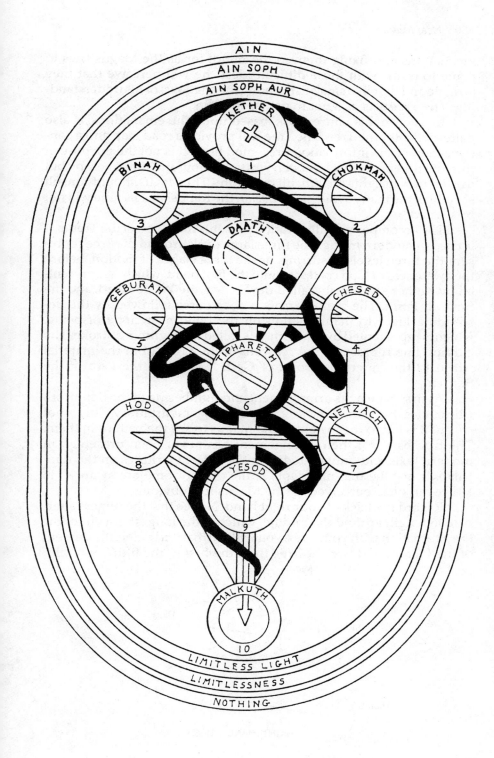

emanations and fixing them in the mind; for as the Magus tries to come to terms with these difficult ideas, he will perceive that they wriggle and dart like small fish among the shadows of his understanding. The Tree acts as a net to gather them in.

In a sense this entire work, based upon the emanations, is also patterned after the Tree. The Tree will provide a road map and a condensation of the information presented here. It is not the purpose of this text to repeat what has been written a thousand times before, but to offer new insights on difficult questions. The Magus should consult several of the many available books on the Kabbalah. His time will not be wasted.

The accompanying illustration presents the glyph of the Tree as it is used in modern magic. The three large ovals around the Tree represent the three levels of stirring, or the three stages of motion, before the awareness of God coalesced into the first point, which is represented by Kether—variously called the Crown, the White Head, and the Smooth Point. The zigzag arrow is the course followed by the descending Light to manifestation on the outermost circle of being, which is represented by Malkuth. It is called the Lightning Stroke. The curving line represents the reascent of the Light from the material world to the innermost point of God. It is called the Path of the Serpent.

At first glance the arrangement and numbering of the Sephiroth (the circles that stand for the emanations) seems arbitrary. This is not so, but it is left to the insight of the Magus to see the pattern in them. The true basis for their arrangement has never been presented in modern texts and only hinted at in the ancient writings on the Kabbalah. It may be that no adepts at the present time are aware of it. However, once perceived by the Magus it is obvious.

Regard the back of your right hand. Notice that the fingers alternate in length around the middle, which is the longest. If you follow the alternation with your eyes, you will see that it parallels the descent of the Lightning down the Tree from the first to the fifth Sephirah:

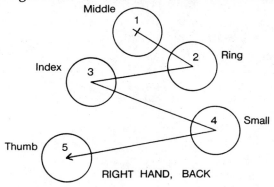

As the Lightning Stroke passes through the sixth Sephirah, Tiphareth, the numbering reverses itself from left to right: that is to say, whereas on the upper half of the Tree the even numbers are on the right side, on the lower half the even numbers are on the left, having been polarized by their passage through Tiphareth.

Hold your right palm over the still waters of a pool or before a mirror, even as the mystics of the Kabbalah must have done in ancient times. You will see the back of your right hand and, reflected in the water, its mirror image. This reflection is also present in imperfect material guise in the palm of the left hand, which because of the bilateral symmetry of the human body is the mirror image, approximately, of the right.

Here is the pattern of the fingers on the palm of the left hand:

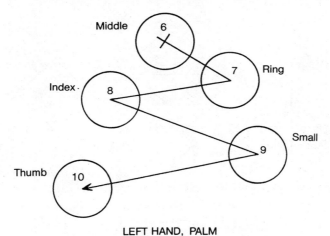

LEFT HAND, PALM

It will be observed that the numbering of the Tree accords with the shape of the reflected right hand, the single deviation being the vertical alignment of the ninth and tenth Sephiroth, Yesod and Malkuth. Why the ninth and tenth Sephiroth have been aligned on the Tree is not explained. Perhaps it was thought necessary to emphasize that all nine of the preceding emanations take on material substance in the tenth, which is thus symbolically the root of the Tree embedded in the earth. Or perhaps it was a device to conceal the seemingly obvious correspondence between the hands and the Tree; if so, it was remarkably effective.

With his left hand the Magus can approximate the lower half of the Tree, if he wishes, by crossing the little finger over the thumb.

When the Magus understands the physical origin of the Tree, correspondences can be made that would otherwise not be apparent. The link between a Sephirah on the upper half of the Tree and its mirror reflection on the lower half is seen to be stronger than is commonly thought. The twofold division of the Tree, which is little spoken or written of, is revealed to be at least equal in importance with the other more accepted divisions—the three vertical pillars, the three triangles, and the diagonal opposites:

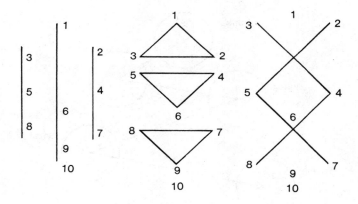

On a practical level the powerful magical symbolism of the Kabbalah is literally placed at the fingertips of the Magus. By relating the powers, angels, demons, and names of God of each Sephirah to one of his fingers, the Magus can make his hands into a temple of the Art. Ritual finger magic, so often hinted at in magical texts but never expounded upon, is given a rational basis.

Although the Tree is the most common arrangement of the Sephiroth, it does not adequately show that all emanations stem from the single point of the center. For this understanding, the Magus must consider a radial model of the emanations. (See diagram on p. 153.)

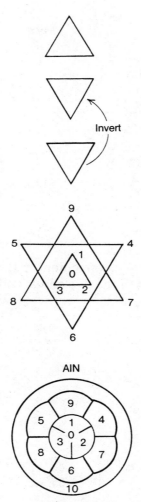

AIN

The Light is the center, and from it go out like the opening petals of a flower the descending levels of emanation. Although the Ain, which is the Unmanifest, is shown outside the rose of emanation it might as easily be drawn in the center of the figure, since it is everywhere and nowhere, separate from creation and yet mingled with it. The Ain is not bordered, since it has no limitation.

The Sephiroth can best be related to the decagram by using the upward-pointing pentagram of the common decagram to stand for the right hand and the downward-pointing pentagram to stand for its double reflection. The Sephiroth are transferred from the fingers to the points of the two pentagrams. They can then be related directly to the unicursal decagram for magical ritual working. (See p. 154.)

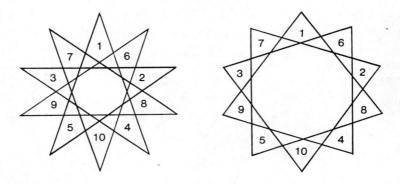

This yields the same arrangement that would result from an interlacing of the fingers of the two hands with the left palm up and the right palm down:

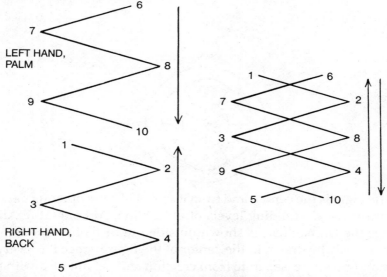

The numbering of the points on the downward-pointing pentagram indicates that the lower five Sephiroth have been reflected both top to bottom and left to right. If the two hands are brought together palm to palm and then opened out from each other so that only the tips of the middle fingers touch, this reflects the Sephiroth top to bottom. If the left is further pivoted so that its palm faces upward, this reflects them left to right. The numbering of the left hand then proceeds from the thumb, which is numbered six, to the middle finger, numbered ten. The odd numbers are placed on the left side, the even on the right—opposite to the upright numbering.

Notice that the points opposite each other on the decagram add up to eleven. This is also true of the Tree of Life—the first and last Sephiroth add up to eleven and so do the second and second-to-last, and so on. It might be wondered why the sum of opposites is eleven and not ten. Mystically this is because the Tree represents, not a perfect harmony, but perfection coupled with its reflection.

By Kabbalistic addition $11 = 1+1 = 2$. Two is the number of polarity and division. That each pair of opposites on the Tree adds up to eleven clearly points to the Tree's composite nature. The Tree is two parts—a heavenly 3x3 embodied by an earthly 1, which is the first Sephirah on the next lower circle of being and which holds within it all other Sephiroth of that world.

In the radial diagram of the Tree, the enclosing Malkuth becomes the center from which stems the next unfolding series of emanations. It is said that certain seeds contain within them an exact miniature of the adult tree they will become. As above, so below—the mysteries are multiplied endlessly in nature.

TABLE OF HENDECAGRAM

	Demon	Function	Substance	Disorder
1	Baphomet	Idolatry	Semen	Delirium
2	Behemoth	Blasphemy	Gas	Hysteria
3	Lucifuge	Pride	Mucus	Narcissism
4	Leviathan	Envy	Pus	Paranoia
5	Zephas	Anger	Adrenalin	Mania
6	Belphegor	Sloth	Bile	Depression
7	Astaroth	Greed	Saliva	Kleptomania
8	Beelzebub	Gluttony	Vomit	Bulimia
9	Asmodeus	Lust	Urine	Satyriasis
10	Lilith	Fornication	Excrement	Nymphomania
11	Abbadon	Soul Death	Putrefaction	Catatonia

HENDECAGRAM

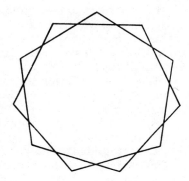

The hendecagram is a star of eleven points. It has two unicursal forms. In the first its line reflects from every fourth point and in the second, from every second point. Both types of reflection suggest aspects of its nature—2 = duality; 4 = materiality. The second, more open form is used when symbols must be written in the center or when the hendecagram serves as a magic circle.

Usually the hendecagram is thought of as symbolizing the relationship 10 + 1 = 11—the number of the complete evolution of emanations plus this rational universe's dark reflection, the dwelling place of perversity and madness. This interpretation is supported by the division of the points into 5 + 6—the number of man exalted and therefore ruling over the number of God, a most unhealthy situation. Yet this is the condition of the modern scientific and industrial society. Man has set himself over God, changing the land, polluting the oceans, and exterminating animal species. The hendecagram might be said to be the symbol of modern times.

Perhaps the most useful numerical division for understanding what the hendecagram means is 9 + 2 = 11. This can also be written 3 + 4 + 4 = 11, which gives a different emphasis. Both equations show the trinity manifesting on the physical circle as duality. Creation is seen as a hostile balance of Good and Evil. This is the world viewed through the eyes of the Persian mystic Zoroaster, who saw it as the

157

divided kingdom of Ahura Mazda (Ormazd) and Angra Mainyu (Ahriman), two equally powerful and independent gods. Zoroaster has Ahura Mazda say:

> I have created a universe where none existed; if I had not made it the entire world would have gone towards the Airjana-Vaeja.
>
> In opposition to this world, which is all life, Angra Mainyu created another which is all death, where there are only two months of summer and where winter is ten months long, months which so chill the earth that even the summer months are icy; and cold is the root of all evil.
>
> Then I created Ghaon, the abode of Sughdra, the most delightful place on earth. It is sewn with roses; there birds with ruby plumage are born.
>
> Angra Mainyu then created the insects which are noxious to plants and animals.
>
> Then I founded the holy and sublime city of Muru, and into it Angra Mainyu introduced lies and evil counsel.
>
> Then I created Bashdi the enchanting, where surrounded by lush pastures a hundred thousand banners fly. Angra Mainyu sent wild beasts there and animals to devour the cattle that serve for man's use.
>
> Afterwards I created Nissa, the city of prayer; and into it Angra Mainyu insinuated the doubt which gnaws at faith.
>
> I created Haroju, the city of rich palaces. Angra Mainyu caused sloth to be born there and soon the city was poverty-stricken.
>
> Thus each of the marvels I have given to men for their welfare has been counteracted by a baneful gift from Angra Mainyu. It is to him the earth owes the evil instincts which infest it. It is he who established the criminal usage of burying or burning the dead, and all the misfortunes which ravage the race of mankind.[7]

Most people today have this view of the world. They see life as a constant battle of happiness with despair, hate with love, and creation with destruction, where there is no hope of victory for one side since the two opposing forces are equally balanced. They pay little attention to the single All-Father since they can see no evidence of his hand in the material world.

This common perception is very limited. The equality of Light and Darkness is only apparent, not absolute. Once the Magus has an understanding of the nature of each pole of duality, they can no longer be treated equally.

The mind cannot conceive of Darkness without Light. If all were

Darkness it would not be perceived as a thing, but would be hidden in the Unmanifest. Similarly, no mind can conceive of Light without the accompanying conception of Darkness. If there were all Light it would not be perceived by the mind as Light but would be perceived as the substance of the true Self, which is without qualities. However, the Magus must not make the mistake of *equating* polarities because of their interdependence. This is the major error of the Western world and a natural weakness of human understanding.

Light is a positive thing, a legitimate and purposeful emanation of the Unmanifest. Light is the intention of the All acting toward its higher purpose. Darkness, on the other hand, is only a semblance of a thing, not real in the true sense of the word but a shadow and deceit. The coming into being of the Light gave rise to the perception that there is such a thing as Darkness. The Light does not pervade the whole of manifestation to an equal degree, and where it is less concentrated is called Darkness.

Satanists assume that the Devil has as much reality, or lack of reality, as God and is therefore an equally suitable object of worship. In fact, Satan is not any thing but is merely the place where God is less evident. Satanists worship a shadow, a dilution of the same power they claim to despise.

Consider the line DCBA:

The right end of the line represents the extreme, or totality, of Light, and the left end, the totality of Darkness. From the perspective of B, A is light and C is dark. But from the perspective of A, B is dark, and from the perspective of D, C is light.

It is not the internal character of the points on the line that makes them Light or Dark since any intermediate point may be both, depending upon the perspective from which it is viewed. Only all Light could contain no Darkness, and only all Darkness could contain no Light— and, as was already pointed out, neither extreme can exist in the material universe.

Man can never escape the apparent duality of manifestation until he transcends the limits of ordinary perception and sees all opposites, not as extremes of a line, but as extremes of the radius of a circle. This is a movement outside the ordinary level of perception, as the transformation of the line into the circle implies a shift from the second to the third dimension:

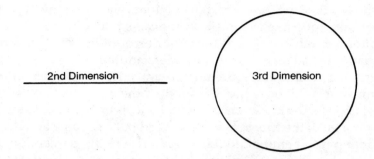

In the second dimension, or Flatland as it is often called, all geometric shapes are perceived as lines. Only when the viewing eye transcends the plane can the circle be recognized. An analogous transcendence is required to see opposites as one.

When this transcendence is achieved by the Magus, the line DCBA can be drawn as the radius of a circle:

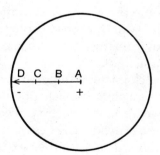

The center of the circle is always the source of emanation, always positive. The circle represents the limit to which this positive emanation has penetrated—the edge of the universe. As the infinite number of radii move out from the center, the concentration of Light diminishes. These are the differing degrees of ignorance and evil that are spaced as points along the radii of Light.

There is never total Light, for this exists only in the infinitely small point at the center, which is not in the universe of manifestation. There is never total Darkness, for this is found only outside the borders of space and time. Outside and inside, as well as all other extremes of opposition, lie beyond the limits of creation and are one and the same.

Darkness was born as a by-product of Light. Evil has its apparent existence as a necessary definer of Good. Hate was an unavoidable condition for the creation of Love. God did not intentionally create Evil. God intended Good. Of course, he was well aware that when he made Good, Evil would come into its sham existence at the same time. This is the inescapable tragedy of manifestation. To create anything, it is necessary, by the very nature of created things, to endure the coming into being of the shadows.

Evil is a lesser degree of Good, not a thing in itself, and certainly not a caprice or whim of the Unmanifest. Under extreme circumstances—the death camps of Nazi Germany, for example—what is thought of as evil by a secure and well-fed person might be considered the greatest imaginable good. God could not banish Darkness from the world without at the same instant banishing Light and all other manifestation, thus destroying all creation and merging it back into the Unmanifest.

It is the most stupid and wicked of impieties to blame the All for deliberately allowing personal misfortune. The All-Father suffers with every ache and cries with every tear. Do not commit this error.

The forces of Darkness wish nothing more than to have humanity accept them as equal in importance to the forces of Light. This is their whole labor, to make mankind mistake the mask for a face and the shadow for a body. Yet all their power is wind and bluster. A single spark of the Light sends them wailing. A single truth shatters all their lies.

In the table of the hendecagram are listed major traditional demonic powers and their associations. Since these demons are degrees of attenuation of the Light, their usefulness is confined to performing tasks that would debase the pure principle of Spirit—in other words, works of evil. The wise Magus never undertakes any magic that would shame him before the face of the Light. The use of demons is mainly confined to those who have renounced the cosmic law (either explicitly or by their actions) and dedicated themselves to doing mischief.

However, demons have occasionally been used in service to the Light for tasks of a grossly material or corporal nature. These might include gaining power for a noble end, injuring an individual to prevent him from committing a crime, and so on. Anyone who employs a demon for material advantage, even if it is altruistic, risks a corresponding loss of spiritual riches and is liable to all manner of self-deception. The more he believes himself to be gaining, the more he is likely to lose. The leaders of Germany believed they could use the Nazis to consume the communists; but when the communists were defeated the Nazis turned their appetites on the institutions of the German state.

In the Kabbalah demons are called Qliphoth, which means "shells." They dwell below the world of Assiah, the material world. The image of the shell is apt because all demonic forces are hollow. With this understanding the Kabbalists named the demonic orders according to their functions—the kinds of evil they cause. These orders may be inversely related to the ten Sephiroth:

1)	Kether	Thaumiel	The Contenders
2)	Chokmah	Ghogiel	The Hinderers
3)	Binah	Satariel	The Concealers
4)	Chesed	Agshekeloh	The Breakers
5)	Geburah	Goloheb	The Burners
6)	Tiphareth	Tagiriron	The Disputers
7)	Netzach	Gharah Tzerek	The Raveners
8)	Hod	Samael	The Liars
9)	Yesod	Gamaliel	The Perverters
10)	Malkuth	Lilitu	The Fornicators

Much can be learned about the nature of the emanations by studying the Qliphoth, since they are the forces of the Sephiroth subverted to the service of Evil. They are the other side of the emanations, the shadows where the light of the Sephiroth does not fall, and their outline is determined by the shape of the Sephirah to which they correspond.

DODECAGRAM

The dodecagram is a star with twelve points. It may be formed in three ways—with four equilateral triangles, with three squares, or unicursally with its line reflected from every fifth point. It is interesting to note that the unicursal decagram reflects from every third point. Since three is a factor of twelve and five is a factor of ten, the decagram and dodecagram are mystically related.

The dodecagram is the most perfectly balanced and harmonious of symbols. The spiritual trinity is repeated four times to show its union with the Earth, and the material quaternary is repeated three times to indicate its heavenly aspect. The dodecagram may be considered as an extension or elaboration of the decagram where the tenth point, representing Malkuth (tangible being), is expanded into a trinity of qualities.

As number symbols increase in complexity, the meaning of single points becomes more individual and concrete, less a simple abstraction. This is the opposite of what might naturally be expected to happen, but it stems from a simple principle. Individuality arises not from essence but from permutation. Three musical notes cannot produce nearly as interesting or unique a song as thirty. It is the same with all things, physical or mental. In simplicity is strength—in complexity is personality.

The points of the dodecagram are magically expressed through

TABLE OF DODECAGRAM

	Sign	Element & Motion	Form	Level	Color	Key
1	Aries	△ —	Wild	Beast	Red	Being
2	Taurus	▽ ○	Tame	Beast	Red-Purple	Having
3	Gemini	△ v	Artist	Man	Purple	Thinking
4	Cancer	▽ —	Land-Water	Creature	Blue-Purple	Feeling
5	Leo	△ ○	Wild	Beast	Blue	Commanding
6	Virgo	▷ v	Priest	Man	Blue-Green	Considering
7	Libra	△ —	Lawyer	Man	Green	Weighing
8	Scorpio	▽ ○	Land	Creature	Yellow-Green	Desiring
9	Sagittarius	△ v	Warrior	Man	Yellow	Perceiving
10	Capricorn	▷ —	Tame	Beast	Yellow-Orange	Using
11	Aquarius	△ ○	Laborer	Man	Orange	Knowing
12	Pisces	▽ v	Water	Creature	Red-Orange	Serving

the Zodiac, a system of twelve archetypal forces loosely related to patterns of stars in the night sky. It should be understood that the symbolic figures and beasts of the Zodiac did not arise from contemplation of the night sky, but were projected onto the star patterns by ancient philosophers who discerned in man and in nature the qualities represented by the Zodiac signs. The heavens served as a convenient place to fix these ideas and contemplate their interaction.

Here are the signs, names, and representations of the Zodiac given in traditional order, proceeding counterclockwise around the heavens:

♈	Aries	Ram	♎	Libra	Scales
♉	Taurus	Bull	♏	Scorpio	Scorpion
♊	Gemini	Twins	♐	Sagittarius	Archer
♋	Cancer	Crab	♑	Capricorn	Sea Goat
♌	Leo	Lion	♒	Aquarius	Water-bearer
♍	Virgo	Virgin	♓	Pisces	Fish

The Tree of Life may be viewed as a terrestrial and human symbol based on the division of fives (the number of man), while the Zodiac can be considered a heavenly and divine symbol based on the division of sixes (the number of God). This distinction is simplistic but can be useful in practical magic.

The Tree is consulted to discover the workings of Spirit in the soul of humanity and used to affect aspects of the personality and correct imbalances. The Zodiac is more useful in delving into the blind forces of nature that constantly surge around and drive human life without being aware of the effects of their actions. The Tree reflects moral qualities such as beauty, wisdom, and severity. The Zodiac reflects the uncaring drives of nature such as being, having, feeling, and so on.

Keep in mind that either of these complex systems is complete in its own right. The Tree also expresses blind forces and the Zodiac, moral qualities, but the distinction above indicates the pervading tones.

The signs of the Zodiac are each assigned one of the four philosophical elements and one of the three kinds of primary motion. This can graphically be displayed by means of a Celtic cross of thirteen squares, with Mercury set in the center and three of the Zodiac signs in each arm. (See the diagram on p. 166.)

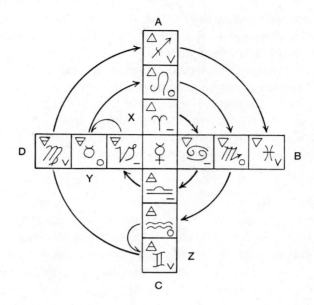

Each arm bears the signs that are ascribed to one of the elements—Fire, Water, Air, or Earth. They are read out from the center of the cross:

> A: *Fire* △
>   Aries, Leo, Sagittarius
> B: *Water* ▽
>   Cancer, Scorpio, Pisces
> C: *Air* ◬
>   Libra, Aquarius, Gemini
> D: *Earth* ⍦
>   Capricorn, Taurus, Virgo

The three concentric circles of four signs each are ascribed to the three kinds of motion—linear, rotary, and vibratory. In astrology these motions are called Cardinal, Fixed, and Mutable. The circles are read clockwise in a spiral out from the center of the cross, beginning with the first sign, Aries:

> X *Cardinal* (linear motion)   —
>   Aries, Cancer, Libra, Capricorn

Y *Fixed* (rotary motion)   ○
    Taurus, Leo, Scorpio, Aquarius

Z *Mutable* (vibratory motion)   V
    Gemini, Virgo, Sagittarius, Pisces

This division into the four elements and the three motions is more commonly shown in astrology by means of the grand symbol of the double dodecagram of four triangles and three squares. (See p. 168.)

Each triangle indicates one of the elemental divisions, and each square points to one of the divisions of motion. When the Magus has gained a solid understanding of the elements and motions, through study and meditation, he will grasp the meaning of each of the Zodiac signs; for it is upon this foundation that all descriptions of the signs are built. As an understanding of the planets is based on the threefold division of the circle into whole (○), half ( )), and quarter (+), so is the Zodiac based on the sevenfold division of the four elements (△ ▽ △ ▽) and the three motions (— o v).

By the combination of its element and motion, each sign is given an individual action. These can be infinitely elaborated, but they can also be summarized in a single word that will act as a key to the memory and call forth a full understanding of the sign when it is spoken or recalled. This catalytic word is for the personal use of the Magus. It should be devised only after careful study of the sign and should be the most evocative of all possible words for the gestalt meaning of that sign.

Here are examples of what these catalytic words might be like; however, the Magus would be well advised to find his own words:

Aries ....Being	Leo.......Commanding	Sagittarius...Perceiving
Taurus ....Having	Virgo......Considering	Capricorn..........Using
Gemini ....Thinking	Libra ....Weighing	Aquarius .....Knowing
Cancer.............Feeling	Scorpio ....Desiring	Pisces..............Serving

No catalytic word will tell you all you should know about a sign, just as no title can convey everything that is in a book. Also, catalytic words can only call up information that has been gathered into the mind through long hours of study—alone they are almost valueless.

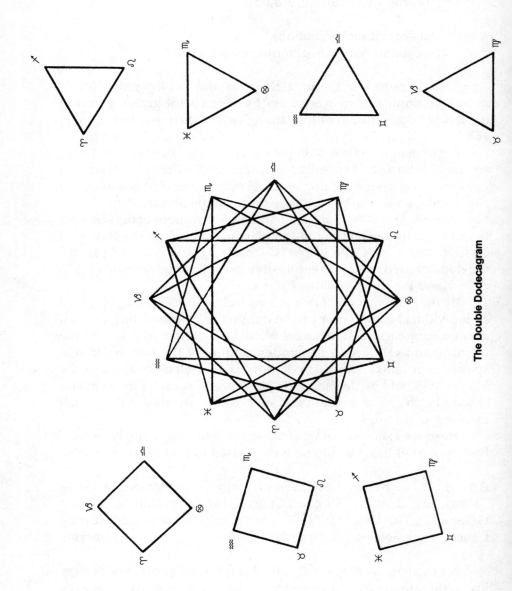

The Double Dodecagram

The powers of the Zodiac are not to be found in the far reaches of interstellar space. The notion that stars and planets physically determine events on Earth is a superstition, a belief that is in defiance of reason. This statement should need no authority to back it up in this day and age, but here is what the writers of the *Rasa'il*, the great book of Islamic cosmology, say on the subject:

> Astrology does not pretend and has not the right to pretend to an anticipated knowledge of events. Many people believe that astrology proposes to study the science of the unseen, but they are definitely wrong. What they call the science of the unseen is really the science of indetermination, the gratuitous pretention of anticipating the future without recourse to any symptom of reasoning, be it causal or deductive. In this sense the unknown is neither accessible to the astrologers, nor diviners, nor prophets, nor sages. It is the work of God only.[8]

Nor are the powers of the Zodiac found in the sky or in some otherworldly place. They are found in the mind of man, which encompasses the universe at its center point. The Zodiac powers were uncontained and formless until the human mind drew circles around them and gave them names. They were drawn from abstraction into being and assigned natures that insured their interaction with humanity. From amorphous nexuses of force they were carved in the same way rough stone is carved by a sculptor, and given desires, hopes, wills, and faces.

This is why the Magus has power over the signs of the Zodiac: they are his children and the children of his race. The Zodiac does not rule man. Man rules the stars. But humanity is asleep and first must be awakened.

There are twelve words of power that call forth and command the forces of the Zodiac. These words have been derived from the permutations of the Tetragrammaton, the fourfold name of God. The forms of the name may be grouped under the elements in order of the increasing violence done to their natural arrangement of letters:

Fire:	*Water:*	*Air:*	*Earth:*
I-H-V-Ḣ	H-V-Ḣ-I	V-Ḣ-I-H	Ḣ-I-H-V
I-H-Ḣ-V	H-V-I-Ḣ	V-Ḣ-H-I	Ḣ-I-V-H
I-V-Ḣ-H	H-Ḣ-I-V	V-I-H-Ḣ	Ḣ-H-V-I

The permutations of the Tetragrammaton display a distinct pattern, which is revealed numerically:

1234	IHVḢ
1243	IHḢV
1342	IVḢH
2341	HVḢI
2314	HVIḢ
2413	HḢIV
3412	VḢIH
3421	VḢHI
3124	VIHḢ
4123	ḢIHV
4132	ḢIVH
4231	ḢHVI

The order of the names given here differs from the commonly encountered order, which seems to derive from an error perpetuated by MacGregor Mathers in the Introduction to his influential translation of *The Kabbalah Unveiled* by Knorr von Rosenroth. Others, accepting Mathers' authority, have copied this error.

Notice that when the names are grouped according to Cardinal, Fixed, and Mutable motion, any letter column spells out the Tetragrammaton in its elemental order if you begin with YOD, read down, then jump to the top of the column:

Cardinal	Fixed	Mutable
I-H-V-Ḣ	I-H-Ḣ-V	I-V-Ḣ-H
H-V-Ḣ-I	H-V-I-Ḣ	H-Ḣ-I-V
V-Ḣ-I-H	V-Ḣ-H-I	V-I-H-Ḣ
Ḣ-I-H-V	Ḣ-I-V-H	Ḣ-H-V-I

These names are assigned to the elemental triangles of the Zodiac counterclockwise in the order given. (See first diagram on p. 171.)

The traditional way of invoking one of the powers of the Zodiac is through the sign of the pentagram that accords with the element under which the Zodiac power falls. For example, in the new system of the pentagram given earlier, the power of Leo would be invoked by

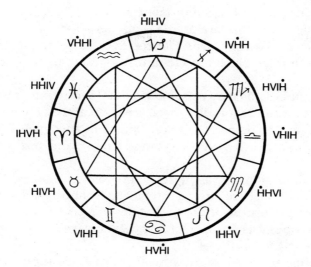

drawing the pentagram clockwise from the point of elemental Fire, then psychically and physically inscribing the symbol of Leo in its center.

When dealing with the Zodiac powers, it is advisable always to use the appropriate form of the Tetragrammaton so that the signs and the fourfold names of God become linked. After the Magus draws the pentagram and forms the sign of the Zodiac in its center, the points of the star should be assigned the letters of the permutation of the divine name in order. The upper point of the pentagram can then be given the Hebrew letter Shin (ש), which signifies the radiance of Spirit. This is equivalent to lighting the mystical lamp and empowers the symbol:

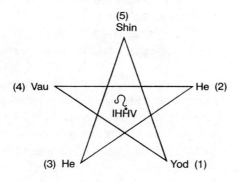

When trying to understand a system of symbols, it is always helpful to break it down into its component parts. The Zodiac has a twofold division into signs that are animal and signs that are human. The animal signs are Aries, Taurus, Cancer, Leo, Scorpio, Capricorn, and Pisces. The human signs are Gemini, Virgo, Libra, Sagittarius, and Aquarius.

The animal signs may be subdivided into four higher beasts, the Ram, Bull, Lion, and Goat and three lower creatures, the Crab, Scorpion, and Fish. The human signs are divided into two male (Sagittarius and Aquarius), two female (Virgo and Libra), and one androgyne (Gemini).

The animal signs are all highly aggressive and sexual. The Ram, Bull, Lion, and Goat are among the most potent beasts symbolically. The Crab and Scorpion are both threatening—the Crab has its claw and the Scorpion its sting. The Fish has always been a symbol of generation and fecundity.

All three of the Air signs appear in the human division. Air is traditionally the element of the intellect and therefore of humanity. Of the four higher beasts, two signs are Fire and two are Earth— opposite elements. All three Water signs appear among the lower creatures because Water is the element of crawling and hidden things.

The symbol of the Crab is its claw, which is grasping and thus female; the symbol of the Scorpion is its sting, which is thrusting and therefore male. The male and female aspects of the lower creatures are reconciled in the Fish, which are outwardly androgynous.

There is a curious and striking balance to be observed in this division of animal life.

The lowest level is presented as a trine—the fish, wholly a water creature; the crab, which lives both in the sea and on the land; and the scorpion, wholly a land dweller.

The middle level is given as a quaternary—two domesticated beasts, the goat and the bull (Earth); and two wild beasts, the lion and the ram (Fire).

The highest level presents the five kinds of human occupation. The Water-bearer is a laborer. The Virgin is a priestess of the mysteries. The Lady of the Scales represents law and social order. The Archer stands for warfare. The Twins are still in their becoming and suggest the higher evolution of the human race as expressed through art. These occupations may also be symbolized by the five magical instruments—Coin, Cup, Rod, Sword, and Lamp.

For the Magus using this breakdown as a guide, it is not hard to construct a model that suggests the three levels of animal life found in the signs of the Zodiac. It will consist of a triangle inside a square inside a pentagram. The Magus may find it useful as a reminder of the relationships between the three motions, four elements, five parts of man, seven planets, and twelve names of God implicit in the dode-cagram:

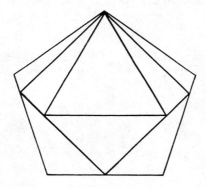

TABLE OF TWENTY-TWO DOORS

Number	Name	Sign	Path	Letter	Kind	Meaning	Trans.	Value*
	Fool	△	11	Aleph א	Mother	Ox	A	1
I	Magus	☿	12	Beth ב	Double	House	B, V	2
II	Priestess	☽	13	Gimel ג	Double	Camel	G, Gh	3
III	Empress	♀	14	Daleth ד	Double	Door	D, Dh	4
IV	Emperor	♈	15	He ה	Single	Window	H	5
V	Hierophant	♉	16	Vau ו	Single	Nail	O, U, V	6
VI	Lovers	♊	17	Zayin ז	Single	Sword	Z	7
VII	Chariot	♋	18	Cheth ח	Single	Fence	Ch	8
VIII	Strength	♌	19	Teth ט	Single	Snake	T	9
IX	Hermit	♍	20	Yod י	Single	Hand	I, Y	10
X	Wheel	♃	21	Kaph כ	Double	Fist	K, Kh	20, ך 500
XI	Justice	♎	22	Lamed ל	Single	Goad	L	30
XII	Hanged Man	▽	23	Mem מ	Mother	Water	M	40, ם 600
XIII	Death	♏	24	Nun נ	Single	Fish	N	50, ן 700
XIV	Temperance	♐	25	Samekh ס	Single	Prop	S	60
XV	Devil	♑	26	Ayin ע	Single	Eye	Aa, Ngh	70
XVI	Tower	♂	27	Pe פ	Double	Mouth	P, Ph	80, ף 800
XVII	Star	♒	28	Tzaddi צ	Single	Hook	Tz	90, ץ 900
XVIII	Moon	♓	29	Qoph ק	Single	Ear	Q	100
XIX	Sun	☉	30	Resh ר	Double	Head	R	200
XX	Judgment	△	31	Shin ש	Mother	Tooth	S, Sh	300
XXI	World	♄	32	Tau ת	Double	Cross	T, Th	400

*Some Hebrew letters have a final form that occurs at the end of words. It has a higher numerical value.

TWENTY-TWO DOORS

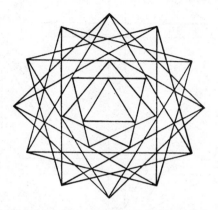

The symbol of twenty-two points is embodied in magic in the Major Arcana of the Tarot. These are the picture cards with individual names such as the Fool, the Hanged Man, and so on. It also acts through the twenty-two letters of the Hebrew alphabet, which link the ten Sephiroth of the Kabbalistic Tree of Life; and through the system of twelve Zodiac signs, seven planets, and three primary motions. The complexity of this symbol is great enough to contain an entire world of meaning. Hebrew uses only twenty-two letters to express the entire spectrum of human understanding. Some alphabets have even fewer letters.

The images of the Tarot are infinitely more complex than individual letters of an alphabet, and their meanings are multiplied to an even greater extent when the cards are combined. Much of what is suggested by the Major Arcana, or Trumps, cannot be expressed in language: it is information with an emotional and spiritual content. Images transcend the barriers of formal speech. A picture can be worth far more than a thousand words: it can carry meanings that no language is able to convey.

The symbol of twenty-two can be looked at through the equation $10 + 12 = 22$, the human and rational plus the divine and spiritual. It is an extension of the heptagram, which combines the heavenly three over the earthly four. The point of observation at the center of the hep-

175

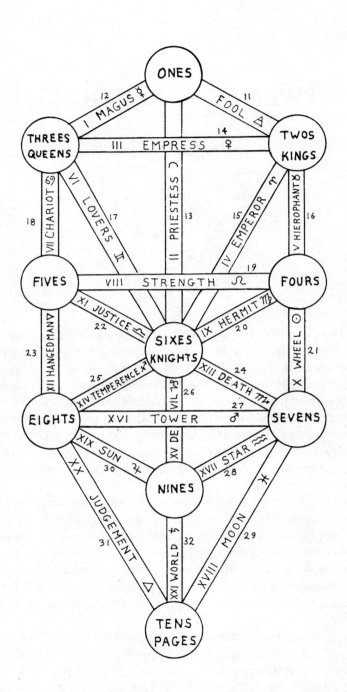

tagram is implied, not explicitly shown. However, in the Major Arcana of the Tarot this observing point is embodied in the card of the Fool, which is without number—not zero, as is so often mistakenly stated. The Tarot Trumps are made up of twenty-one cards—a threefold multiplication of the heptagram $[(3\times3) + (3\times4) = 21]$—plus the unnumbered Fool, which as the point of observation is free to move throughout the deck.

In divination with the Tarot, where the cards are related to the life of a specific individual, the abstract observing Fool is replaced by a Significator, one of the court cards of the Minor Arcana that is supposed to approximate the qualities of the person whose fortune is being read. The Significator does not figure directly into the reading, but all other cards are related to it as the fixed center of the personality the reading is about.

In a general sense the Fool is the Significator of the Tarot. This is why the meanings ascribed to the Fool are so many and varied. The Fool takes his shape from his environment. As the Fool reacts against each card, it colors his nature. The diviner looks over the shoulder of the Fool as he moves through the circular universe of the Major Arcana, and as the Fool enters into each card in turn, it becomes a door and opens inward on the subconscious of the diviner.

Traditionally the Fool was placed between the twentieth and twenty-first cards—the Judgment and the World. It was obvious to occultists that this had been done not for any useful reason but simply because the early users of the Tarot did not know what else to do with him. It then became fashionable to place the Fool at the end of the deck. This practice changed when it was generally assumed that the Fool carried the number zero and therefore should go at the front of the Major Arcana.

Today you will find the Fool, bearing the number zero, at the beginning of most modern desks. However, the older placements of the Fool are still being used.

The positioning of the Fool is essential not only to an understanding of the Tarot, but of the Self as well. All popular placements are incorrect. The Fool properly belongs *outside* the Major Arcana, which is a set of twenty-one consecutively numbered cards. This set of twenty-one is not in a line but in a circle. Like the serpent with its tail in its own mouth, it ends where it begins. After card XXI (the World) comes card I (the Magus). The Fool is the center point of this circle, and he interacts equally with each of the twenty-one cards of the

Major Arcana when the deck is in a passive, or unshuffled, state.

For convenience the Fool may be placed at the beginning of the Trumps. This is useful when one is relating the Tarot to Hebrew letters and to astrological symbols. However, it is equally permissible to put the Fool at the end or anywhere in-between. Perhaps this explains why the Fool traditionally was put between cards XX and XXI. The placement is so arbitrary it suggests the absurdity of trying to fix the Fool between any of the numbered cards.

Understanding the role of the Fool is the single most important step in learning Tarot symbolism because the Fool reveals the dynamics underlying this philosophical machine. The reader and the Fool are one, but the reader is colored by various shades of prejudice and bias, whereas the Fool is as clear as water. The reader stands with the Fool in a great circular chamber with twenty-one glass windows of different colors. As he approaches a window, the light shining through it casts over him a certain hue, and he is enabled to experience life from that color.

Since he has colors in his own personality, however, he can never experience the light shining through the windows in its purity. To do this he must first become clear like the Fool, which he must make his model if he is to delve deeply into the patterns and shades of life. As the sages of the East say, only the still waters reflect a true image. Only the Fool perfectly understands what each card means, because he knows nothing.

None of the many modern Tarots that have been devised in the last few hundred years are of more than passing value to the serious student of the occult. All are derived from the Tarot of Marseilles, the oldest and most perfect of the Tarots. Although older individual decks of other styles exist, the Marseilles Tarot is the one from which magic draws its inspiration. Its history is certainly more ancient than the examples of it that have survived in museums. The Magus should always refer to the Marseilles deck whenever a confusion of symbolism confronts him.

This chapter is not intended as a complete guide to the Tarot. Many books have been written on the subject and the serious student should certainly read at least several of them. It is true that most of the books are incomplete and contain many errors. It might be said with some seriousness that in fact only one book on the Tarot has been written and that all the published volumes contain a few pages here, a few pages there, of that single uncollected book. A study of the Tarot involves wading through hundreds of tedious, repetitious pages to gain a single new fact or insight. Almost all books on the Tarot merely parrot what others have said or written.

Here is a mnemonic for the beginner that presents in rhymed form a single key word for each of the cards of the Major Arcana:

I The Magus *Wills* with bolts of fire.
II The Priestess *Shapes* her hidden desire.
III The Empress *Births* beneath the Sun.
IV The Emperor *Rules* the four as one.
V The Pope *Blesses* the narrow way.
VI The Lovers *Tempt* by night and day.
VII The Chariot *Conquers* with iron mind.
VIII The Balance *Weighs* and pays in kind.
IX The Hermit *Lights* the right-hand path.
X The Wheel *Turns*, the gods laugh.
XI The Strength of *Faith* shuts savage jaws.
XII The Martyr *Bows* to heaven's laws.
XIII The Reaper *Frees* the souls from earth.
XIV The Alchemist *Blends* and fines true worth.
XV The Beast *Tests* with earthly blow.
XVI The Tower *Falls* if built for show.
XVII The Star gives *Hope* of things to be.
XVIII The Moon *Warns* of the dangerous sea.
XIX The Sun *Warms* the world with joy.
XX The Trumpet *Wakes* the sleeping boy.
XXI The World *Combines* the all in One.
    The Fool's *Road* ends where it's begun.

The numbering of the cards presented in the above rhyme is different from that of the modern occult decks. The true and absolute numbering of the Tarot is one of the great unsolved questions of Western magic. Like the search for the square of the circle or the philosopher's stone, it may have no concrete solution.

The difficulty lies in rationally relating the Trumps to the twenty-two letters of the Hebrew alphabet and then to the symbols of astrology and the paths on the Tree of Life. The Hebrew alphabet is not subject to changes in ordering. Neither is the Zodiac. Both are fixed by ancient tradition. The letters of the Hebrew alphabet divide into twelve simple letters, seven double letters, and three mother letters (so-called for the way they are pronounced). These groups are assigned the signs of the Zodiac, the seven planets, and the three motions. The motions are usually represented by the elements Fire, Water, and Air.

The task then becomes one of shifting the symbols of the planets, the motions, and, to a lesser extent, the Trumps so that everything forms an integrated whole. What results is not perfect and is never likely to be so. However, it is surprisingly elegant and useful, considering that the men who devised the various systems of symbols never intended that they should be put together. It works because all of the systems are true and because all are based on a single reality.

In the table at the start of this chapter are the correspondences used in modern magic. They have been tortuously arrived at over a period of more than a century and are still open to dispute. One or two small changes have been made that seemed necessary. For instance, it is usual to match the astrological Sun with the Tarot Trump XIX (the Sun) and to match the planet Jupiter to the card X (the Wheel). It seems more reasonable to put the astrological Sun, which is, after all, a great wheel symbolically, with the Trump X (the Wheel) and to put the astrological Jupiter—ruler of the world—with the Tarot Trump XIX (the Sun). It should be pointed out that the card of the Moon is never assigned the astrological Moon.

Also, since the traditional numbering of two of the paths on the Tree of Life seems illogical, paths twenty-five and twenty-six have been interchanged in the diagram, along with their accompanying Tarot Trumps.

The major accepted change in the numbering of the Tarot—the interchanging of cards VIII (Justice) and XI (Strength)—is made necessary by the fixed order of the Zodiac signs. Obviously Libra suits Justice and Leo suits Strength better than the other way around. The Fool has been placed at the beginning mainly because any other placement seems to destroy the correspondences of the other cards, but also because it is generally assumed to be a zero card.

This merging of astrology, the Tarot, and the Kabbalah into a single system is the great achievement of modern magic. It is perhaps the only aspect of magic that the modern world could teach the ancient. This the modern Magus has, and previous adepts did not.

Here is a brief presentation of the meanings of the Trumps listed in their modern magical order. It is intended to be suggestive only:

Fool—Wanderer. Watcher. Fool on the hill. Speaker of riddles. Dweller in the desert. Mirror of life.

I Magus—Male potency acting in the world. Craft. Guile. Deception. Aggression. Power behind the throne.

II Priestess—Guardian of the mysteries. Knower of secrets. The whisperer. The diviner. Wearer of masks and veils. She preserves what is too fragile for the light.

III Empress—Earth mother. Pregnant nature. Horn of plenty. Cup of cheer. The hills are her breasts, and the lakes her eyes.

IV Emperor—Father of Life. Lawgiver. Ruler. He who orders the way of things. Natural law.

V Hierophant—God's interpreter. Hidden currents of divinity harnessed for the benefit of social man. The role now imperfectly filled by the scientist.

VI Lovers—Hermetic union of opposites. From the mire arises fine gold. The necessary prelude to creation.

VII Chariot—A fresh rain that washes old sediment aside. Wind of change. Conquering hero.

VIII Strength—Spirit ascendant over the tyranny of flesh. Faith. Victory of martyrs. The mouse confronting the lion.

IX Hermit—Search for truth. The urge to return to the Light. Desire to know the right and to follow it. Recognition of the futility of the world.

X Wheel—Cycles of life. The way force acts in nature. Reciprocation. Motion in a spiral.

XI Justice—Regulator of the Wheel. The Will of God acting in the world. She is often pictured as blind because she does not share human perceptions, but she sees well enough in her own way.

XII Hanged Man—Absolute futility. Resignation to events. Negativity—no pain, no trouble, but no hope or will either.

XIII Death—Decay necessary for rebirth. The dead must be absorbed into the earth before new shoots can sprout. Serpent in the skull. Flower on the grave.

XIV Temperance—Blending of opposites. The search for balance. Dynamic tension. The golden mean.

XV Devil—Inertia in matter. The shadow, the vacuum, the mask, the bag of wind, the bluff, the bully, the lie.

XVI Tower—Pride. The tower of Babel. All castles in the air that are overgrown with time. The vanity of human wishes. Denial of natural law.

XVII Star—Light in darkness. Heart's ease in heart's sorrow. Hope. The voice of angels. What makes the stumbling man look up.

XVIII Moon—Waters of despair. Tears. Light that vanishes in a dream. Will-o'-the-wisps. False prophets. Indifference at the gates of success.

XIX Sun—Blood of life. That which vitalizes all things. Positive thoughts and feelings. Good actions. Truth. Strength. Purpose.

XX Judgment—Emergence of the butterfly from the chrysalis. The last will be first and the first will be last. Things seen for what they are.

XXI World—All the world's a stage. The universe as the theater of being. The backdrop for all actions of the divine Spirit. The contrasting ground against which God observes himself.

The numbered cards and the face cards of the Tarot should more properly be considered under the decagram and the square, respectively. However, their meanings can be briefly set forth.

The ten numbered cards are the ten emanations of God that brought the universe into being. The suits stand for the four Kabbalistic worlds:

> Scepters: Atziloth (Emanation), Fire
> Cups: Briah (Creation), Water
> Swords: Yetzirah (Formation), Air
> Coins: Assiah (Action), Earth

Each of the forty numbered cards stands for one Sephirah in one of the four Kabbalistic worlds. For example, the seven of cups symbolizes Netzach, or Victory, in the world of Briah, Creation.

The sixteen face cards belong to the philosophical elements in this order:

> Kings: Fire
> Queens: Water
> Knights: Air
> Pages: Earth

Since each suit also corresponds to an element, the face cards have a greater and a lesser elemental quality. For example, the queen of scepters is of the Watery nature of Fire. The title of the face card provides the active element, and the suit provides the ground against which it acts.

The uses of the Tarot in magic are too many to list. Each individual card can be the object of fruitful meditations. Cards can be used as talismans, as instruments of ritual workings, as patterns for god-forms, and as symbols of power. Above all else, the Tarot is a tool for examining the Self and its relation to life.

The use of the Tarot for divination is a debasement of its higher purposes. Many adepts who study it cease altogether to use it for divination as they come to feel that such a trite use of the symbols affronts the Light. However, the Tarot is not a piece of cloth that can be soiled. The mind that abuses it may be degraded—the symbols can never be other than what they are.

After the Magus lives with the Tarot of Marseilles for a year or two, it will be time for him to make a personal Tarot for his own private use. This must be drawn and painted by his hand, and it must be original—not merely copied from other decks. When used for magical workings, these handmade cards are always more potent than a printed deck because they are so personal. Each symbol is absolutely unique in all the world, the most powerful interpretation of the Tarot Trump possible for the mind that created it.

A model useful for understanding some of the relationships of the Trumps can be constructed in the shape of a cubic cross—a cross made of five cubes, one at the center and one forming each arm. The cubic cross is a three-dimensional figure with twenty-two outer facets.

Here is an exploded view of the cross with the cards assigned to their proper squares:

			2			
		3	5	4		
	8		1		18	
7	10	6	0	16	20	17
	9		11		19	
		13	15	14		
			12			
			21			

Each of the triform points of the cross wraps in upon itself to make one of the outer cubes. The lowermost square forms the back-center of the cross.

The cubic cross reveals divisions of the Tarot that are not often considered—into pairs, indicated by opposite sides of the cubes; and into fives, indicated by each cube. It shows the central importance of the Fool, who is placed at the front-center of the cross, and the Fool's opposition to the World, which is placed on the back-center square. It suggests the pivotal importance of the cards numbered five, ten, fifteen, and twenty; each of which sums up the meaning of the four cards that precede it.

For example, the Magus is opposite the Priestess on the top cube. These cards are active and receptive aspects of Spirit. The Empress and the Emperor are also opposite on the first cube. They suggest the nurturing and ordering forces of the material world. The capping card on top of the cube is the Hierophant, who is hermaphroditic and embraces both the Spirit and the world. The fifth card joins the preceding four cards physically in the model as it links them symbolically.

If the symbols of the astrological powers, the Hebrew letters, and the numbers of the paths on the Tree of Life are added to the cubic cross, it becomes a useful reference tool.

Part Two

MICROCOSM

MAGIC

A GREAT MANY misconceptions exist about magic, not the least of which is that it should be spelled with a *k*. Most people reject the word without even knowing what it is they are rejecting. Others, with only the vaguest ideas about the object of their adoration, blindly embrace magic for such shallow reasons as power and romance.

Magic is the art of affecting the manifest universe through the great Unmanifest. Many techniques called magical that never cross the Veil of Unknowing are really no more than sleight of hand and fascination, in the same category as the tricks of the stage magician. Their effects are predictable and measurable and will eventually come into the domain of science. Hypnotism is one such technique. By the same token, many activities thought of as commonplace are really magical in the true sense of the word. These include the creation of art and the projection of personal beauty.

The Veil is often crossed by ordinary people in their daily lives. The crossing liberates a power that makes them special for one reason or another, depending on how the power is manifested. It is responsible for genius and for the moments of glory that light up otherwise drab lives like blazing stars. It is also responsible for the acts of inspired evil that have too often shocked the world. Einstein was a natural magician. So was Hitler.

White magic is the Art of making the healing and life-giving powers of the Light manifest on the circles of human perception. It will never become science because science, by its inherent nature, must deny the existence of the Light. Science deals only with that which is measurable and predictable. Magic is controlled by the inner human condition and not at all by outer circumstances—that is, by the spiritual Self and not by the perceived forms. It acts through a distortion of probability, varying the way and order in which events commonly happen. Magic makes the unlikely occur.

In the Unmanifest all things are possible because none are actual. The Unmanifest is a great sea of potential. Nothing exists there, not even the ideas of things that will be; but everything is there potentially, waiting to be conceived into the manifest universe.

Picture a dozen monkeys typing gibberish for eternity. This is an often quoted model used to demonstrate aspects of chance. The laws of probability state that eventually one monkey will type the complete works of Shakespeare letter-perfect. Of course this would not likely occur in the near future, but eventually, with all eternity to choose from, the plays of Shakespeare must be typed, simply because it is possible; and in eternity all possibilities must be realized.

In the universe this scenario is absurd because the universe itself is finite. However, the Unmanifest is an infinitude of possibility outside of finite time and space. Magic taps the bottomless lake of potential that is within everyone, as everyone is within it, and calls into being that aspect of potential that concerns the Magus. It may be likened to dipping a vase into the waters of the sea and giving discrete form to that portion of the water held in the vase, except that the Unmanifest is never diminished when forms are drawn from it.

The form created may be as noble as universal love or as material as winning a lottery prize. In the first the Light is exalted. In the second it is degraded. The Light is the Will of the All and is symbolic of the central purpose that gave rise to the manifest universe. It is cosmic order and the grace of God.

The universe is a balance between the positive actions of the Light and the negative reactions of the Darkness. What man regards as normal probability results from the dynamic balance between Good and Evil. This balance is not always the same, nor is it fixed into place. It rocks periodically, creating the cycles of history. And it can be tipped.

Humanity walks with its eyes closed along a tightrope over a bottomless pit without realizing its precarious position. Only when someone's foot slips momentarily does that person open his eyes and look down into reality, realizing with a sudden rush of emotion how close he has lived to the edge of disaster all his life without knowing it.

Each time you step off the curb to cross the street there is a chance you will not reach the other side. Usually you do because the odds are in your favor. Your reflexes are good, you are aware of the dangers, and your senses are keen. Even so, you would die if any one of a thousand unforseen events were to take place. A car's accelerator might run wild, or its steering linkage fail. You might trip and fall under the wheels of a bus. You might suffer a heart attack or a sudden fit. You might even be hit by a meteorite or a falling piece of an airplane passing overhead.

All of these things do happen, some with regularity and others only rarely. They did not happen to you when you crossed the street the last time, but they may the next. All it would take to cause your death at any time and under any circumstance is a simple act of what is called "bad luck." It might be only a little thing, such as your car key breaking off in the lock when you are in a lonely parking lot late at night while three thugs are approaching, or a cut from a broken bottle that simply refuses to heal.

The vital realization is that life is possible only in the narrowest band of probability that mankind has come, through custom, to regard as the norm. If the odds of life tipped against anyone only a fraction of one percent, he would not live long. Sooner or later his streak of bad luck would prove fatal. Gamblers know this great truth because they live with it from day to day, but most men and women go through life with their eyes tightly shut. It requires a stinging slap on their faces to make them peek out at reality, and then they shut their eyes again as quickly as they are able.

To tip the scales of probability is the awesome power of magic: to dip a hand into the bottomless sea of the Unmanifest and draw through the mirror surface something rich and strange.

Black magicians use this power to harm others and to increase their personal wealth and power. What they fail to realize, or choose to ignore, is that the balance of fate eventually rights itself. If it did not, Chaos would rule and the Will of the All would be overthrown. The evil these black magicians work always returns on their heads, although they may be so blinded and perverted by their material lives that they fail to recognize the evil for what it is and open their arms to their own destroyer.

Drugs have been the executioner of many of fate's harsh sentences against foolish or evil adepts. Inflated egos and delusions of godhood have insured the obscurity and ridicule of others. Insanity prevents still others of this class from harming their fellow men. The mill of the gods turns slowly but grinds exceedingly fine. The black magician may for years be the king of the petty world he surveys, only to find himself at the last naked and alone, his words ashes in his throat.

Practitioners of the black arts vainly believe they can deflect the reflux of cosmic law away from themselves and onto some innocent human or animal. This view betrays an appalling crassness of intellect. No one can blind the eye of God, which sees all and knows all because it is All. Innocents never suffer in ways that are outside divine law. Without question there is evil in the world, and the black adept can work wickedness that in his limited vision leaves him better off; but in the eye of God he has gained nothing.

The Magus should bear these thoughts in mind and resist the impulse to use his increasing knowledge for petty personal gains, even when the temptation is great. To do so is to turn away from the face of divine love that is his only guide to true happiness and peace.

It is permissible for the Magus to alter probability in specific personal matters if it harms no one, not even himself; if it helps move him forward along the path of his one true destiny; and if it does not seek something for nothing in defiance of cosmic law. But beware of self-deception! It is all too easy to mistake selfishness for piety.

This is the lawful zone of magic. Elements in the balance of life can be rearranged for better effect. The balance can even be momentarily tipped so long as it is righted afterwards. The Magus may use his power to pierce the Veil to aid in the achievement of his own destiny and to assist others to walk the narrow path that leads to their personal Great Work, the purpose of their lives. He may not load the balance wantonly like a child, disregarding the effect this will have on the cosmic order.

When the Magus bends probability to accomplish a certain end—for example, to bring about a meeting with another person—this is not to suggest that the end will be realized outside the boundaries of physical law. The individual will not simply pop out of the air or be levitated into the presence of the Magus. Such wonders are not impossible (just ask a nuclear physicist), but magic always takes the course of least resistance: or to state it another way, it tips the scales of fate as little as it must.

The Magus may encounter the person in the street seemingly by complete coincidence, or happen to read of the person's whereabouts in the paper and be forced to take the initiative and travel to the place where the other is staying. More often than not, magic in action looks very much like luck, which of course it is. It is seldom spectacular because it seldom needs to be. Almost any goal or desire can be naturally realized with only a few tugs at the hand of fate. All men either gain or lose their heart's desire by the narrowest of margins.

This is what would-be sorcerers cannot, or will not, understand. They want crumbling mountains and slavering demons. Only the greatest of adepts can do such tricks, and people of such high attainment have better matters with which to occupy their minds. Rarely will a Magus of attainment put on a show for the vulgar. In the first place it is far easier to act through the mind of the observer and make him believe he has seen something he has not. But the prime concern is that to use the Light for such petty ends is to risk losing it forever.

The Magus can achieve all his goals and desires by manipulating only those forms of manifestation that he regards as his physical and mental self—that is, his perceived self. Every man and woman has it within themselves to be wealthy, successful, loved, and honored—all the Magus need do is use his Art to bring into prominence those characteristics of his personality that will serve him best in society.

Grandiose displays are not needed. Magic is most effective when it is turned inward and used to shape the landscape of the perceived self, because it has less obstacles to overcome. The Magus does not easily believe that his Art can move mountains. However, he does believe that it can affect his personality because the false gods of science have assured him that this is possible. In fact, changing the inner landscape is more difficult than changing the outer, but it appears easier.

Bearing in mind that every action brings about an equal and opposite reaction, the Magus will use his power to tilt probability with circumspection. He will not expect a direct physical solution to a problem unless it is the only possible answer. Most important of all, he will never seek pleasure through the pain of others lest his own agony become a source of amusement for the masses at some future time.

The prime symbol of the balance of fate occurs in the mythology of ancient Egypt. It is the great scale of judgment that is presided over by Osiris. On it he weighs the heart of the newly dead person, symbolizing the sum of the person's actions in life, against the cosmic law, which is represented by the single ostrich feather of Mayet (Maat), goddess of justice and truth. She stands guard against the forces of Chaos. If the heart of the dead is filled only with Light, it will weigh less than the feather. But if the heart is defiled with only a trace of materialism, the love of form, it will tip down the delicately hinged scale.

The jackal-headed Anubis adjusts the balance to insure absolute honesty. The god of the scribes, Thoth, records the list of sins. Nearby waits the monster Ammut, the Devourer (part crocodile and part lion), to seize the souls found unworthy of admittance into the presence of Osiris and grind them to nothingness in his massive jaws. For the damnation of the Egyptians was not hell but eternal oblivion. Souls that had defiled themselves were not fit to merge with the Light. Their life experience was so much chaff, good for nothing but to fuel the fires of the world.

If the soul was found worthy, then great Thoth would speak thus:

> His heart hath indeed been weighed, and his soul hath born witness concerning it; it hath been found true by trial in the Great Balance. No evil hath been found in him, he hath not wasted the offerings in the temples, he hath not done harm by his deeds, and he hath uttered no evil report whilst he was upon earth.[9]

It should be obvious at once that St. Peter, who waylays souls at the gates of heaven and opens his book to affirm their worthiness before admitting them, is analogous to the Egyptian god Thoth. The book of Thoth, with sins listed on the left and good deeds on the right, has itself become the great scale. Heaven is the inner chamber of Osiris. Hell has been granted a reality it does not merit, since it is born of shadows and its true nature is oblivion.

The Egyptians understood the dynamic aspect of the balance of life—that every action was part of the final assessment of the soul. A deed could be balanced but never erased. Nor could anyone escape the ultimate judgment as to the worth of their existence. Cosmic law is a machine that is not subject to prejudice or affection. It always weighs true.

Although the norm of society is the sum of the good and bad fortune of all its members, it is an error to think that everyone has the same degree of luck. In fact, just the reverse is true—every individual has his own level of luck that is not shared by any other person. For most people, the middle point between good and bad luck is about in the same place. The differences are usually too minor to notice, since the fortune of every man is normal to him. Only when a person's fortune is wildly out of harmony with the mass of humankind are they singled out for notice, receiving either envy or pity depending on whether their luck is very good or very bad.

Someone enjoying especially bad fortune may be the object of a magical attack. Of course, there is no physical way to demonstrate that this is so. Even if the intent to injure could be proved, and the magical practices documented, there would still be no certain cause-and-effect relationship between the ritual to do evil and the evil fortune of the victim.

The balance of fate has a tendency to right itself. Very good luck is often followed or preceded by very bad luck. A lottery winner may lose his family in a car accident. A black Magus who sends evil intent out to others may find that similar evil is returning to him. Happiness is met with happiness; anger with anger; scorn with scorn. The average man is a cog in the great wheel of cause and effect, action and reaction. He initiates little in the world and spends most of his time simply reacting like a machine to the broader currents that swirl around him.

The Magus seeks to elevate himself above the level of a machine. He knows that the probabilities of his life are not chiseled in stone. He strives for the center of the balance, neither hating when he is hated nor loving when he is loved. He uses his Art to make the good of his destiny occur where it is most needed and desired, and to make the evil fall where it will do the least harm. So long as he does not try to move the center point of his destiny, he has committed no act against the Light. If he is foolish enough to imagine he can gain something for nothing and improve the totality of his fortune beyond what the All set down at his conception, he will be rudely disillusioned. No mortal can cheat God.

The Magus may use his powers to fulfill his destiny—a great achievement and a rare event in human history—but he can never gain, through Art or guile, a higher destiny than is rightfully his. This is what Faust desired and what Mephistopheles promised, although he knew full well when he made the promise that he lacked the power to fulfill his word.

In the final analysis, the only worthwhile use of magical attainment is in service to the Light. The good and evil of a life are weighed against each other in the great scale, and the direction the pan tips determines whether the life was lived in vain, in mockery of God and therefore also in mockery of the true Self, or whether it has contributed in some small way to the progress of the Light. Life lived for the Light has value and purpose. Life not lived for the Light is rudderless, without hope of any description.

INITIATION

INITIATION IS BOTH the first step on the path to magical attainment and a never-ending process of becoming that lasts a lifetime.

In primitive societies, initiatory rites are common. However, in the modern Western culture they have been virtually eliminated in their overt forms. It may be argued that they still exist below the surface as the unstructured and spontaneous actions that welcome an individual into any group—a professional sports team, a fraternity, a military service—yet as a definite and clearly expressed rite of passage, initiation is largely suppressed. This impoverishes Western culture and is a symptom of its sickness.

Initiation is a ritualized event that marks a person's exit from the common world in which he has lived and his entry into an elite circle of the chosen. In its highest form it symbolizes the death of worldly man and his rebirth as spiritual man. Initiation can be received voluntarily or involuntarily, depending on whether the candidate seeks to enter the circle—the quest—or is called to enter by higher spirit forces—the calling.

In the quest the candidate recognizes consciously the value, material or spiritual, of the hidden wisdom that the members of the circle possess and resolutely sets out to attain the benefit of that wisdom and power for himself. Tennyson's poem, *Sir Galahad*, suggests the spirit of the quest:

> "O just and faithful knight of God!
> Ride on! the prize is near."
> So pass I hostel, hall, and grange;
> By bridge and ford, by park and pale,
> All-arm'd I ride, whate'er betide,
> Until I find the holy Grail.[10]

In the calling the candidate has no wish to enter the circle—often just the opposite—but the secret currents of his life conspire to lead him continually to the gates of the temple. No matter how hard he strives against them, there is no rest or happiness for him until he accepts his destiny and submits to the initiation. The mystical poem by Robert Browning, *Childe Roland to the Dark Tower Came*, gives an example of the unwilling spirit of the calling:

> For, what with my whole world-wide wandering,
> What with my search drawn out through years, my
>   hope
> Dwindled into a ghost not fit to cope
> With that obstreperous joy success would bring,—
> I hardly tried now to rebuke the spring
> My heart made, finding failure in its scope.[11]

By its nature initiation implies there is a circle of people that is of special value within the larger all-encompassing circle. In its spiritual form this special circle is one of wisdom. The wisdom is either hidden from the mass of the population, as was the case with the Egyptian and Greek mysteries, or it is simply unobtainable by those who have not been transformed and prepared to receive it, as with the shamanic initiations of the American Indians.

Generally speaking, the long and involved rites of initiation in primitive societies begin with the preparation of the sacred circle, or ground, where the ceremony is to take place. The candidates (usually men but sometimes women, only very rarely both) are taken away from their family and friends. While segregated, they are given secret instruction and prepared for the rite. This preparation often involves the scarring of the skin or other mutilations. The candidates must endure hardship, wear special dress, eat only prescribed foods, and obey all other taboos.

The rite of initiation takes place within the circle with dancing and music, often with drugs or alcohol, to lend a heightened mental perception of the event and set it apart from the everyday reality. Here the candidate is ritually slain and buried in his old name, then magically resurrected and given a new name to signify his rebirth into the secret circle. His nakedness of birth is covered up in robes that accord with his exalted status. He is given the most secret and holy wisdom of the society compressed into emblems and parables.

Occult initiation is patterned after this model. Since first it descended from the Eleusinian mysteries of the Greeks, its rough edges have been softened, and ritual scarring and mutilation is not customary; although in the rites of black magic these practices still go on to satisfy the sadism of the initiators. True magical initiation is the highest form—the death of the material and the rebirth into the spiritual life.

The actual rite of initiation into a magical group occurs when the candidate is without great knowledge of occult matters. Usually the actions and symbolism in the rite are a complete mystery to him. If he has imagination he may see a hidden, spiritual meaning—the glow of the Sun through a veil of clouds. On the other hand, if the candidate is a fool he will see only empty words and gestures, and will soon repudiate the circle he has sought to enter. Since he is convinced he has learned nothing, he can do no harm.

The heart of magical initiation is death and rebirth. Symbolism of mystical rebirth is found throughout the literature of mankind. The story of Jonah and the whale is an example of rebirth through the calling. Aboard a ship during a raging storm, Jonah has no faith in divine protection. His spiritual center is overpowered by the brute instincts of the flesh. Cast into the sea, he is swallowed by a whale—symbolic of his death where his flesh becomes the brute flesh of the sea creature. Yet he does not die. Jonah sees that his fears were needless, that he is protected by his heavenly Father. He perceives that the seemingly cruel act of his being cast overboard is a part of the plan for his salvation. After three days and nights he is set safely on shore, symbolically issued from the whale's womb transformed by his new faith and understanding.

Another ancient symbol of initiation is the maze, or labyrinth. Pursuing his quest, the seeker Theseus enters the twisting darkness where lurks the monster of his bodily fears and desires waiting to devour him. Yet with courage he overcomes the Minotaur and follows the threads of Ariadne, his faith, into the light of day. He has been transformed and elevated from the man he was, who remains entombed within the bowels of the Earth.

These legends bear on the initiation into a modern magical school. No seeker can enter a true secret lodge so long as he lives in the material world of conceits and delusions. The philosophy of the world is material; the philosophy of magic is mystical. The two are oil and water. They will not mix.

True, the trained Magus is able to take his place in the world, even as he is able to adapt his mind and body to all mundane occupations; but this is no longer his real life. He recognizes a higher existence more precious than the dreary forms and motions he is forced to enter into in the material world. Whereas before, his occupation was his reality and the concerns of his Spirit were delusions; now the work he does to maintain himself physically is the dream, and the matters pertaining to his spiritual development are the true reality.

Therefore the old personality of the initiate must die before a new self can be born. He must be wiped clean of all the graffiti that has been scrawled and scratched on the slate of his soul over the years, in order that a new Word may be written on it.

He may be asked to simulate the physical act of dying, through such gestures as lying in a coffin or being elevated on a cross in a dramatic recreation of the crucifixion. Through trials of courage, he may be tested to determine that he is serious enough to treat the symbolism of the rite with respect, and strong-willed enough to keep from betraying the secrets of the lodge. Usually these tests are symbolic in nature, although made to appear terrifyingly real, and physical injury is not permitted to happen in a responsible group.

The 19th-century French occultist Paul Christian, purporting to describe the Egyptian mysteries, tells how the candidate is led to a dark passage and told to crawl in. The candidate has no assurance that he is not crawling to his death. As soon as he has passed the threshold, the heavy bronze door of the passage is dropped with a clang, and the candidate hears the terrible words: "Here perish all fools who covet knowledge and power!"[12]

The candidate faces an agonizing quandary. Should he wait for release, or go on into the threatening darkness? He has been given an oil lamp by his guides, but the oil will not last forever. Gathering his courage, he crawls down the sloping passage and eventually comes upon a great abyss. On the side of the pit is an iron ladder that leads down into the impenetrable darkness. With the lamp in his teeth, the candidate descends the ladder.

Abruptly his foot swings on empty space. The ladder has ended on nothingness, and the bottomless darkness of the pit still beckons below. Hopelessness grips the candidate. He inwardly curses the foolishness and pride that led him to such a circumstance. There is no going forward and no escape behind. The lamp flickers.

Then suddenly he notices a small aperture in the side of the pit near the ladder, just wide enough to admit the body of a man. Hope surges within him. Can this narrow avenue lead to salvation? With a trembling and thankful heart he pulls himself into the opening, which ultimately leads to the inner temple and the place of the initiation ritual.

Whether this is a true description of the Egyptian initiation or is wholly fanciful does not matter. The meaning is clear. The clanging door is the gate of Death. The sloping dark passage is the birth canal, and the dark pit is the abyss that every soul must cross when it moves from one life to another. Had the candidate hesitated, the lamp—his hope—would have flickered and failed, and he would never have seen the narrow doorway that led to his salvation. Instead, he would have hung suspended, trapped between the past and the future, until through weariness he fell at last into the dark of oblivion.

Having ritually died, the candidate is reborn into the circle of initiates. Life is breathed into his body. He is given fresh robes to clothe his spiritual nakedness. He is christened with a new name to impress upon his mind that he is not the man he once was. The name is secret, known only to the group or to a chosen number within the group. It is symbolic of his new life, and he remains as yet vulnerable as a newborn infant and must be protected from the malefic forces of the larger world. Those intending him harm could use his magical name as a key to open the door of his turbulent subconscious and inject poison into his forming awareness.

Often some other symbol is given to the initiate—a geometric sign, or the image of an animal or plant. This acts as the nexus around which he builds his new magical Will. In modern magic the symbol is a motto chosen by the initiate or chosen for him. At least for the immediate future, he will pattern his life around his new name and motto, for when their usefulness has been exhausted, the initiate will choose or be given others that will help him attain a still higher level of wisdom.

At the time of the rite, the rebirth is more in word than deed. As yet the initiate is much unchanged. His new name means little or nothing to him, however he may reverence it. The elements of the rite are confusing and seemingly without meaning.

In effect, the ritual of initiation compresses into a short span of time a process of becoming that requires years to bear fruit. As the Magus grows in wisdom and acquires the basics of his Art, the real rebirth takes place—a slow miracle, like the growth of a tree, so slow that it is barely discernible in the short run but is readily apparent over a large stretch of time.

If the candidate is initiated into a lodge or other established circle, he has a relatively easy task. He is told what to do, and provided that he is of average intelligence and courage, he will readily be able to accomplish what is expected of him. It is not the desire of any lodge to turn candidates away, but to find those who will bear refinement and tempering into a useful instrument for the Light. How far the candidate will advance in the Art is another question, but he should have little difficulty with the physical aspects of the initiation rite itself.

If, on the other hand, the would-be magician is utterly alone, learning the elements of his Art from books and, it is to be hoped, guided by his intuition, his task is more difficult. This is all too often the case in the Western world. It is not that secret organizations offering initiation do not exist, but it is seldom worth the while of the Magus to join them. Too often they are theaters of conceit where the rocks and twigs of learning are guarded and hoarded up jealously with magpie zeal, as though avarice alone would transform them into precious jewels.

The Magus should seek out a circle he feels may have something to teach him, but should not join from desperation a social club for the self-deluded. It is far better if he constructs his own initiatory rite, baptises himself with his magical name, and takes upon himself a motto to act as a staff for his development. But to do this he must possess a clear concept of what the rite is intended to accomplish.

Solitary initiation is seldom as beneficial for the development of the Magus as group initiation, for a number of reasons. Group initiation partakes of the dramatic effect of a pageant. At its best it is awesome and meaningful. Also, groups support the individual over difficult passages, giving advice and examples. And an established group rite with tradition and years of practice behind it is almost certain to be more complete and better structured than any rite created by an individual in his early stages of attainment.

Yet if the solitary initiate is resourceful and possessed of a strong artistic sense, a rite of his own composing can be of greater meaning to him than any public ritual. This only happens when the elements of the personal rite have been inspired by the Light. Then it is of extreme potency, for it strikes a resonance in the deepest core of the subconscious mind of the initiate.

Each person must seek into the secret depths of his being for his initiatory ritual, bearing in mind the necessary components of segregation, purification, death, rebirth, and christening with a new name and a motto. It is best for the beginner to work with the simple tools of the Art—circle, ray, pentagram, elements, guardians of the quarters, wave, spiral, Light, and the names of God. These are seldom hurtful if intelligently used in harmonious combination.

First you must purify your mind and body. For the mind, set yourself apart for a period of several weeks. The time of an annual holiday is perfect for the rite of initiation. Go to a place where you are not known and where you have no material business, such as a quiet place in the mountains or beside the ocean. As much as possible, avoid the frivolous company of others unless they are directly a party to your initiation and are working with you toward your goal.

Establish a rigid regime of prayer and meditation and stick to it despite the distractions that will surely arise to make this difficult; for you should know that the forces of Evil will not placidly allow you to abandon them and dedicate yourself to the service of the Light. Strive to learn your strengths and weaknesses by rigorously examining your past life. Strive to rid your mind of all hatred to anyone whatsoever, no matter how terrible their treatment of you has been—that very hatred is the power they, and through them the forces of Evil, hold over you. Likewise eliminate all spite, jealousy, fear, and other petty emotions.

Do this not by trying to suppress them but by allowing them to rise up unchecked within you while you observe them dispassionately as from a great height, as though they belonged to another person you hardly know. Listen to the stream of your thoughts as though it was the ceaseless chatter of a foolish, bigoted old woman, and for the first time, see your thoughts for what they are—vain, arrogant, and futile.

Pray and meditate at least twice a day, once in the morning and once in the evening. Three times—once at noon—would be better. Four times—waking yourself every night at midnight—is better still.

Prayer and meditation always go together. In meditation you open yourself to currents in the subconscious mind. Prayer is your shield of protection. Pray before and after the period of meditation. Of course, prayer alone can be done anytime and under any conditions without harm. Pray for purity and the coming of the Light.

Through this constant prayer and a regular, pure lifestyle, the physical surroundings in which you live will be cleansed and made ready for the descent of the Light. The prayer creates a circular barrier around your living space through which Evil cannot pass unless you foolishly invite it to enter. Within this temple built of prayer and pure aspirations, it is safe to open your innermost heart.

For the purification of the body you must sleep only so much as is strictly necessary for health on a hard bed or upon the floor. Rise at first light of morning. Eat no more than three meals—two is better—and these composed of light but nourishing foods, with many grains, fresh fruits and vegetables, and little meat. However, the Magus is cautioned not to attempt to alter his diet too greatly as this will surely result in sickness, and the entire period of initiation will be wasted.

Care for your physical appearance as though you were making yourself ready for an introduction to a very important and special person with whom you desire to leave a favorable impression. Wash your body regularly and thoroughly—teeth, hair, nails, and any part where sickness is resident. The study of the physical aspects of yoga will provide the best techniques. As with all other things, the rule here is moderation. The cleansing is for your benefit, not for the benefit of the All, to whom one part of the physical realm is much like another. Drink only clear, cool water. Do not smoke. Do not drink alcohol. Do not indulge sexually. Exercise for a fixed period every day until your body is tired, but not to the point of total exhaustion. Swimming and running are ideal.

Persist in this regime for at least three weeks. Six months would not be too long. Direct all your thoughts and desires and actions to one purpose: the preparation of your soul for death, where it will be weighed in the great scales and found either acceptable or lacking.

During all this time the ritual has been prepared and memorized. Illuminations brought about by prayer and meditation will certainly necessitate modifications, but the basic format should be fixed before the initiation is begun, the result of months of study and thought.

At the time of the rite, which must take place apart from interruption, wash and anoint yourself with clean oil. Don a robe you have handmade of clean white linen. Draw a circle of protection about yourself and invoke the guardians of the quarters—the Angel, Eagle, Lion, and Bull. Purify the circle with fire and water. Create a vortex at its center by dancing or walking clockwise and call down the divine Light of holy Spirit. Offer your heartfelt prayers to the All and state clearly your intention in carrying out the ritual.

These are the preliminaries, which are the most important part of any ritual as they prepare the way for what is to follow. If they are not properly carried out, the essential symbolic message of the ritual will not reach its objective, no matter how elegantly it is constructed or executed.

The actual ritual of dying and rebirth must be constructed of visual symbolism that you can act out with your physical body and picture within your mind. It is not the purpose of this work to present particular examples. However, one avenue is the symbolic destruction of the old name by fire and its return to the earth, followed by the consuming of the new magical name that has been written on some edible substance. The Magus must kill and bury, symbolically, all that is connected with his old way of life, then give birth to and exalt his new magical identity.

When the magical name has been assumed, and along with it some physical mantle or object of dress that signifies its attainment, and the Magus has spoken the motto upon which he will base the central motive of his new life, it is a good occasion to invite the Light to offer its unique contribution by some sign or understanding given to the Magus that he will cherish and seek to interpret fully for perhaps years into the future. If the ritual has been truly carried out this sign is seldom refused, though it may sometimes be overlooked due to the ignorance of the Magus, who often expects it to be delivered in sheets of flame and words of thunder.

The ritual should be composed as a piece of art offered to God, with its movements a dance and pantomime, and its sounds song and poetry. Always it should be a beautiful experience.

Initiation is ended with a prayer of thanksgiving. The vortex is closed and the circle cleansed of all lingering evil influences lurking outside it, then reabsorbed into the mind of the Magus. The final act for the initiate is to center himself in his universe, using his new magical name for the first time in addressing the All.

It is well for the beginner to practice the movements of the rite beforehand until he is letter-perfect. For him to forget an integral part during the performance gives pleasure to the forces of Darkness. The Magus should be confident that he can conduct the ritual perfectly from start to finish, even should his mind enter an exalted state of awareness. To commit errors in the mechanics of the rite, regardless of good intentions, shows that the initiate lacks the necessary sincerity and dedication.

Once you have completed your initiation, never talk about it to others. Never reveal your magical name no matter what the social temptation may be to induce you to do so. It is sometimes hard to keep from talking about things in which you justifiably take great pride, but you must resist and keep silent. This in itself is a testing. It will strengthen your Will. That which only you know and revere will remain forever pristine and undefiled.

There are two sides to magic. There are the general principles and common wisdom that should be freely given to all who seek it. This is the common coin of the Art, which is both used and abused. But the other, hidden side of magic lies in the personal rites and symbols that are intimately bound to the individual and are a part of his innermost subconscious being. To reveal the first is the duty of every seeker after the Light. To betray the latter is both foolish and dangerous.

Remember the Hermetic maxim—Know, Dare, Will, and Keep Silent.[13]

INSTRUMENTS

THE INSTRUMENTS OF magic are only the physical basis for the forms that are created in the psyche of the Magus. These psychic, or mental, forms are in turn the rational basis for forces that exist below the level of cogitation.

Magic works in two directions. Material instruments generate psychic forms that in turn call into operation the superconscious forces. This is magic from the outer to the inner circles of being and is the Way of the Serpent. Sometimes forces beyond the conception of the human mind cause ideas and images to appear in the psyche of the Magus, who then uses these images to make material instruments of the Art, as in the case of intuitive sigil making. This is magic from the inner to the outer circles and is the Way of the Lightning.

In practice neither of these operations is pure; both are related and interdependent. Before the instruments can be used to invoke the Light they must first be obtained. And in order to facilitate the descent of the Light, instruments and ritual methods must be used. Magic is therefore an upward spiral of increasing knowledge. Each new insight becomes another rung in the ladder that leads to the Great Work. There is a flux and reflux of Spirit between man and God.

The traditional instruments are few and simple. They are based on the magical principles presented in the first half of this work.

The four main objects that are the foundation of the Outer Temple are the elemental weapons—Rod, Cup, Sword, and Shield. They are to be found as the emblems of the suits in the Minor Arcana of the Tarot and in a host of other places.

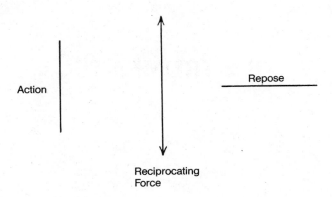

Rod

Also known as the Wand, the Scepter, the Staff, and the Club. It is the instrument of impregnation and suggests the phallus. Since it represents balanced or reciprocating force, it is the instrument of rule, or order, and in another form is commonly said to represent the Will of the Magus. Its element is Fire.

Magically the Rod is used to issue directives, to construct ritual forms, and also to project positive forces.

Held upright it symbolizes action; held horizontally it indicates repose.

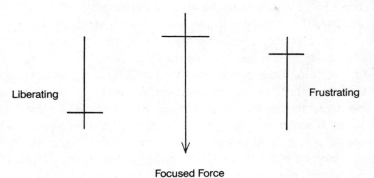

Dagger

Also called the Sword, the Knife, and the Pin. It is the instrument of violation. It suggests thrusting and piercing and thus represents unbalanced force. The guard of the Dagger is akin to the small arm of the Christian cross, which is off-center and directs the primary force of the vertical ray out its longest segment. Its element is Air.

Magically the Dagger is used to command through threat of punishment. It can cause discomfort to psychic entities, as can all pointed steel or iron objects. Generally it symbolizes justice and retribution.

Held with the point up, it is the symbol of liberation. Held point down, it is symbolic of frustration and waste.

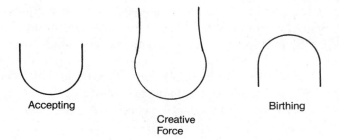

Accepting

Creative
Force

Birthing

Cup

Also called the Chalice and Grail. It suggests a seed unfolding new life and a womb ready to issue forth its contents, which it has nurtured and protected. Growth, love, protection, and creation—all are represented by the Cup. Its element is Water.

Magically it is used as an instrument of nurture. Strength may be drawn from the Cup, and evil influences washed away in its waters. Love may be spread through its sharing.

Held upright, it is the open womb waiting to receive the impregnation of the Rod or the vessel about to give form to what is poured into it. Held inverted, it is the symbol of birth and realization: that which has been nurtured is released into the world.

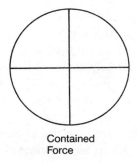

Contained
Force

208 / New Magus

Shield

Also called the Disk, the Pentacle, and the Coin. It is the only one of the four elemental instruments that is radially symmetrical. It suggests completeness, and thus sterility. It is self-contained, giving nothing, and taking nothing. The Shield symbolizes frigidity, aridity, and inertia; the virgin and the maidenhead. But the other side of the Coin is resistance, persistence, and a cold, remorseless strength. Its element is Earth.

Magically the Shield is used as a protection against hostile forces. It imposes a freeze similar to that associated with the equal-armed cross. The Shield neither moves nor can be moved, although it can be shattered if sufficient force is applied. The Dagger rapes and violates the Shield.

Since it has no top or bottom, it cannot be changed by inversion. Consider an apple; it begins small and green, then grows larger and gets red; it goes from sour to sweet—yet always it remains an apple. This is the power of the Shield.

Each of the four instruments represents the nature of one of the elements. For this reason they are most effective when applied to their own elemental spheres. Two are male (Rod and Dagger) and two are female (Cup and Shield). The Rod-Cup form a natural pair of the Light; the Dagger-Shield form a pair of the Darkness.

All the instruments must be consecrated before they can be used. Consecration drives away any lingering base associations and prepares the instrument to act as a channel for the Light. Consecration of the instrument is accomplished in a separate ceremony of prayer and purification by means of the element associated with the instrument. For example, the Rod is purified with Fire, and the prayers for the rod are directed at the Fiery aspect of the All.

The shape of the instrument will vary according to personal taste. However, these general guidelines should be followed. The Rod is a shaft of hardwood about a foot long and as thick as a finger, tipped with steel or brass caps. The Dagger is a short steel knife with a handmade wooden hilt. The Cup is a goblet of any convenient material of a size to hold about eight ounces. The Disk is of hardwood an inch thick and small enough to hold inside the spread fingers of one hand (about five inches in diameter).

It is usual to write the names of the angels and spirits associated with the instrument on it in the appropriate elemental color. Some of these names are to be found in the table of the square. However, it is not necessary to write the names provided the Magus knows them by heart.

There are two general instruments of a masculine type used to direct and command magical powers. They are the Wand and the Sword.

Wand

The Wand is similar in shape to the Rod and shares many of its characteristic functions, but applies them generally to all the elemental and other magical forces. The Wand rules and directs all magical operations. It is the single most important instrument and is said to embody the Will of the Magus. It should be of hardwood, hand-carved and consecrated at the least with the four names of God—IHVH, Eheieh, Adonai, AGLA—and with the four elements. The general rule is to consecrate an object in those areas where it is to be used. Since the Wand is used in all aspects of magic, its consecration must be all-encompassing.

It should be in length from the fingertips to the armpit and in thickness like the thumb. Sometimes one end is divided to signify a male and a female end, but this is not common. The wood of Mercury, the hazel, is recommended.

Sword

The Sword is similar to the Dagger, but applies its qualities throughout the realm of magic. It is used in all matters where command, threat, or punishment is necessary. For this reason it is seldom used in works of white magic.   .

It should be made of good steel and equal in length with the Wand, preferably hand-forged by the Magus. Where this is impossible, at least the hilt must be fashioned by the Magus. When not in use it must be kept wrapped in clean white linen. This applies to all the instruments.

Several other objects are used to form the basic Outer Temple. These are the Altar, the Lamp, the Circle, and the Gate.

Altar

Ideally this should be made from a single block of natural stone, unhewn in any way, about two feet square and flat at the top and four feet high. Since this is usually not possible, a block of natural stone should be used as the top of the altar or at least enclosed within it.

The Magus does not worship the stone. Nor does he worship the Earth through the stone. He worships the Light through the Earth, which is represented by the stone.

The Altar is always the focal point of the ritual and where possible, should be placed in the center of the Circle. The ritual instruments are placed on top of the Altar when used, and when not in use, are kept inside it. The Altar must be kept safe in a place where it will not be touched by the hands of the profane.

Lamp

Usually the Lamp is made of brass. It should be hung over the Altar or set upon the Altar top, and should burn throughout the ritual. Often it is lit during the ritual preparations, which may take days or weeks, in order to gather psychic force for the ritual. It must never be allowed to expire through neglect.

A colorless, odorless oil is used that will harmonize with the Light of Spirit, which the Lamp represents. Electric Lamps are not suggested as they are usually discordant. The major objection is that they are too easy—a ritual should be a work of care.

Translucent shades can be made to fit over the lamp in the colors of the elements, planets, and Zodiac signs. These shades are used when the ritual is specifically directed at one element or astrological power.

Circle

The ritual Circle should be large enough to accommodate comfortably the number of people who will occupy it and should be drawn in a number of units that is harmonious with the ritual purpose. For the Magus alone, usually it is six feet in diameter; for the Magus and the ritual Altar, nine feet in diameter.

If the ritual is conducted out-of-doors, the Circle is scratched into the earth with the Dagger or Sword. It may then be filled with oil and set alight so that the Magus is surrounded with a wall of flame.

If the ritual is done indoors, the Circle may be marked on the floor with fluorescent tape or paint, or a ritual carpet unrolled that has the Circle woven into its pattern. In any case it is best to make the physical Circle anew each time a ritual is conducted, then erase the physical Circle after the ritual is ended.

The Circle may be as simple as a single line or more complex with pentacles and names of power inscribed on it. This is a matter for the good taste and discretion of the Magus.

Gate

The Gate is a symbolic doorway set up inside the Circle, usually through the use of two pillars—one black and one white to suggest the duality of manifestation. A thin veil of silk is hung between the pillars.

The Gate is the physical representation of the aperture that is to be opened into the point of Self. By passing through it the Magus signifies to his subconscious that he has crossed the Veil of Unknowing.

It may also be represented by a hoop that is large enough to pass easily over the body. Stepping through the hoop will symbolize penetration of the Veil.

In addition to these outer instruments, there are certain objects that are always carried on the person of the Magus during ritual events. These are the Robe, the Sash, the Cap, the Crown, the Pentacle, and the Ring.

Robe

This is of simple white linen, with sleeves loose and ending at mid-forearm and the hem falling between the knee and the ankle. It symbolizes purity and the protecting cloak of the Light that enfolds the good purposes of the Magus. It must always be kept spotlessly clean. Decoration is left to the vanity of the Magus, who should remember that only sincerity of motives impresses the All.

Sash

The Sash binds the robe close and bars unfavorable influences. It is the symbolic lock on the door. It should wrap around the middle of the Magus three times and tie in the front. It is about two inches wide and made of seven colors arranged in lateral strips. The middle strip is white. The three upper strips in order going outward from the middle are red, blue, and yellow. The three lower strips going out from the middle are colored green, orange, and purple.

The Sash can be used to measure the magic Circle by driving the Wand into the earth and tying one end of the Sash to it, then inscribing the Circle with the Sword at the opposite end, with the Sash acting as the radius. This is most often done when the ritual involves a group and is conducted out-of-doors.

Cap

Ideally the Cap should be tall and conical. However, this shape has been so often mocked through history by the Church that the Magus may be embarrassed to make use of it. The conical Cap symbolizes the descent of the Light from out of the point of Self into the awareness of the Magus.

The best color for the Cap is light blue, signifying a passive and gentle descent of the Light. It should be made of paper or stiffened cloth. Leather can be used, but it must be taken from a virgin animal, a kid or lamb. If using paper, make sure it has no recycled fibers.

Crown

This is a circlet worn around the brow that is made of brass, silver, or gold in the shape of a serpent swallowing its tail. The head of the serpent is worn to the front.

It symbolizes the inward spiral, or the descent of the Will of the Magus from the world of perception through the Veil to the Unmanifest. The Crown is the opposite of the Cap—the Cap symbolizes the outward flowing of the Light; the Crown symbolizes the in-streaking of the Will. They stand for opposite movements across the Veil.

Pentacle

This is the personal symbol of the power of the Magus, and it depicts his knowledge and attainment. It does not remain fixed throughout the life of the Magus, but evolves to keep pace with his learning.

The Pentacle is worn on a chain or ribbon about the neck. It is the size of the center part of the palm and may be inscribed on metal or painted on wood. It rests over the heart of the Magus, which is his natural body center.

In times of great distress the Magus will use the Pentacle to command unruly spirits, as a weapon of last resort. The Pentacle is more personal to the Magus than even the Wand. It is constructed out of his magical name even as the sigils are based on the magical names of the spirits.

Since it is so much a part of him, the Magus must never allow the Pentacle to be seen or touched by another being as he will be extremely vulnerable to its misuse.

Ring

The Ring is the natural balance to the Wand. It corresponds to the Cup in the set of elemental weapons. It releases creative and protective forces and can be used to draw power to the Magus, to help others recover from illness, to still anger, and to promote good feelings.

The Ring is almost always worn on the index finger of the left hand because it is passive by nature, and it balances the body of the Magus with the Wand, which is always held in the right hand.

It must be handmade and consecrated in the same way as all the other instruments. It may also be inscribed with symbols and names appropriate to its uses. The master symbol of the upright pentagram should be cut on its face. When it is worn with the top-most point of the pentagram facing inward, it draws favorable influences and wards off evil from the Magus.

The donning of the Ring is akin to inserting the Rod into the Cup—an act of impregnation. In an emergency, force can be focused along the index finger and projected through the ring's axis by putting the ring onto the right hand. This inverts the powers of the ring. However, it is more usual to focus force by means of the Wand and Sword. The putting on of the magic Ring marks the actual beginning of the ritual, and the taking off signifies the ending.

The Ring should not be worn casually or be seen or touched by others. Like all the instruments it is sacred and must be kept apart, wrapped in clean white linen when not in actual use.

In addition to the simple instruments enumerated above, a more complex magical tool may be constructed and used in rituals. This is the personal Tarot, each card of which must be drawn and painted, then consecrated by the Magus. The personal Tarot is actually an entire Outer Temple all to itself, and correspondents for the magical instruments will be found among the cards.

There is always a strong temptation to elaborate and decorate when making the instruments. This should, for the most part, be resisted. Such detailing merely distracts the mind away from the basic principles behind the instrument, which are always very simple and straightforward. At the same time, the instruments should not be made and consecrated with carelessness. This indicates a contempt for the Light, which may be overt or subconscious.

The answer is to make the instruments simple and plain, but as perfect as is humanly possible and from the best carefully selected materials. For example, the Wand should be little more than a straight shaft of wood; however, it should be the very best wood without warp or knot and of an even and beautiful grain, planed and sanded until its outer surface is as smooth as glass and hand-rubbed with oil to a deep luster. This same guide applies to all the other instruments.

THREE TEMPLES

WHEN A PSYCHICALLY sensitive person enters a large church he is first struck by the coldly inhuman atmosphere. The stones and stained glass seem to have nothing to do with puny humanity and its insignificant hopes and fears. It is a great hollow place where many speak, but few listen. And it is empty. Even when filled with people, there is a sense that something necessary is missing, as though a reception has been prepared for a very important dignitary who failed to arrive, and the embarrassed guests were painfully going through the motions.

That missing guest is magic. Without magic, religion is a farcical mockery. All religions are magical in essence. They must be. God is a supernatural being. All religions are based upon the worship of God. To deny magic in religion is to deny God. The church then becomes a social meeting house, a useful place for carrying out archaic customs such as marriage and christening, but devoid of any central reason for being.

It is no outrage when a church is sold and turned into a theater or a private dwelling or a barn. The offense was committed long before by cynical priests and indifferent congregations who cast the magic out and left a hollow shell. The churches of the West are corpses that provide no sustenance for the maggots that infest them.

Houses of worship are called by many names—church, synagogue, and mosque. A term that embraces them all is temple, which means a place set aside for communing with God. The development of a special house for prayer is the outgrowth of a fixed society rooted to the earth by agriculture. In ancient times and among primitive hunting and foraging tribes, devotions were often tied to special days of the year, and a temporary temple of dancing human bodies and flaming bonfires, or colored lines drawn in the sand, was erected as the focus for magical forces.

The modern rebirth of Wicca (a conscious attempt to revive the deification of nature) shows a regression to the nomadic type of magical worship, where the temple is formed by convening a group of worshipers, often but not necessarily thirteen in number, on the eight major feast days of the year. Worship takes place out-of-doors with only the magic circle to act as the walls of the psychically erected temple.

Modern pagans, because they welcome uncritically the forces of magic and because they are fiercely devoted to their beliefs, usually succeed in filling their temples of the imagination with Light. However, it can happen that Wiccan covens become mere social clubs or, what is worse, sexual theaters of the absurd. When this occurs, their magic circles are as empty and as useless as the cathedrals in Rome. The Sabbats are mockeries of the Deity, however it may be conceived.

There is a third kind of temple that is never entered except by the faithful. It cannot be profaned because when its worshipers pass out its doors, it ceases to exist. It is without a name because it belongs to no set place. All peoples of the world worship in it together, yet it is only large enough to accommodate a single soul. A man can stray away from its roof, and always it is with him. Eternally new, it is as old as time. No man may buy it, but it can be freely given. This magic place, which once seen is never forgotten, is the temple of the Spirit.

Hermetic magic, with its characteristic love of synthesis, has tried to integrate the best features of all three temples into its own temple of the Art. Its design is reminiscent of the caskets of the Egyptians, which often contain a box within a box within a box. The Outer Temple of magic is a physical place, usually a room or a building but occasionally a grove or a field. The Middle temple is an imaginary setting that often bears little resemblance to the physical surroundings of the Magus. The Inner Temple is entered with the descent of the Light into the magic circle, and its characteristic is joy.

Paradoxically the three temples are constructed from the outside in, even though they are vitalized from the inside out. The Outer and Middle temples have no reality without the temple of Spirit, yet it is through them that the Inner Temple is reached. Thus the construction of the Outer and Middle temples is an act of faith that may or may not be ultimately rewarded. They must be carefully considered and made, for the magical life of the Magus depends on their efficacy.

Outer Temple

Also called the Temple Material. This must be a place where, above all, the Magus can feel relaxed and secure from interruption on any level of being. The air should be healthful and quiet, free from odors, discordant noises, dampness or smoke. The chamber that is to contain the Outer Temple must be secure from the intrusions of strangers. The emotional atmosphere should be pleasant or, at the least, neutral.

For these reasons the heart of a city is a poor place for the Outer Temple. However, since many people live in cities, oftentimes the best must be made of a bad situation. Cellars are well insulated from chance comings and goings, as are attics and outbuildings. Such disused spaces can often be made to serve provided they meet the subjective needs of the Magus.

It is a good idea to locate the place of ritual and worship as far away as possible from other human beings, even when no threat of intrusion exists. Otherwise, when you carry out a ritual you will discover that the waves of power you are sending out will disturb your neighbors. Few people can sleep when a ritual is being conducted anywhere nearby. Animals, particularly cats, will also be affected.

Once you have located a suitable environment, you must consider the ritual space itself. It should be a room of at least 10 x 12 feet with a hardwood floor and a high ceiling, no windows and a single door opening in the north wall. If it is accurately aligned with the points of the compass, so much the better. Since windowless rooms are uncommon, shutters should be made in the inside to completely seal the windows. These can be left open during the day and closed for ritual work at night.

There must be adequate lighting in the room so that in an emergency the chamber can be brightly lit at the touch of a switch. A large tilt-style switch that can be easily located and operated in the dark should be installed. The walls are best left plain and featureless, and the same goes for the door. Walls, door, shutters, and ceiling are painted a neutral gray. Some adepts suggest black, but this tends to be oppressive. Red should not be used, as it is the color of Satanism. The temple should never be painted any one particular color since it would influence all successive rituals.

Study of the interior design of traditional Japan will suggest the ideal the Magus should strive for. The chamber must be simple and balanced, neither forbidding nor inviting. When the Magus has entered it, he should feel as though he belongs there, yet when he leaves and looks back, he should not get the impression that anything is lacking.

Ventilation is necessary as sometimes large amounts of incense are burned in charcoal fires—during certain evocations, for example—and carbon monoxide poisoning could be a possibility were the chamber sealed tightly. Ideally the floor should have some spring so that prolonged standing and walking may be done without fatigue.

Before the chamber is used it is purified and consecrated. Some adepts maintain that the magic circle is not necessary when magic is done in a consecrated chamber. This is true when dealing with the forces of Light. The odor of sanctity will keep away any prowling demons. When calling upon the forces of Darkness however, a circle is always used. The very fact that such entities are summoned into the chamber defiles its purity and thus it is no longer a protection.

Middle Temple

Also called the Temple Astral. This is the imaginary landscape that satisfies the emotional needs of the Magus, as the Outer Temple met his physical needs. It is created in the mind through a stepped process of visualization that requires many hours of intense meditation. It must be as clear in the mind of the Magus as a stereoscopic technicolor movie, as clear as the inside of his dreams. If group magic is conducted, the imagery is reinforced by a verbal interchange describing the details of the temple. In this way all members of the group are sure to visualize much the same setting.

Middle Temples can be drawn from personal experience, mythology, dreams, even travelogues. Often an ancient temple site that agrees with the magic being worked is chosen and recreated in the mind. For example, an adept might picture himself conducting his ritual in the Parthenon or within the ring of Stonehenge. Or a natural setting such as the shore of a Tibetan mountain lake or a shadowy grove of ancient oaks might be used. Even settings that have no correspondence on Earth make successful Inner Temples. The Magus might imagine himself standing on a flat black disk that floats in interstellar space.

The unifying factor among these diverse visions is that they must uplift the consciousness of the Magus out of its ordinary state. However he chooses to see his Middle Temple, it must inspire him with wonder and a sense of awe. His purpose in erecting it is to create a religious rapture. Therefore its every association must be positive and powerful.

It is within the Middle Temple—not the Outer Temple, as is commonly believed—that magic is performed. Even simple ritual actions such as prayer are done within the grandeur of the temple built in the psyche. The Magus must be able to enter and leave it more or less at will if he hopes to make his rituals effective. To stand inside the Middle Temple is to be halfway to the state of exaltation that permits the parting of the Veil.

Inner Temple

Also called the Temple Spiritual. Little can be said descriptively about the temple of the Spirit because it has no perceivable qualities. It cannot be seen or heard or touched. However, entry into it is akin to opening the door of a brightly lit room before a man lost in the night. To experience it engenders a reaction of unutterable joy. It is the ecstasy of mystics, the rapture of saints.

The Inner Temple houses the lamp of Spirit and the secret Torah that contains the knowledge of God. It may be described as the interior of the vessel that holds the first emanation. This is as close to God as any manifest thing can approach without itself becoming God.

To stand within this Temple Spiritual is the goal of every true Magus. The mystic wishes to dwell within it forever, but the Magus seeks to come and go at will in order that he may carry the fires of heaven to Earth. No true magic is possible unless the Inner Temple is at least touched, no matter how briefly. Through the doors of the Inner Temple the Light of God issues out to illuminate the outer circles of being.

It is a fact of human nature that most aspirants after magical knowledge begin to practice the Art before they understand what they are practicing. They construct detailed, lavish Outer Temples without knowing how to erect a temple in the mind, let alone a temple of the Spirit. The result is a place of worship as lifeless and as hollow as any Christian cathedral.

Many are discouraged at this stage when they attempt material rituals in their material temples and get no results. However, the few persevere in striving to understand their errors and to rectify them. Like children unraveling a ball of string, they begin to travel inward, moving past the outer pageantry to the emotional meaning of the symbolism on which it is based. Finally they begin to touch the walls of the Inner Temple, where the potencies that give the symbols meaning dwell. Only after establishing contact with the Light can they turn outwards once more and, with confidence, create rituals based on cosmic law.

RITUAL

RITUAL IS THE vital heart of magic. It creates a communication between the phenomenal world and the point of the Self that is the doorway to the Unmanifest. The information gained from the Self helps make the mechanics of ritual more effective, which in turn results in a more positive transfer of knowledge. Each pole strengthens the other. In this way the Magus grows, by relying on his initial attainments, to win ever greater command over his personal universe.

Through a series of words, gestures, and movements a mind-state is induced that opens a door through the Veil into the Unmanifest and guides the outward streaming of the Light toward a specific objective. The mechanics of the ritual act as a kind of filter, allowing only that aspect of the infinite possibility that is the Unmanifest through the door that is of practical use to the Magus and is not destructive of the Light.

The Magus makes a series of physical gestures that resonate as symbols in his conscious mind and enter his subconscious as directives. The force of Will, acting through the lever of symbolism, opens the vortex door in the deepest well of the Self and allows the Magus to tap the milk of Hathor (the Light of the Unmanifest), which pours forth as a raw power and is shaped for its specific ritual purpose the instant it enters manifestation in the forge of the subconscious. The conscious mind then becomes aware of this potency on the mental and physical levels through its action. Consciousness monitors the success or failure of the ritual as it occurs, and if necessary, sends a ray of Will to change its direction through the medium of the subconscious.

It should be made clear that "subconscious" is only another word for ignorance. It is the catch phrase made popular by nineteenth-century psychiatrists talking about those aspects of the psyche that could be observed only through their actions, never directly by the conscious mind. The reason the subconscious cannot be observed by the conscious mind is because it is closer than consciousness to the center of Self. For the conscious mind to observe the subconscious would be like the eye trying to look at itself directly. The eye can only observe itself indirectly through the physical mediation of a mirror or some other device. In the same way, the conscious can only observe the subconscious through its effects. The subconscious can be observed directly, but only from the point of Self, which is a vantage not obtainable by normal consciousness.

Several elements are prerequisites for any successful ritual:

1) *There must be a rapport between the conscious and the subconscious.*

In order to be effective the ritual must reach the subconscious levels of the psyche. The subconscious can be opened through the practice of meditation and autosuggestion so that certain universal symbols can be made to resound over its deepest levels.

If the elements of ritual do not reach the subconscious, they will have no power. Just as when two people look at a work of art and one is moved while the other feels nothing, so can the same symbol be meaningless to one man and potent to another. The conscious mind is capable only of dissection. Dissection kills a living symbol. To be effective, symbols must be experienced intuitively and emotionally.

This process of becoming attuned to symbolism is a slow evolution that may take years. However, some people possess a natural sensitivity to symbols that intellection can only retard. Individual reaction to symbols is the only sure guide.

2) *There must be a strong Will.*

The Will provides the initial push that injects the set of ritual symbols into the subconscious. It acts as a ray that pierces the artificial barrier separating the two levels of mind. The force of Will primes the pump, so to speak, so that a greater river may flow out from the subconscious sea.

3) *The ritual must be composed of symbols.*

The subconscious works on the level of symbols that are below the level of language, and only through the subconscious can the Magus tap the potencies of the Unmanifest, which is forever barred to direct access by the conscious mind. The conscious can experience the effects of the Light, but cannot summon or direct it except through the mediation of the subconscious.

A ritual where the Magus simply recited in a dry tone his desires would be completely ineffective. Even if through an immense act of Will he succeeded in sending his words into his subconscious, words have only a limited power there. Words are symbols, it is true, but symbols of a second level abstracted away from the symbolism of the natural world. The subconscious would be forced to translate the words into its own vernacular of sensory symbols, which are mainly visual, and most of the power of the initial impulse of Will would be lost.

4) *The ritual must be externalized.*

Physical expressions of the symbols, such as the magical instruments, hand gestures and body motions, sounds, colors, scents, tastes, textures, and images, should be employed wherever possible. This gives the conscious mind (the awareness of the Magus) a tangible input through the five senses that it can hold onto and use to guide the ritual on the subconscious circles without lapse. The ritual must be brought into a mental existence before it can be sent to reverberate on the Self. The physical side of the ritual helps make its mental side more complete and clear.

Actually the physical and mental are one and the same thing, but because modern man is so used to crediting what he gains through his senses and ignoring what occurs solely in his mind, a physical externalization of rituals is almost a practical necessity.

After the Magus has attained a high degree of proficiency in creating mental images and, more importantly, learned to believe in their objective reality, he may dispense with the external show of ritual.

5) *Ritual requires an ability to make the mind absolutely tranquil.*

The Magus must be able to make his inner being like the surface of a lake at twilight. After the pulse of Will, loaded with its symbolic directives, is sent into the subconscious to act on the Self, the Magus

must turn his mind to a receiving or passive mode so as not to interfere with the fruition of the ritual. Often the hopes and fears that arise
in the mind after the active part of the ritual are more potent psychically than the carefully expressed intentions of the Magus, because they
arise spontaneously from the depths of his being. These undirected
emotions can wreck the working of a ritual by interfering with the
current from the Unmanifest.

The Magus must be able to calm his mind after the physical work
of the ritual is done and refrain from fretting over the outcome. A firm
unshakable faith that the ritual will succeed has the effect of washing
out small but destructive doubts and fears. This faith cannot be gained
merely by wishing for it; it grows from experience and an understanding of the way magic works. Until faith has been achieved the Magus is
best served by striving for tranquility and refusing to react to doubts
when they arise. Trying to suppress doubt only serves to strengthen
it.

6) *The ritual must be protected from the forces of Darkness.*

Any properly performed ritual puts the Magus in a vulnerable
position. All manner of strange and dangerous entities can use the
channel he has bored through his subconscious to gain access and
take up residence there. He must employ symbolic filters to insure
that only those forces he actively summons come into his personal
universe.

The subconscious has two circles. There is the vast sea where all
manifest beings and forces dwell—those that are good, evil, and indifferent to mankind. It is sometimes called the racial memory, but this is
only a small part of it. The minds of all humanity, and of all other
beings and things, touch its edge.

Then there is the personal circle of the subconscious, which is
like a small inlet of the greater sea. This is the part of the subconscious
that affects the individual. It has its own inhabitants that are used to
interacting with a single human being. Generally an uneasy truce
exists between the beings in the personal subconscious and the will
and desires of the individual. Madness, suicide, or destructive behavior
results if the balance is disrupted.

Through ritual the Magus summons the creatures of the depths
up through the levels of shadow to enter his little pool of subconscious. These may be great benevolent whales or savage sharks. It is in
the interest of the Magus to keep the sharks out while letting the

whales enter. There are several magical methods the Magus uses to insure this.

a) *Purity*

The Magus must cleanse himself physically before each ritual; at the same time he is inwardly washing his soul clear of all stains. The physical washing is itself a mini-ritual. The Magus washes out all vanity and spite and other polluting emotions, then dons clean robes that have been kept pure for ritual use. All his instruments are likewise pure. Nothing is used that is physically or psychically soiled.

b) *Prayer*

Before, during, and after the ritual the Magus earnestly prays to the Light for strength and wisdom. He prays that the purpose of his ritual will be lawful. Moreover, he prays that the ritual will fail if he has, through weakness or ignorance, undertaken it for unworthy motives. He surrenders himself to the Light body and soul. By subordinating his Will to the All, he puts himself in harmony with cosmic law. He becomes an active instrument of evolution and derives a reflected authority from his service.

c) *Names of Light*

All evil fears the Light. By its nature the presence of the Light instantly destroys Darkness. The names of the principle emanations of the Unmanifest, which are names of God, have power over hurtful spirits when spoken with sincerity. The Tetragrammaton is especially useful when rightly understood. Traditionally it was said that a true uttering of this name would give the speaker power over all the world.[14] This is the power of perfect devotion undefiled by the smallest particle of ego. Such a devotion does not exist in our time. Its power would be beyond measure.

d) *Signs and Words of Power*

These are the least potent form of protection, but are the easiest to charge with meaning and therefore the most reliable for fallible humanity. These are the symbols that do not directly represent the Light, such as the pentagram, the cross, the triangle, the four guardians of the quarters, the magical instruments, curses, chants, and banishments that do not include the names of God.

Signs of power do not directly invoke the Light but rely on the authority that has been created in them by their form and function in the mind of the Magus. Spirits submit to the signs for the same reason electricity runs along a wire instead of through the air: it is their nature to do so.

e) *The Circle*

An invariable feature of any ritual, the circle is drawn around the Magus physically and at the same time mentally to separate his perception of self from hostile forces. The circle is impassible by an entity unless the Magus himself breaks its boundary or willfully invites an entity to come in. In everyday life the boundary is established at the limit of the physical body and a bit beyond, but when, during the ritual, the Magus consciously projects what are considered to be elements of his psyche outward into the greater world—externalizing his mind—this natural boundary threatens to become indistinct and must be reinforced by the circle.

Listed below in their correct order are the essential parts of any ritual. Because all true rituals are personal in nature, the descriptions of the steps are generalized. They should be used as a guide for the construction of particular rituals tailored to the needs and desires of the Magus.

1) *Purpose*

Before beginning a ritual the Magus should have clear in his mind the reason for conducting it. The longer he reflects on the object of the ritual, the more powerful its effect is likely to be. A period of several months for reflection and meditation is not excessive for important rituals.

2) *Withdrawal*

Before performing the ritual the Magus should live apart for a time, avoiding as much as he may the company of other people. There is no set period for withdrawal; ideally it will correspond with the gathering of purpose. If prolonged withdrawal is impossible, the Magus should at the very least be alone and silent for several hours before beginning. During this time he can make the necessary physical preparations.

3) *Purification*

The Magus cleanses himself solemnly with awareness of the importance of the act, like a bride preparing for her wedding night. He realizes that he is making himself ready to face his God. It is traditional to bathe, run fresh water and put consecrated salt into it, then bathe again while repeating a prayer of purification; finally the body is anointed with consecrated oil.

Here is a cleansing prayer drawn from Psalm 51:

> Have mercy upon me, O God,
>   blot out my transgressions;
> Wash me thoroughly from mine iniquity, and cleanse me
>   from my sins;
> Purge me with hyssop, and I shall be clean;
> Wash me, and I shall be whiter than snow;
> Create in me a clean heart, O God; and renew a right spirit
>   within me.

A similar prayer was used by adepts in ancient times. The angel of cleansing is said to be Tahariel.

4) *Robing*

The Magus puts on clean garments that have been kept solely for the purpose of ritual, never seen or touched by anyone outside the circle of initiates. These garments (usually a robe and slippers) are handmade by the Magus. They should be of high quality, yet simple and without ostentation. A short prayer is said over each article as it is put on, asking that it may perform its function. In addition to the robe a cap, circlet, and sash may be worn. The personal pentacle and magic ring are put on last.

5) *Arming the Altar*

Upon the top of the altar are set all the instruments and materials that will be used in the ritual. These will depend on the purpose of the working. The altar should never be cluttered, nor should the Magus be in danger of knocking something off if he passes near it. Each instrument should be kept wrapped in clean linen and tied with a seal of its power. As it is taken from its resting place the Magus kisses the seal, removes it and unwraps the instrument, then kisses the instrument and raises it to the East, saying "This instrument is sacred in your service, O Lord; may it never be defiled."

6) *Quieting*

The lamp has been lit. The instruments are arrayed on the altar. The Magus is properly robed. Now he stands in the ritual chamber facing the East and calms his mind for the task ahead, his back straight and his hands at his sides, his eyes closed. He recalls briefly the words and gestures of the ritual that he has previously memorized. This takes five or ten minutes.

7) *Centering*

The Magus emphasizes his central position in the universe. With his wand held in his right hand, he indicates a vertical axis through his body from his brow to the pit of his stomach. This he visualizes in red light. Turning the wand sideways, he then traces a horizontal axis from left to right that passes through his heart. He pictures this in blue. Finally he points the wand to the East with the base directed at his heart to make a third axis from his front to his back. This is visualized in yellow. The intersection point of the three axes is his heart center. It is pictured and felt as an intensely blazing white star.

This prayer is spoken while forming the cross:

> Thine (touching the brow) is the kingdom (touching the lower stomach), the power (touching the left shoulder), and the glory (touching the right shoulder), forever (pointing East with the wand), Amen (raising the wand into the air overhead).

8) *Circling*

A circle of protection is drawn clockwise with the wand at the level of the heart while walking around the altar. This circle is visualized as extending from the wand to hang glowing with white light in the air. It must be seen clearly and held in the mind. It may correspond to a circle of similar diameter drawn on the floor with chalk or paint. If the chamber is small the Magus may draw the circle by rotating on a point, thus making himself the center and, if need be, the altar.

9) *Cleansing the Circle*

Usually the circle is cleansed of unwanted influences by Fire, Water, and Air. Symbols of the elements can be used, but it is more effective to use physical representatives. Fire is indicated by a candle or lamp; water is sprinkled with the fingers or often a pinecone; and Air is usually signified with the smoke of an incense stick or sometimes a feather—however, it is better to indicate Air with the breath.

Each element or its symbol is taken from the altar and carried once around the circle clockwise, pausing at each quarter to display the element and invoke the powers of that element to cleanse and guard the circle. The sign of the element is traced in the air at each quarter with the symbol or object that represents it. The element is then returned to the altar.

10) *Opening the Door*

This is done by spinning on a point or walking inward clockwise to create a vortex in the magic circle. The vortex opens the point of Self onto the Unmanifest. The number of rotations made is usually three, but it may be five, seven, or twelve, depending on the nature of the working. If the ritual is intended for evil, the rotations would be eight or eleven.

11) *Invoking the Light*

A prayer is spoken to the Light, calling it down into the circle that has been prepared to receive it. Traditionally the Light is pictured as streaming down from a point over the center of the circle. Invoking the Light is akin to catching the eye of God.

12) *Statement of Purpose*

The Magus acknowledges the presence of the Light and states his purpose for conducting the ritual as clearly as possible. This is mainly to get it clear in his own mind, as simple statements have little effect on the subconscious.

13) *Invoking (or Evoking) the Spirits*

Signs and words of power are used that call forth the spirits or blind forces to be employed in achieving the purpose of the ritual. When they are invoked, they are summoned inwardly and transform the personality of the Magus; when evoked, they appear outside the circle as tangible beings. In either case their obedience is assured by binding them in the name of God.

14) *The Working*

This is a set of symbolic actions that plays out in dramatic form the realization of the Will of the Magus. It is the heart of the ritual to which all that went before tended. The working is the most individual part of a ritual and should always be unique, since it is tailored for the specific purpose of the Magus. Usually it takes the form of incantations in original verse combined with a kind of pantomime play where the ritual desire is symbolically attained. The Magus should be in a heightened mental state at this step, concentrating intensely on his desire. The visualizations must be quite real in his mind, or the working will lack effect.

15) *Thanksgiving*

The Magus offers thanks to the Light that the purpose of the ritual has been achieved. He must be filled with faith in the success of the ritual, or at least inwardly tranquil, or he will destroy the working with his doubts and fears. This prayer releases the Light from the circle and returns it to the Self, where it cannot be profaned by careless actions.

16) *Closing the Door*

A reverse vortex is created by outwardly circling the altar counterclockwise the same number of times used to open the door to the Light. This seals the aperture in the Veil of Unknowing and is a necessary step to avoid possession or mental illness. It also symbolically represents the realization of the ritual purpose. The Will was projected into the Unmanifest by the clockwise inward spiral; the counterclockwise outward spiral manifests the returning pulse from the Unmanifest.

17) *Banishing*

Any spirit or blind force that may have been attracted to the perimeter of the circle (as sharks are drawn by disturbances in the water) must be sent back to its rightful sphere before the Magus dares abolish the circle. This is done through a general banishing formula composed by the Magus for this purpose, usually relying on the authority of one or more names of God. It might be something like the following:

> All spirits or entities attracted to the outer edge of this magic circle, depart now, for you have no lawful business here. Go! In the holy names Yeheshuah and Yehovashah: yet go in peace and fare you well.

18) *Erasing the Circle*

It is not good to leave the magic circle hanging in the air and simply step through it as though it did not exist. Such disregard severely weakens its protective power. At the close of each ritual, the psychic circle should be reabsorbed into the personal self of the Magus by reversing the actions that extended it. That is, it should be drawn in through the index finger of the left hand, or through the wand held in the left hand, as it is retraced counterclockwise. This restores the circle of protection to the aura of the Magus and returns the ritual chamber to its neutral polarity.

19) *Centering*

Once again the Magus crosses himself through the heart with the three axes of colored light, speaking the short prayer to the Light as he does so. He reaffirms his position at the heart of the universe.

20) *Ending*

The ritual is clearly and unequivocally stated, aloud, to be over by the power of the Tegragrammaton or other name of God. The wand is struck against the floor sharply four times to indicate the earthing of all magical potentials. Then the wand is set on the altar, and the magic ring removed.

Immediately after the ritual is concluded, the instruments are reverently wrapped and put away in the reverse of the manner they were brought out. They are elevated to the East and kissed, then covered and sealed, and the seal kissed. This demonstrates the humble respect of the Magus for the Light.

When a ritual has been improperly performed, there will be a reaction. This may occur during the ritual, but more often it happens after the ritual is concluded and the Magus has relaxed his guard. After any ritual the Magus should strive to clear his thoughts of occult matters for the space of several hours. It is not the best idea to go directly to sleep after a ritual unless sleep is a specific part of the working. Bad dreams and hypnogogic images are likely—indeed, almost certain— to occur. Noises, sudden breezes and chills, voices, and other psychic jetsam are common after a powerful ritual as the potencies invoked leak past the protective barriers the Magus has erected around himself.

If his protections are rightly made, these aftereffects will be of no great consequence, and the Magus should not be overly concerned about them. On the other hand, if the Magus is badly shaken after a ritual he had best give himself some weeks to recover before attempting another. Sanity is a fragile balance. During his convalescence he should look searchingly at his motives and his manner of working to see where and why he failed.

Those who utterly reject the power of magic will not believe that anyone can be seriously hurt merely by mumbling a few arcane phrases and waving his arms about in the air. And indeed, these skeptics would be fairly well protected from harm by their circle of contempt. Unfortunately for them, their shield is also their prison. Protected from many of the ill effects of magic, they are at the same time barred from its good. And because their subconscious minds are not skeptical in the least, eventually they will burn themselves if they dabble in ritual long enough.

INSPIRATION

IT HAS BEEN said in the true grimoires that to achieve a mastery of magic the Magus needs nothing beyond a pure heart and prayers to God. When rightly called, the Light will manifest itself and instruct the Magus in all manner of signs and words necessary to achieve his ends. This should uplift the heart in times of discouragement. All magic lies within the Magus. Books, symbols, and names are only vessels that may or may not be useful in evoking the true magic from his inner being.

This is why the pentacles and sigils of magic have a finite life span and why they gradually lose their power as they grow older. Symbols above the elementary level are made to serve an individual, a class, a race, or a period in history. As the human circumstance changes these symbols lose their relevance, and new ones must constantly be created under the guidance of the Light by the adepts of the new age from the simple symbolic building blocks.

No Magus can progress in meaningful ways without the inspiration of the Light. The very word "inspiration" refers to the life-giving breath of God that infuses vitality into dead forms. It is the Light that confirms to the mind what books are valuable, which teachers speak wisdom, and which thoughts of the Magus are worth remembering. The Light is the touchstone by which everything is tested. It is the very soul of truth, one point of a trinity whose other two points are beauty

234 / New Magus

and goodness. The truth is the one from which beauty and goodness spring.

The general magical symbols presented here are only the framework upon which the complete house of the Art is erected. It is necessary to understand such symbols, but in themselves they are not enough. After grasping the bones of ritual, the Magus must then seek the enlightenment that will supply him with specific tokens keyed to the depths of his unique subconscious. Before the Light will dwell within him long enough to teach him the secrets of the Art, he must suffer the considerable pain and doubt that comes from completely renouncing his material mode of thinking and living. These hard-won secrets will be his alone and will have great power, but they will be wasted if he tries to share them with the larger world.

In legends the Norse god of magic, Odin, is said to have undergone this kind of personal sacrifice to achieve his illumination. In a beautiful and powerful excerpt from the *Havamal,* an unknown bard takes on the voice of the god in order to sing of his trial and achievement:

> I trow that I hung on the windy tree,
> Swing there nights all nine,
> Gashed with a blade,
> Bloodied for Odin,
> Myself a sacrifice to myself—
> Knotted to that tree,
> No man knows
> Whither the roots of it run.
>
> None gave me bread
> None gave me drink,
> Down to the depths
> I peered
> To snatch up runes
> With a roaring scream
> And fell in a dizzied swoon.
>
> Well-being I won,
> And wisdom too,
> I grew and joyed in my growth—
> From a word to a word
> I was led to a word,
> From a deed to another deed.[15]

Besides being of great beauty, this ancient poem has much to teach the modern Magus about the way to acquire the favors of the

Light. It is evident that the Magus must make a significant commitment in his life to seek wisdom, despite the very great hardship this may entail. The tree upon which Odin willingly hangs himself is the Kabbalistic tree of emanations, known in the North as Yggdrasil, the eternal ash whose roots reach down into hell and whose branches hold up the heavens. It is symbolic of the material order, the cosmic law, of the manifest universe. There are parallels to the cross of Christ.

The nine days are the nine primary emanations that are reflected in the physical world. Odin is said to remain tied to the tree for nine nights. Obviously he could not have gone anywhere in the physical sense. His peering into the depths was a vision of the secret depths of his own being. His reaching down to snatch up the runes was an act of Will to liberate the wisdom of the Light in symbol form from beyond the Veil of the Unmanifest. The opening through which the god stretches his hand is his point of Self, which both encompasses the entire universe and is every point in it.

His sacrifice was threefold. First and most important was the loss of his freedom. To the Norseman, bondage was slavery, and slavery was truly a fate worse than any death, no matter how horrible.

Second was the spilling of his own blood. This was a magical act for the Vikings, done to empower their symbols and weapons. It is the true form of bloody sacrifice. The slaying of an animal or another human being is a foolish attempt to trick God by substituting the blood of another creature for the lifeblood of the worshiper. Only the spilling of his own blood can commit the worshiper wholly to the keeping of his deity.

The third act of sacrifice was the nine-day fast Odin endured, during which he took neither food nor drink. To go nine days without food is comparatively easy. To endure nine days without water is a hardship that would cause the death of all but the strongest. The Norsemen were a physical race constantly pressing the boundaries of their endurance. One of the runes supposedly given by Odin is Nyd (ᚾ), which means "the necessity to endure." They would have appreciated full well the meaning of nine days without water. Interestingly, there is a Japanese Buddhist initiation that requires the priest undertaking it to go nine days and nights without water or food. This is still practiced today.

What is the inner meaning of the sacrifices of Odin? To be bound to the tree entails the curbing of the animal will to strike out in passion or hatred as soon as the impulse comes to mind. To mutilate one's own flesh is to proclaim to the depths of being that the pleasures and pains of the body are of secondary importance to the union with the Light. Finally, to go without food or drink is a symbolic repudiation of the worth of mere material sustenance.

Taken together the three sacrifices are a cleansing of the three levels of being—bondage thwarts the mental impulses; self-mutilation opposes the emotional and sensual impulses; and fasting thwarts the physical needs of the body itself.

When Odin peered into the depths of his own being after the nine nights, the effect of what he saw was almost overwhelming. To look into the face of the unshielded Sun is to court blindness. Madness and death are all too often the bitter fruit of the pursuit of enlightenment.

Only the briefest glance was necessary, for the center of Self is timeless, enfolding eternity in an instant. At once Odin saw the knowledge he wanted, and as he drew it past the Veil of Unknowing, it cast itself into symbolic forms that he could manipulate and work with in the world of forms.

The final verse of the poem is interesting because it reveals the close kinship between the word and the deed in magic. An action is a shell for the underlying reality it represents. The soul of the action is the pattern upon which the actual act bases its structure. Likewise, the word or words for the action are also only forms, or shells, of the underlying reality. The mystic sees no significant difference between the word and the deed, the name and the object—both are illusory cocoons spun around the reality that is directly manifested from the All.

In practical terms, the signs the Magus wins from the Light through his personal seeking will act as the basis for his further meditations, and while only a few signs will be given at the start, the acquiring of the elements of the Art will have a snowball effect. These signs from the Spirit are not abstractions but are concrete tools by the use of which the Magus can sculpt his personal universe. Words are powers. In this view the Norse were very close to the Hebrew Kabbalists, who also perceived that words truly spoken have a vitality all their own.

Odin is said to have given his knowledge of runes to his people, but of course he could not have done so. Even had he been a historical personage, he could only have given a translation of the runes he snatched from his subconscious, which would have been a pale shadow of their reality—a name for a name. He could never give the runes themselves because they were a part of his unique personal universe.

The attainment of personal magic is a secret that few professed adepts know and fewer teach. It is well worth acquiring because all magical paths open to the Magus with divine inspiration, and no mere human or other entity can bar them: for the gift of knowing comes from the highest authority, the Light of the Spirit. No magical secret can be withheld in its essence from one who is right in his heart. Only the shell of the secret can be concealed; the inner nut becomes the property of the Magus.

The other side of this coin is that no amount of lying or stealing or book study or travel can gain a would-be adept the wisdom of personal magic if the Light has closed its ears to the defiled adept's hollow promises. The All gives or withholds as it judges fit. It is the highest court. Neither demons nor angels can gain wisdom from across the Veil if the All chooses to withhold it. What is freely and effortlessly given to a child or a savage tribesman may be withheld from a university professor with access to the British Museum Library.

Because the symbols of personal magic are unique to everyone, they cannot be described here. Only the way of attaining them, should the Magus be worthy, can be suggested. It follows the immutable principles given earlier in this work.

Meditation is the most fruitful method of gaining access to the Light. This is a learned technique of stilling the mind so that the Light can speak if it chooses to make itself heard. The din that echoes continuously in the skull of the average modern man or woman makes it utterly impossible for the Light to express itself at a safe volume. It is always possible for the Light to flood the mind of a human being to the exclusion of all other sensory signals but this can result in madness and only happens in circumstances of dire necessity. The Islamic mystics of the Middle Ages wrote that the voice of God can clearly be heard at all times and in all places and that it is only the willful stupidity of mankind that obscures it.

When the Light speaks to an individual on the personal level, it does so through the mediation of a perceived form that the individual's mind is able to deal with. When the message is purely emotional and spiritual, this is often only a pearl white luminescence that can appear anywhere. It brings a feeling of bliss, comfort, love, occasionally fear and awe, and may be accompanied by a musical tone like the ringing of a crystal bell and by a sweet perfume.

However, when the Magus seeks concrete symbols of power for the working of the Art, the Light, in order to please him, may assume a more fixed and solid shape capable of gesture and speech of a kind. This is not absolutely necessary, but it may be the easiest way of transferring the necessary knowledge. Traditionally this shape is thought of as an angel personally concerned in the welfare of the individual. Since it is this personalized aspect of the Unmanifest that watches over the soul, it is called the guardian angel. The Guardian is treated more fully in a following chapter.

Some schools of mysticism like to abstract the Guardian one step away from a discrete and self-aware being, preferring to call it the genius, or highest spiritual level, of the human mind. This is splitting hairs. What the Guardian is, it is, and it does not change with human ways of conceiving it, although those conceptions may color human perceptions. It is a natural act of the mind to project a sense of personality and identity onto other manifestations. Since it is so natural, to do so is likely closer to the truth than to attempt to abstract and objectify them through an act of mental juggling.

The process of attaining a magical symbol of personal significance is threefold. First the Magus clears and quiets his mind by sitting passively in a place specially devoted to ritual and meditation. He enters a state similar to auto hypnosis, opening a channel to his subconscious mind. Second, he concentrates all his faculties on the question that confronts him—for example, a wish for a sign with which he can effectively control the elementals of Fire. This is akin to sending a ray of desire to the center of Self. Third, he makes his mind a blank slate and awaits the reply of the Light.

This reply is seldom in the form of words and is rarely delivered by the discrete, perceived entity called the guardian angel. Rather, it is symbolic and arises in the conscious mind in the same way that any other thought or desire arises—spontaneously from somewhere else. The symbols that come are not a cloak for the truth, as psychologists might put it, but are a plainer statement of the absolute truth than is possible using the clumsy instrument of language. Through them the Magus gets more in his answer, not less.

At first his inspirations will be sporadic and unclear. The Magus will receive answers to questions he has not yet asked and will only realize that they are answers when the questions at last occur to him.

The Light cannot be ordered about. It will reveal what the seeker is ready to receive—neither more nor less. What the Magus may believe he is fit to receive in his human conceit and fraility is of no importance to the Light.

If the meditations are working, he will get the strange impression that he is somehow thinking forward in time and coming to know things before he has learned them. He will find that his inspired knowledge is often confirmed months after he first acquired it. Reading a book of some authority, he will see in it ideas that are already laid out in his head. It will be as though he had intensively studied the book months or years before, even though he has never opened it before that moment.

Eventually the Magus will learn to accept with prayers of thanks anything the Light sees fit to bestow upon him, whether he comprehends its purpose at the time or not. He may make mistakes—the Light never.

Black magicians often delude themselves into believing they can take shortcuts and "cheat the devil." It is true they gain much magical expertise in dealing with material matters. They even attain personal magical symbols of a kind. What must be understood is that the source of this understanding is not the Light. Such understanding is tainted. It may work effectively, but it is not lawful in the eye of God. Such understanding has no wisdom.

The impatient and irreligious adept may think he is willing to sacrifice the grace of the Light in order to achieve his ends, but it is not so simple. By their inherent nature evil entities (those psychic beings on the shadowy limit of manifestation) are eager to expand into regions where the Light chooses to withhold itself. They thrust understanding of black magic onto those utterly unworthy of the Light, and the result is that the black magicians destroy themselves. They cannot manipulate the forces they presume to command. They fail, not through cold-bloodedness or animal courage—for these things they have in abundance—but simply through an ignorance of cosmic law. Cosmic law is the way things work in the universe. By denying the Light the black magician closes his eyes to cosmic law. He is like a blind man trying to drive a car through a crowded city. He can only blunder along so far before disaster strikes.

The black magician lives a few pitiful, worthless years in self-delusion, glorying in his material power and his illicit learning, and all the while he decays inwardly until he passes the point of no return, when he is forever lost to the Light. Once the demons of Darkness are sure of their human prize, they desert him and leave him to die in madness or squalor, either from drugs or directly by his own hand.

The legend of Faust has much to say on this matter. As Faust discovered, in the early stages the demons in the pit of the subconscious wear the masks of angels. They reveal, or promise to reveal, knowledge of real value and set the Magus lusting for more. As he progresses in his descent from the Light, the demons become more gross in their presentations. Although the erring magician might still save himself with a single word spoken from his heart, that word becomes ever more difficult to pronounce. Ultimately it cannot even be remembered.

How is the Magus to guard himself from deception when seeking the inspiration of the Light? By remembering the part of cosmic law that says nothing is for nothing. Whenever the Magus finds himself trying to profit by what he has not earned it may be assumed that he is in danger of straying into the shadows. All black magic is a vain attempt to cheat destiny and gain more than the allotted portion.

In ritual magic the Magus should use the names and symbols of the Light, excluding from the circle of protection anything that is disharmonious to the Will of the All. When these symbols of Light are linked in the mind of the Magus to a true understanding of what the Light is, they will act as a sure protection. But remember, "The signs and symbols of Light, when abused and perverted, become the signs and symbols of Darkness."

Any adept who willfully uses the sacred names and symbols of the Light for wicked and purely personal ends, thinking thereby to protect himself from the natural consequences of his transgression, soon renders them tarnished and unfitted to represent the Light. They become vehicles for the forces of Evil, and only the foolish magician himself has any doubts as to their meaning.

INVOCATION

INVOCATION IS THE drawing forth of the powers and qualities of spirits into the perceived self, where they work a mental, emotional, and sometimes physical transformation. The coming of the spirit into the circle is felt as an inner change in the personality. The invoked spirit is usually visualized by the Magus as surrounding him, like a cloak of light, and sinking into the depths of his being. It is a kind of voluntary possession similar to that experienced by mediums, who are taken over by their spirit contacts, and by Voodoo worshipers, who are mounted and "ridden" by their loas. However, in Hermetic magic the Magus always retains a center of self-awareness and control.

Invocation is used mainly to get control of the powers of a spirit for a time. In the same way that primitive warriors once ate the hearts and brains of their defeated foes to gain their cleverness and courage, the modern adept takes into himself the essence of a spirit so that he can harness the virtues of that entity for his own purposes.

For example, if the Magus faced a difficult mathematical problem he might invoke Thoth and contemplate the problem through the eyes of the Egyptian god of learning. If it were necessary for a female adept to dominate a social function, she might invoke Aphrodite, Greek goddess of love and beauty.

Usually invocation is made to meet a specific situation or perhaps

241

to briefly experience life through the personality of a god and thus grow in wisdom. Sometimes, however, a single spirit is invoked repeatedly. In this way the Magus can, in a sense, become the spirit. Through constant association his identity is slowly made more like that of the spirit. During the invocations he actually becomes the spirit, and when they are over, some of the qualities of the spirit remain with him.

The dangers of invocation are many. Spirits enjoy putting on flesh. It lends them a vitality they were not meant to possess. Consequently spirits of the lower type are reluctant to leave after the ritual is ended. The Magus may believe he has banished the spirit, only to find later that he is acting in ways not natural for him. When confronted with a situation of emotional intensity, he may do something completely alien to his personality. This reveals the previously invoked spirit, which is still struggling for control of his body.

An added threat exists. When the spirit assumes control of the Magus, it may change him without his being aware of the change. Generally everyone assumes they are exactly what they want to be. Remember Jekyll and Hyde. Jekyll loathed Hyde—but only when he was Jekyll. When he became Hyde, he reveled in evil. Without question, many of the senseless, brutal killings that occur are the work of evil spirits possessing those who have a weak sense of self and those who play with Ouija boards and magic circles.

Even when an invoked spirit is benign, too often the Magus becomes intoxicated with his strange and novel sensations and forgets the reason for conducting the invocation. John Dee, the great Elizabethan magician and philosopher, suffered this impediment when seeking to scry with his jet shewstone. The spirits he invoked were willing to share the knowledge he sought, but he became hopelessly intoxicated by their presence. Finally he was forced to employ Edward Kelly as his seer and write down the things Kelly related to him.

Invocation relies on standard ritual methods. The spirit is called into the circle by means of its associations, which the Magus experiences through the avenues of his senses. These include the visual symbols of the spirit, its colors, its substances, its names (both exoteric and esoteric), its scent, its emblematic plant or animal, and perhaps appropriate music. The Magus must be able to experience these qualities or they are useless. For example, a colorblind adept will gain nothing by using the color associated with a spirit during its invocation because spirits have no eyes; they see through the eyes of the Magus.

Remember that the circle is the extended self. Anything called into the circle becomes a part of the Magus, although he may external-ize it as a voice, a light, or some other phenomenon. The key distinc-tion between invocation and evocation is that in invocation a spirit is called forth inside the circle, while in evocation it is manifested out-side the circle. All other distinctions stem from this fact and are secondary.

The safest way to avoid possession, the loss of Will to a spirit, is to only invoke benevolent spirits. This is the reason good spirits are invoked and evil spirits evoked. There is never danger in invoking the Light or the angels of Light. Simply calling a spirit forth in the name of the Light will insure that no deception takes place. The invocation is worded to set necessary conditions for the appearance of the spirit:

> I charge you _____ who are an angel of Light and bound in
> the service of the one true God, who is above and before all
> things, descend into this magic circle, etc.

With the pagan gods you cannot be too careful. They are cunning and powerful, and their moral code is not Christian. They will not hesitate to deceive if it suits them. This applies to the majority of pagan gods. Therefore you must have a method of discomforting them if they refuse to depart. One way is to subject their sigil, a geometric image of their secret name, to fire or other elements. This should not be necessary, but the sigil should be kept wrapped in a safe place for emergencies. The sigil may also be pierced with the magic sword, which will wound the spirit itself, or put under pressure until the spirit yields.

A simpler and more effective way is to earnestly invoke the Light. The Light will drive out any possessing god or demon, for it is all powerful. When your heart is filled with Light, there is no room in it for evil. After the possessing spirit is expelled, the aura can be strengthened and defended against its return, and a magical image made for the binding of the spirit should it persist in bothering you.

It is a common error to assume that invocation is less dangerous than evocation. Just the reverse is true. In invoking a spirit the Magus willingly allows it to enter past his personal defenses. If it then chooses to make mischief, he will be in trouble unless he has prepared for such an eventuality. In evocation the spirit is kept outside the circle, at arm's length where it cannot do harm. During invocation there is always the danger that the Magus will deceive himself and change his personality in destructive ways without being aware of it.

Early in his development a certain adept tried to invoke the powers of Mars through Geburah. Seemingly the working was a failure. He abolished the circle and left the ritual chamber in disappointment. Later that day he found himself in a constant state of suppressed fury. Several times he almost flew into violent, uncontrollable rages over insignificant incidents, and it was only with the greatest difficulty that he restrained himself. All at once he realized that the invocation had not been completely lacking in effect.

This litle fable, which happens to be true, should act as a warning to beginners. Invoke often—but be careful what you invoke.

EVOCATION

THE MOST NOTORIOUS act of magic is the evocation of spirits. It has been mocked often enough in literature and on film so that everyone is familiar with it. The magician dressed all in black reads, in a tremulous voice, from an ancient book bound in human skin and waves an anemic wand. There is a puff of sulphurous smoke and the devil appears, ready to do his bidding.

Critics single out evocation as the ultimate absurdity of the occult. They point out that the devil is made to materialize from thin air, which defies the laws of physics. Something cannot be produced from nothing. And if demons and spirits can be tangibly conjured up to see and touch, why are there no accredited photographs or witnesses of them?

Such critics cannot be answered in the materialistic terms of science. Science contends that there is a measurable, observable world of natural phenomena where if a thing is so it is always so, and that there is a mental, subjective world of dreams and delusions where nothing is tangible or real in the least degree.

This distinction is simplistic. What is called the real world and what is called the mental world are, in an absolute sense, the same thing. Each person creates his inner and his outer world and, more importantly, himself draws the dividing line between them. What you apparently see in front of you at this moment is actually happening

245

inside your mind, and what you call your innermost private thoughts are in no way removed from the image of the outer world you contemplate.

This is not to suggest that reality in human terms is an illusion. But the underlying manifestations of the All (the dreams of God, which to feeble human awareness are the absolute reality) are much more immaterial and transitory than human beings can hope to imagine. Everything in the universe is being created and destroyed countless times per second. What is perceived as motion and life is an infinite series of tableaus akin to the frames on a reel of cinematic film. The human mind can never directly experience reality, and in this sense everything perceived is unreal.

Some hint of the true nature of the world can be gained by considering a newborn baby. What appears to adult eyes as the orderly, rational universe is chaos in the eyes of the infant. What to the adult is so clearly outside and inside is to the child all on the same side. Babies have no sense of the limitations of their bodies. They attempt to alter the greater world to suit their desires, and when they fail, they react with outrage and frustration.

Only as the child gets older does it appreciate that there is a world it rules (its perceived self) and a greater world over which it has very little control. All of life then becomes an attempt to extend the boundaries of the self into the greater world. The larger the sphere of total control gained by an individual, the greater his measure of success in society. Man spends his entire adult life trying to break down a barrier he himself erected in the cradle.

The view of the child is not the illusion. How could it be, when the child is newly issued from the womb, newly come from the bosom of the Unmanifest? No, what the child sees of the world is much closer to the root of reality than the distorted view of the adult. The child sees with clear sight while the adult looks through the lens of his fears and prejudices. The adult constructs a dreamworld where he can live in comfort and security without losing his reason. Only the child can stand to look upon reality, because he does not know how to look away. The adult cannot bear it; he is too naked, too vulnerable, so he erects a wall around himself, calling one part of his being inside and the other part outside.

In this manner the adult cuts himself off from even the possibility of affecting the outer world in other than the accepted material ways. The child, on the other hand, instinctively recognizes his godlike power and is upset when he finds that he cannot exercise it. The shock makes him withdraw inwardly and form an island of self where his will rules.

The Magus seeks to return to the initial perception of childhood believing that the inner and outer worlds can be recombined if only they are seen with unprejudiced eyes. With his greater wisdom he hopes to rule his personal universe as he does his perceived self. Thus when the Magus evokes a spirit, he realizes that it is both as real and as unreal as the floor upon which he stands. Since it is of his personal universe, it may not be visible to others who look upon it, but it is no less real to the Magus on this account.

What a person living in society sees is what he has agreed to see beforehand. This is not to say that the peoples of the Earth hold a giant convention and legislate what will and will not be seen. It merely means that the members of a society share certain conventions of perception. No one ever sees anything really unexpected. Try to imagine a creature that bears no resemblance at all to anything you have seen—it is impossible. You may conceive a composite of parts from all corners of nature, but can never picture anything truly new. This is because you alone have made your world what it is, and something novel has no place in your preformed perceptions.

Variations within the conventions of social perception are most noticeable over a large span of time. To modern eyes, the woodcuts of the Middle Ages that depict the human figure seem crude. The features are unsymmetrical. The length and size of the limbs are distorted. The modern observer can be forgiven if he automatically assumes that the medieval artists had no knowledge of perspective and no ability to convey the true appearance of a human being.

The actual explanation is that what was perceived as the form of man at the time of Dante and what is perceived today are not the same. Man is still man, but the way human seeing assembles his details has changed. What medieval man found beautiful about the body is what modern man finds ugly. The religious artists of the Middle Ages emphasized aspects of human form a modern realist would not. But the difference is not a matter of choice: it stems from the way the two artists see.

The Magus must treat with utter seriousness his evoked spirits. To him they are as real as wood or stone. When he uses his Will to lend solidity to an entity, it gains power over his personal universe. It becomes at the same time more useful and more dangerous. And because the secret depths of all people are linked, that power can extend to other human beings.

Evoked spirits can be watched. Evil spirits are always evoked. Good spirits may be evoked when the Magus has need to send them over a distance to perform tasks. Spirits with questionable motives should be evoked initially, as a precaution. It can then be determined if it is safe to invoke them.

Spirits have no forms or bodies of their own. However, they have natures that harmonize or clash with elements of the natural world that are transformed through the mind of the Magus. That is why angels often carry with them pleasant odors. The spiritual reaction of the Magus to the scent of flowers is in accord with the quality of angelic being. The resonance created in the spirit of the Magus by rose incense, for example, is perceived as desirable by angels and attracts them; conversely, the spiritual quality of angelic nature is translated into sensual terms familiar to human perception—often an agreeable scent.

Since spirits have no fixed body, they can be evoked in whatever form the Magus chooses. Demons may initially come as monsters with loud voices and disagreeable odors. These things accord with their nature. But the Magus need not endure these forms. He can command the demon to transform itself into a less noxious shape. He should bear in mind that a demon forced to put on too pleasing a body may suffer great pain, because beauty is out of accord with demonic nature. A neutral shape should be chosen, such as the simple form of an animal or a man.

Spirits are always evoked outside the magic circle. The circles of evocation given in the grimoires are needlessly complex. The only additional element necessary for evocation is the triangle. This is to be drawn on the floor or ground two feet away from the standard nine-foot circle. It is to be equilateral, three feet on each side, and should point away from the circle. Its apex marks the degree of the compass that is the abode of the spirit. As with the circle, it is necessary to retrace the triangle at the beginning of each evocation. It should also be traced vertically in the air with the wand from inside the circle.

Into the triangle is placed a manifesting medium, such as a bowl of water, a smoking brazier, or a magic mirror, intended to give the spirit something to form its body around. Also put into the triangle is the character, or sigil, of the spirit, which draws the spirit into the triangle, and any symbols or natural materials agreeable to the spirit.

Holding the magic sword with his right arm, the Magus can reach the triangle but should never in any other way break the circle with his body during evocation. The power of the sword will protect his hand, though he may feel a slight shock should the spirit touch the blade.

The triangle provides a focus for the spirit to materialize. It is not a cell to bind the spirit, although the spirit will instinctively remain within it because all the associations of the spirit are gathered there. The triangle represents the vortex issuing from the Veil, and it is pictured as descending vertically through the air, although it is represented horizontally on the floor or ground. The spirit comes into being from out of the point of the apex and expands toward the base.

Usually its body does not appear in a completely solid form. It can be made so, but the doubts of the Magus tend to keep the body of the spirit insubstantial—smoky, or misty. In former times it was believed that a spirit needed fresh blood to shape itself, that there was some vital fluid within the blood that acted as a foundation for the body of the spirit. This is nonsense. The body of the spirit is founded on the faith and Will of the Magus—nothing else.

Therefore the manifesting medium is likewise unnecessary, except that it is symbolically useful and aids the imagination of the Magus. The same is true of all the physical materials of ritual. They are only needed due to human weakness and doubt.

In order to evoke a spirit the Magus must possess perfect knowledge of it. He must have a firm expectation of what will appear. Interestingly, the actual form of the spirit often differs from his expectation in many ways, but the solid image held in the mind at the beginning aids the evocation. Once a spirit has been evoked, it will always assume the same shape in later evocations unless ordered to change by the Magus.

The ritual of evocation is begun in the regular fashion. The purpose to be served by the spirit is decided upon, and the words and gestures of the working and evocation are composed. The Magus undertakes a period of fasting, prayer, and purification to ready himself. He robes and lays out the instruments in the ritual chamber, paying particular attention to the symbols, materials, and manifesting medium in the inscribed triangle. The sigil of the spirit is laid in the triangle, wrapped loosely in silk. If the spirit is good or neutral, the silk should be blue; if it is an evil spirit, the silk should be black.

The Magus centers himself and traces the circle clockwise; then, from inside the circle, he uses the wand to trace the triangle. With fire and water he cleanses the circle. A vortex is created inside the circle, establishing communication with the Light. He invokes the protection and favor of the Light and states his purpose for conducting the ritual. At this point he must feel the presence of the Light and be in a state of high excitement.

In resonant tones the prepared evocation is chanted while the Magus focuses his Will upon the manifesting medium in the triangle. He should have the sword in his right hand. The words of the evocation should be original and composed by the Magus. Here is an evocation from the *Key of Solomon* that is intended to serve only as a guide:

O ye Spirit_____,ye I conjure by the Power, Wisdom, and Virtue of the Spirit of God, by the uncreate Divine Knowledge, by the vast Mercy of God, by the Strength of God, by the Greatness of God, by the Unity of God; and by the Holy Name of God EHEIEH, which is the root, trunk, source, and origin of all the other Divine Names, whence they all draw their life and their virtue.

I conjure ye_____by the indivisible Name YOD, which marketh and expresseth the Simplicity and the Unity of the Nature Divine.

I conjure ye_____by the Name IHVH ELOHIM, which expresseth and signifieth the Grandeur of so lofty a Majesty.

I conjure ye_____by the name of God EL Strong and Wonderful, which denoteth the Mercy and Goodness of His Majesty Divine.

I conjure ye_____by the most powerful Name of ELOHIM GIBOR, which showeth forth the Strength of God, of a God All Powerful, Who punisheth the crimes of the wicked, Who seeketh out and chastiseth the inequities of the fathers upon the children.

I conjure ye_____by the most holy Name of ELOAH VA-DAATH, which signifieth Vanquisher of God.

I conjure ye_____by the most potent Name of EL ADONAI TZABAOTH, which is the God of Armies, ruling in the Heavens.

I conjure ye_____by the most potent Name of ELOHIM TZABAOTH, which expresseth piety, mercy, splendour, and knowledge of God.

I conjure ye_____by the most potent Name of SHADDAI, which signifieth doing good unto all; I conjure ye by the most holy Name EL CHAI, which is that of the Living God.

Lastly, I conjure ye_____,ye rebellious Spirit, by the most holy Name of God ADONAI MELEKH, which Joshua invoked, and stayed the course of the Sun through the virtue of Methratton, its principal Image; and by the troops of Angels who cease not to cry day and night—Holy, Holy, Holy, Lord God of Hosts, Heaven and Earth are full of Thy Glory; and by the Ten Angels who preside over the Ten Sephiroth, by whom God communicateth and extendeth His influence over lower things, which are KETHER, CHOKMAH, BINAH, GEDULAH, GEBURAH, TIPHERETH, NETZACH, HOD, YESOD, and MALKUTH.[16]

The original evocation is considerably longer, but the above should serve as a sample. The evocation is designed to inflame the heart of the Magus and fire his Will. The one given here follows the descent of the Light from the Unmanifest to the material world, using the names on the Tree of Life as words of power. This is a reasonable and effective form, but many other forms of evocation are possible.

In general, the ancient evocations are too wordy and too much occupied with externals. Modern evocations tend to be much shorter and may be repeated many times for a cumulative effect. The Magus must be moved emotionally by the evocation, or it is useless, no matter how well constructed.

Evocations should be "vibrated" for maximum effect—that is, spoken resonantly from the depths of the chest so that the throat and back of the nose vibrate with the force of the sonic waves. This technique is well known to singers and stage actors, who learn it of necessity. If done properly, the words of the evocation will penetrate and have a ringing quality even when they are not spoken loudly.

At the end of the evocation, the Magus uses the tip of the sword to uncover the sigil that is resting in the triangle. The sigil is traced with the sword in the air over the triangle inside the psychic triangle previously formed with the wand. The smoke or water vapor, whichever is used, will begin to coalesce within the glowing psychic triangle. Usually the face of the spirit is the first to emerge. If the Magus is using a magic mirror, only the image of the spirit will appear in the depths of the glass.

It may be necessary to repeat the evocation, which should be spoken in an even more compelling tone. In any event, the Magus must never lose his temper. This is what evil spirits wait for, in the hope of using the anger of the Magus against him. If still no spirit presents itself, the Magus must command by the holy names of God that any being within the triangle instantly show itself. If an evil spirit has been concealing itself, it will at once become visible.

The very fact that a spirit has appeared confirms the power that the Magus has over it. No evil entity willingly humbles itself before a human being. The Magus may direct it with confidence that his orders will be obeyed. However, if the Magus acts very unsure of himself, the spirit may feel bold enough to put on a sham front of defiance. It will roar and bluster, hoping to make the Magus lose his nerve and his common sense; but it cannot harm the Magus inside the circle, and compelled by the authority of the Light, it must at last obey.

In reality, demons have little power over human beings. They cannot kill on their own authority, and this is why they form pacts with foolish human beings. Even the lowest man or woman has free will and can deal death. The devil pretends to rule the man who has sworn an oath to it, but without the man it treats as its slave, it is ineffectual. Through intimidation the devil causes the man to do its evil for it. The man can even license demons to kill other men in his own name, and all the consequences of these actions fall on the damned soul of the man.

Once the spirit has been sent on its mission, the sigil is carefully covered once again with silk, by means of the sword. The aperture of the cirle is closed, and all lingering influences in the outer darkness are most carefully banished. Then the ritual is concluded in the usual fashion, with the Magus taking care to put the sigil of the spirit in a secure place.

Failure in evocations is always attributable to the lack of preparedness on the part of the Magus. He must be confident of success before he begins. Even so, the usual reaction on first evoking a spirit is disbelief followed by terror. The Magus is never utterly convinced the spirit will manifest until he has seen it with his own eyes, even after all his study and preparation. This is why it is so much easier for a beginner to work with an established group: his initial lack of confidence is less of a factor. Once a spirit has been evoked successfully, future evocations are much easier because the wall of disbelief has been breached.

Eventually evocation becomes an instrument of accomplishing ritual desire, just like any other. But the Magus himself is inwardly transformed after evocation. His perception of reality has been broadened, and he will never again see the world in quite the same way.

GUARDIAN

THE GUARDIAN IS a noncorporeal entity, commonly called the guardian angel, whose task according to tradition is to watch over and protect the human being to whom it has been assigned by God. This tradition exists among many diverse cultures. In the far East the Guardian is assumed to be the ghost of a departed relative. In Catholicism the role has been partially filled by the patron saints.

Two constants emerge from the legends about the Guardian: 1) It represents the personal intervention of spiritual forces in the life of the individual. 2) It serves as a mediator between ordinary human consciousness and the unknowable mind of the All.

The Magus who is liberated from the burden of superstition (which is belief without reasonable cause) will not make the error of thinking of the Guardian as a physical being with wings and a halo. Nor will he go to the opposite extreme and mistake the Guardian for a mere fantasy. As in so many cases, the truth lies where these two opposite views merge.

The Guardian is a psychic entity in that it exists in the rooms and corridors of the subconscious and usually reveals itself through the doorways of dreams, visions, and impulses. However, as has already been suggested, the subconscious is a vast house that extends far beyond the boundaries of the individual mind, reaching even to the Veil across the face of the Unmanifest. What lives in the subconscious can have more objective reality—significance in the evolution of the universe—than the parasitic manifestation called consciousness. The Guardian may be more real, in an absolute sense, than the average conception of self.

The Guardian has been recognized as being of the highest importance to Western magic for centuries. The ancients rightly understood that without the conversation of the guardian angel, or the communication with their highest awareness, nothing was possible; but with the conversation of the Guardian, all was possible. The Guardian is the personalized response of the Light to human needs. It is the medium through which the All expresses its omniscience at the level of the individual.

Cut off from the Guardian, all learning would be no more than dry book study devoid of inspiration. Ritual acts would be like batteries unable to hold a charge. The symbols of magic would be as empty and foolish as science believes them to be. Contrarily, once the Guardian has been fully reached and a reliable channel of communication with it established, all magical acts become easy to accomplish. The Magus is wrapped in Light and is capable of miracles. He has no further use for books or teachers since he finds there only the things he already knows.

It is exceedingly rare that a perfect communication with the Guardian is established. Equally rare is an utter lack of communication. All except the lowest dregs of humanity have at least flashes of awareness that something larger than themselves is concerning itself with their lives.

The Guardian has been described as the higher genius. This is perhaps an unfortunate description as it conveys the impression that the Guardian is nothing more than a hidden level of the personality expressing itself through consciousness—no more than a metaphor for the noblest aspirations and most exalted thoughts. Such a view is true as far as it goes, but is limiting.

The Guardian should not be thought of as a discrete being, for humanity needs no third party to carry its prayers to God. Rather, it should be thought of as a living personification of the mediating aspect of man that links him with the Light. Humanity exists both in the manifest and the Unmanifest at one and the same instant. The Guardian bears the messages of God and casts them in human terms so that the fallible sons and daughters of Adam can, in some part, gather meaning from them. Since God cannot exist uncontained in the manifest universe without destroying it, he needs many servants.

In the same way the Magus molds his telesmatic images from the natural forces outside his perceived self, he shapes the Guardian from the directing power of the Light within. By personalizing the energy that is the Guardian, he gains some measure of control over it: he can speak to it and expect an answer, and he can call it forth and hope to see it.

Usually the Guardian is visualized as a human form of the opposite sex that has refined beauty and is bathed in light. A male adept would see a female Guardian, and a female adept, a male Guardian. Traditionally the Guardian was sometimes said to be of the opposite color: a white female might be watched over by a black male. The reason for this opposition is that the Guardian represents the spiritul spouse and therefore communion with the Guardian is the magical union of man and God.

The similarity between the guardian angel and the winged god, Mercury, will at once be apparent. The Guardian is a personal Mercury. Mercury is an abstraction of all the Guardians; for in truth there is only one Guardian, who is diversified in several billion human consciousnesses. All angelic visitations, such as the one that came to the shepherds at the birth of Christ, are visitations of the Guardian in different guises. Each man and woman conceives the Guardian uniquely. In a sense there is only one angel, who takes a different name and face for each new task.

In magic the prime use of the Guardian is to gain instruction in the right mode of living in harmony with the Light. On a more mundane level, the Magus uses the Guardian to learn the mechanics of a personal system of magic that does not violate cosmic law. The Guardian is relied on to remove psychic blockages and to unstop the springs of power so that the symbols of the Art can be used with practical consequences. The Guardian also provides guidance in times of great trial and confusion.

The conversation of the guardian angel and the direct inspiration of the Light can be distinguished in that the Guardian meets the immediate personal needs of the Magus, usually through his senses, while the Light tends to be more abstract and careless of time. The direct inspiration of the Light and the conversation of the Guardian are two aspects of the same process of enlightenment, but the Guardian is an instrument that focuses divine knowledge on particular human needs.

The Magus should never get the notion that he is manipulating the Guardian to serve his own ends. Quite the reverse is true. The Guardian only manifests its power with the authority of the All. It is completely subject to the Light and is without effect in matters apart from the Light. The Magus can never compel it to do what it is not intended to do. For a time the Magus may think he is making use of his Guardian, but he will eventually comprehend that all the while his Guardian has been using him, poor clay that he is, to execute its mandate from the Unmanifest.

The Magus ignores the advice of his Guardian at the peril of his soul. Once rebuffed, the Guardian is slow to speak again. It must be courted assiduously; all its dictates followed to the letter, and its presence never taken for granted or else it will be gone. Yet, understand that the Guardian, who is intimately bound to the Magus, cannot actually leave him. Foolish disregard of the words of the Guardian creates a barrier in the mind of the Magus. The Guardian is no less willing to guide him, but the Magus blinds himself with his own conceit.

Nor should the mistake be made of ascribing human motives to the Guardian. It may make no earthly difference to the angel if its human host is run over by a truck. This event may be in harmony with the All. Do not rely on the Guardian to act as a personal watchdog. It will protect you if that is its appointed task—if it will not intervene if there is no higher purpose served by your continued existence. If it did, no man or woman would ever die, and the Earth would be awash with humanity.

Only when man acts as an agent for higher forces can he elevate himself above his petty, material life. Only when he seeks to be a receptacle for the Light will these forces interest themselves actively in his physical welfare. This seems harsh but it is true. Of course, different people serve the Light in different ways. If the service is through magic, the Guardian will speak of magical things. If through poetry, the Guardian will play the Muse and open a fountain of beautiful words. If through mathematics, it will speak in numbers. To obtain the conversation of his guardian angel, the Magus need only make himself a pure vessel.

Think of the voice of the Guardian as a whisper and of all manner of evils as loud pounding noises. When even a small amount of noise is present in the psychic ear of the Magus, the whisper cannot be heard, although it continues to speak all the while. Evil can take many forms: thoughts, acts, words. Such things as the worry and bother of daily business are not thought of as evil, yet they drown the voice of the Guardian.

This is why medieval woodcuts show little devils pricking the common folk with pitchforks as they go about their futile activities— gossiping, lying, gambling, speculating—because the artists intuitively grasped that Evil uses small acts to distract the mind away from the Light. Why else show devils tugging on ears and tickling noses? Such useless and time-wasting activities as fill the lives of average people are the stones that build the Tower of Ruin.

Have you ever wondered why you curse God when you drop something, or cut yourself, or trip? The momentary distraction of your will allows a tiny tendril of evil to slip past your defenses, and in that instant of distraction, you are made to serve as an instrument of Darkness.

Make a simple test. Sit in a quiet place and try to listen to your own inner stillness. In Zen terms, strive to hear the sound of one hand. Do not allow your attention to fix on any extraneous thing. Ignore all sounds, movements, sensations, and thoughts.

Unless you have trained for quite a long time, you will not be able to do it. The little devils with pitchforks will prevent you from concentrating on the silence. You will itch. Your tongue and lips will become dry. You will swallow. You will shift about in your seat. Small noises will soon be magnified into thunder. Your mind will race like an engine out of control. And any time you focus your attention on these matters you will be turning away from the voice of your Guardian.

The grimoires lay down various harsh regimes for the aspirant who wishes to attain the conversation of his Guardian. To become inwardly still requires that the seeker set aside the world and, in effect, become a holy man totally dedicated to the Light, for a time at least. All forms of stimulation must be avoided, even those seemingly harmless, because they distract the mind from truth.

You may not wish to hear that the only way you can obtain the conversation of your guardian angel is to renounce the world and live apart. You may be waiting to learn the easy trick that will let you get around this task. There is no trick, no shortcut. If you are unwilling to devote yourself utterly to the Light, perhaps for a period of months, or even years, be assured you will never attain the conversation of your Guardian or see the angel face to face.

The way to purity and inner stillness has been given in the chapter on initiation and will not be repeated. At the end of the preparatory process, the Magus must conduct a master ritual of evocation which is based on his knowledge of the Art, to bring the Guardian into a material presence before him. This ritual serves to forge a bond between the Magus and the angel that allows easier communication thereafter, provided the Magus does not turn away from the Light. When the Magus returns to live in society, he carries the conversation of the Guardian with him.

It is not the purpose of this work to recommend texts, but the Magus will find the second part of the *Book of the Sacred Magic of Abramelin the Mage* particularly useful for these questions. It is a true book, descended from the ancient mysteries. In it is given a system of living that has been effective for attaining the conversation of the Guardian. It should not be copied, but used as a pattern and guide. The spirit names and magic squares in the book belong to the writer, Abraham the Jew, and should not be used by the Magus, who must rely on his Guardian to provide him with his personal hierarchy of spirits.

At the highest level of attainment it is possible, though extremely rare, to invoke the Guardian into permanent active being. This is usually done intuitively, with no conscious beginning or end, by religious mystics. In such instances, the holy man becomes his guardian angel incarnate, in constant and unimpeded communication with the Light. No wonder such men rise above the mass of humanity, yet the one constant among them is compassion.

As there is an opposite to all manifestations, so is there an opposite to the personal angel. This is a being charged with the purposes of evil and given a form by the individual's hates and fears and lusts. The common image of a man with an angel on his right shoulder and a devil on his left is based on this truth. Unlike the Guardian, the personal devil speaks in a voice that is loud and unceasing. It prefers to remain invisible so that the thoughts of its host will not dwell on its foul nature.

Mankind can be divided into three parts based on their interaction with their personal angels and demons. The lowest order of humanity go through life guided entirely by the voices of their devils, without a single doubt or question about the futility of their little, ugly lives. These are the lowest of the low, who cannot even be compared to beasts without outraging nature. They are beyond change or help, knowing and caring to know nothing but material things.

The middle class of mankind, which are the majority, are guided for the most part by the strident voices of their devils, but on occasion they give heed to the quiet voices of their Guardians, usually when their devils have momentarily failed to keep them entertained. The great power of the Guardian is that it speaks truth. The devil yells and curses and pounds the floor for attention, but always it speaks lies. After a long time, some men grow weary of lies and turn with determined hearts to seek the truth. Most, however, find it easier to pretend the lies are true and the truth, lies, turning the universe on its head and coveting a bag of common stones as diamonds.

Finally there are the third class of humanity who seem to recognize the voice of their angels from birth and are never misled by their personal devils, who in these rare cases seem to be mutes. How such people come to be born is one of the mysteries. The Magus should envy them their innocence, yet at the same time pity them, for they have no need to strive against adversity and no chance to acquire the inner strength that only comes through transcending obstacles. These people are like pampered house cats that never hiss or scratch and, for this reason, are treated with kindness wherever they go. Occasionally they find themselves cast out into the snow by circumstance; and then they quickly perish, for they have no way to defend themselves.

It is assumed that the Magus comes from the second, greater mass of mankind. When he attempts to summon his Guardian, he would do well to insure that he does not inadvertantly call up his personal devil in its stead. When the Magus is striving to contact the ultimate Good, there is always the danger of reaching, by mistake or foolishness, the ultimate Evil. Only purity will protect and guide the Magus—purity of thought, purity of Will, and purity of hope—for purity, after all, is his Guardian.

GOD-FORMS

THERE IS ONLY one God who is without form or attribute, who is nameless and faceless, the beginning and the end, the first and last, who was and is and will be. The lesser gods of myth and legend are limited emanations of the single true Deity. For this reason they are treated with respect, but never with reverence or worship.

The Magus must not commit the sacrilege of praying to a lesser god. The gods are tools to be used by him with the authority of the Light. Since the Light is the primary emanation, all things are subservient to it. Man need kneel to no being with a name and a form, regardless of how terrible it appears. Such awesome shapes melt like wax when struck by the Light. Their essences are dreams of the Unmanifest, as their forms are dreams of humanity.

God-forms are never the creation of an individual; they are always the work of the group mind of a culture. For this reason no single mind can comprehend them completely. Although shaped by the will of a people, the gods are not mere illusions but are aspects of manifestation the culture has recognized and magically circled, thereby crystallizing them into discrete forms with comprehensible motives.

Consider the pagan god Thor. Some believe Thor to be a figment of the Nordic imagination, a god without a trace of real existence. Others would say that while it is true Thor was created by the concentrated will of a people, he now exists on some elusive but real level of being and will continue to exist so long as the mind of man conceives him. Still others might maintain that the minds of men had nothing at all to do with the creation of Thor, who exists independently of humankind in every way.

All these views betray a faulty understanding of the natures of the All and the manifest. Men do not create but are creations of God. What men call their creations are creations of the Light from the Unmanifest acting through men, as light shines through a prism, on the manifest universe.

When men began to worship Thor, they did not invent the attributes of that deity—the thunder and lightning, strength, courage, fury, destruction—but recognized the common principle behind those qualities and focused it into a form with a name and a human shape. Thus the god Thor existed before the race of homo sapiens, although he was not symbolized as a warrior with wild black hair and fiery eyes who carried a hammer. By the power of the All that is within them, men drew this symbol from the Unmanifest in order to harness and control the forces of the god. Men did not create the underlying reality. What they did was provide a vehicle through which the pre-existing forces could express themselves to the human race.

In ascribing to Thor a human form, the Norsemen gave those forces qualities they would not otherwise have possessed. The pre-human Thor was not concerned in the affairs of humanity. It was not a fleshy being with memories of a past and hopes for the future, but was a principle of nature, a natural concourse of forces that, when cast into the mold of a man, could be addressed in human language and might respond on the human level.

The numerous god-forms—which are all gods bearing a name or form by which men have limited and defined them—are both more and less than men. They are less because they have no free will and can never evolve or develop into something more than what they are. They are more than men because they embody immense powers in nature and are eternal and indestructible in human terms. Even if all men cease to remember a god, that concourse of forces that provided the focus for the god endures, ready to receive a new name and symbols from some future culture.

Men do not create the gods, they name them—but through the names they gain power over the god-forms. The complex name of a god embodying its form, its desires, its attributes, its abilities and limitations, is a kind of magic circle that binds the god to the will of the group that gave it expression. This is why it is often said that the gods are dependent on the worship and sacrifices of their followers, without which they would fade away. The people that name a god are its servants yet also its masters, since through neglect they can send the god back to the oblivion of blind natural forces from which it arose. The relationship between man and the gods is symbiotic and mutually dependent.

The process of forming the gods was a subconscious one for primitive peoples. They did not reason it out; and therefore they often lost sight of the fact that the gods were only creations of the All and ascribed the highest place to the lesser gods. Many times, anthropologists investigating native societies discover they possess a supreme deity that they have nearly forgotten, a deity with few or no characteristics that has been thrust from its supreme position by younger, more human god-forms.

This is a degeneration of religion and is a great evil when it is committed by those who should know better. Men shame themselves when they worship idols of brass or wood, and they also shame themselves when they bow before any god with a name or a shape. Indeed, there is no difference between the two offenses—only a matter of degree.

God-forms gain or lose in power depending on how they are looked upon and worshiped by their people. Many gods who at one time were principal deities have, through conquest, become absorbed into the pantheons of other races and have descended in status. For example, the god Ptah was supreme in the city of Memphis in the early days of Egypt, but when the pharaohs of the Nile moved their palaces southward to Thebes, Ptah lost much of his authority.

God-forms were created because they are useful. They allowed men to reach hidden powers and direct them according to human purpose. For this reason god-forms are still being created today in civilized Western culture. The forms of the Worker, the Consumer, the Scientist—all are personalizations of the general forces that exist and have always existed, but which, when given a symbol-name, can be used by mankind for questionable ends.

The god-forms of any culture reveal its health or sickness. Culturally, this is not a happy age in which to live. The great Moloch of the present is Mekanos, the cold, remorseless god of steel and wire and glass. His image is embodied and worshiped in the glass sky-

266 / New Magus

scrapers of every modern city. He is even more powerful and insidious because he has not yet been overtly recognized as a god. He is a god of Darkness and cares nothing for the sorrows of humanity.

In magic the common way of utilizing the power of the gods is by putting them on, like a cloak or mantle, over the perceived self. This is called assuming the god-form and is a kind of invocation.

If the Magus wished to become more attractive, through this method he or she might create a ritual to take on the god-form of Apollo or Aphrodite, and view the world through the eyes of that lesser god for a time. If done correctly and repeatedly, this would give the Magus great personal charm and beauty of a combined physical and psychic character. The hidden forces of beauty channeled through the Magus by the focusing lens of the god-form would transform the personality of the Magus by reaction and alter the physical body as well.

Beauty would be inevitable. Its exact quality would depend on the assets and defects of the Magus, both physical and mental, for magic always seeks the easiest course to its objective. If the Magus were crippled or deformed, the beauty would take on a predominantly mental and emotional character. The physical handicap might become lessened through surgery or other treatment. Magic uses mundane means to reach its ends as readily as the more esoteric means. Magic makes no distinction between the physical and the psychic—these are human distinctions.

Another function of assuming a god-form is that it better enables the Magus to issue commands to the spirits and forces that fall under the rule of that god. In becoming Thor, the Magus will command the storms; becoming Pan, he will rule the woodlands; becoming Neptune, the sea.

Before attempting to assume a god-form, the Magus should have a thorough knowledge of the basics of magical workings, the ability to compose a personal ritual of invocation that is viable, and a complete knowledge of the gods of mythology (their strengths and weaknesses, associated materials and colors, familiar animals, symbols, scents, and so on). It is best to practice by assuming the forms of the angels, as these are unlikely to prove harmful. Then the more benevolent gods should be assumed first.

Invocation of a god-form is a type of voluntary possession. For a period of time limited by the protective safeguards of the ritual, the Magus allows his normal personality to be submerged into the character of a god. Depending on the nature of the invoked god, this can be a pleasant or unpleasant experience, but it is always dangerous. Personality is at best a feeble flame that flickers and dims in every psychic wind. By voluntarily forsaking it the Magus takes a risk. He is prepared to do so because the wisdom and power that can be gained in this way are of great value.

The Magus always builds certain weaknesses that he can control into his personal conception of the god. These must be true weaknesses based on a careful assessment of the nature of the god, not merely arbitrary words and signs. In the construction of the ritual, these weaknesses are used so that when the Magus commands the god to depart, the god cannot dispute it. Such weaknesses are often found in the old literature, particularly regarding the demonic gods that are very dangerous.

To assume a god-form, the Magus prepares himself and draws a magic circle in the presence of the attributes and associations of the god. He wears a symbol of the god next to his skin over his heart. An image of the god is upon the altar. The symbol and the image of the god should be formed in part from a common substance connected most closely with the god; they are then, in effect, two parts of a whole. To summon Isis, for example, the symbol and the image of the goddess might be cast from the same piece of silver.

Calling upon the god to descend into the circle, the Magus offers the inducement of appropriate food and drink. Here a sacrifice of the blood of the Magus may, in certain cases, be made. The Magus fixes his gaze upon the figure of the god on the altar and wills the god to merge with him. Success is often signaled when the symbol over his heart becomes warm or animated. At the critical moment, the Magus gives expression to his transformation, declaring his identity with the god and recounting at length the complex name of the god with its relations and correspondences.

After the task of the ritual has been accomplished, the god is dismissed by the authority of its ruling deity. For example, if it is Thoth, god of Egypt, dismiss him by the authority of Osiris. If the god assumed is the leading deity of a pantheon, dismiss it by the authority of the Light.

It may happen that the god refuses to leave the body and mind of the Magus. Then it must be threatened through its image on the altar, which it simultaneously inhabits, with its natural weakness. Most gods have an affinity with one of the four elements, and the opposite element will affect them unpleasantly. Mercury, god of airy motion, can be compelled by the threat to imprison his image in clay; however, Mercury is a most tractable deity and will never betray the Magus.

If it happens that the Magus has been very foolish or careless and the invoked god-form has gained the upper hand, remember that all manifest beings are subservient to the Light. Earnest prayer is the one action no demonic force can directly prevent the Magus from performing. He should open himself without reservation to the divine Spirit, which will wash through him like a cool stream and carry away any corruption.

The god-forms of Egypt are particularly useful in magic. Since the Egyptians were themselves great magicians, they personified all the natural forces around them so that those forces could be used magically. This personification resulted in a diverse pantheon of hundreds of deities. These gods must be studied individually so that the Magus will know precisely which is most appropriate for his specific purpose.

The gods of the Greeks are less abstract and more human than the Egyptian gods, and for this reason, more complex. Their motives are not always so easy to determine beforehand. It is hard to predict exactly how a Greek god will act in a given situation. However, they are generally more sympathetic to human needs because they share them, in part. For more material purposes it might be better to use a Greek god rather than an Egyptian. You will get a more flexible response.

The gods of the Germanic peoples (the Saxons, Germans, Norse) are dangerous. There is no more polite way to phrase it. By modern standards, many would be classed as demons. They represent the crudest of elemental forces and are very difficult to control once invoked. They have a disturbing tendency to lose their reason and commit general mayhem. A person possessed by Lok, Thor, or Wotan could easily become berserk and go on a killing rampage if the power of the god were not contained. Because of their nature these Northern gods are often used for evil purposes. Although not evil themselves, they care nothing about human suffering—just the opposite, they delight in seeing the human will struggle against adversity, and view human disputes and wars as sport.

These are the three main pantheons used in modern magic. However, any god-form from any culture, once thoroughly understood, can be invoked and assumed. It is usually safer and more effective to rely on those gods from civilized societies with which the Magus has a personal affinity. For a white man in the West to assume an African tribal god would be foolish, unless he were completely African under the skin. For the same reason, a black American would be better off assuming the gods of Egypt or Greece, since his culture has become Westernized over the centuries. The true affinities of the Magus must always be left to his personal judgment.

TELESMATIC IMAGES

IN EVERYDAY MAGIC it may be necessary to conceptualize and empower an entity for a specific function that is beneath the dignity or outside the province of the god-forms. These lesser spirits may be distinguished from the god-forms in that they are the creation of one or several minds rather than an entire culture acting over generations.

To be perceived, all spirits must be created. A spirit does not exist unless it is conceived in some way. This process of creation can be voluntary or involuntary. It can begin from existing traditional features or be wholly new. It can be the work of one person, or several, or many. The existence of the spirit can be brought about on the mental, astral, or physical circles of being.

All spirits emanate from the Unmanifest. Their unity is basic, their differences superficial.

A *god-form* is a spirit of great power created by a society.

An *angel* is a spirit wholly dedicated to the service of the Light.

A *demon* is a spirit dedicated to the service of Chaos, or Darkness.

An *elemental* is a spirit formed of and bound to a single philosophical element.

A *planetary spirit* is a spirit formed of and bound to the qualities of a planet.

A *Zodiacal spirit* is a spirit created from and bound to the qualities assigned to a particular degree of the heavens.

A *larva* is a spirit created by the strong emotions of an individual or group.

An *elementary* is a spirit created by an individual as a personal servant.

A *ghost* is a complex type of larva.

A *homunculus* is a spirit created by an individual in the shape of a human being and infused into some material substance.

A *vampire* is a spirit that draws vitality by force from living beings.

A *succubus* is a sexual vampire in female form.

An *incubus* is a sexual vampire in male form.

All forms of spirit can, in theory, act on all levels of being. However, the identities of some types are bound by tradition to certain levels. Ghosts are popularly defined by their appearance on the astral circle: they are visible and audible, sometimes tactile, but they seldom leave material evidence of their presence. A homunculus, on the other hand, would not be a homunculus unless it had a physical body of human shape.

The formation of a spirit may be completely unconscious as in the case of larvae, or deliberate in various degrees. The most highly conscious method is the telesmatic, where the spirits are built up from simples into complexes through a rational process of correspondence. The creation of a telesmatic image can be compared to the process of life. It begins with an initial impulse, goes on to the gathering of useful raw materials, and then an involved pattern is constructed from these basic building blocks.

Telesmatic images are alloys of forces, desires, and emotions that have been given a form by the creative Will of the Magus. They have their own identity and a sense of purpose that revolves around the task they were created to fulfill. Once given life, they fear death and will use all their limited abilities to avoid being dispersed. The longer they live, the stronger and more complex they become, for they continue to draw identity from the Magus. They are not creatures of the ego of the Magus alone however; they take some of their nature from his godhead.

These spirits may become so concrete over time that they are clearly perceived by other people who know nothing of their existence. In Tibet, before the coming of the Communists, the creation of telesmatic images was a part of the training of magicians. It was said to be not uncommon to encounter these manufactured spirits while walking along the empty mountain trails at twilight.[17]

The traditional method of forming a telesmatic image involves the use of a spirit name. The name is translated into Hebrew letters. Each letter has a certain set of symbolic associations. The first letter of the name is used to form the head of the image; the second letter, the shoulders, and so on. Bit by bit the spirit is built up, like the Frankenstein monster, until an integrated figure is obtained. Throughout the formation process, the Magus relies on the symbolism of the letters for guidance.

To illustrate, here are the attributes of Graphiel,* the intelligence, or good spirit, of the planet Mars:

G	Camel	Priestess	Moon
R	Head	Sun	Jupiter
A	Ox	Fool	Air
Ph	Mouth	Tower	Mars
I	Hand	Hermit	Virgo
A	Ox	Fool	Air
L	Ox Goad	Justice	Libra

The first column after the name is the Hebrew meaning of the letter; the second is the Tarot Trump connected with it; and the third is the astrological power. There are many other associations for each letter, and each of these symbols has many associations of its own. Thus the variety of figures, personalities, and qualities that can be extracted from this group of symbols is virtually infinite. The Magus must rely on his intuition to find the best figure for his needs.

This traditional method of deriving spirits has certain limitations. The Magus is bound by the symbols attached to the Hebrew letters, and these may not always be right for the purposes he has in mind. He is restricted by a limited number of names for angels, demons, and so on. In other words, he must try to fit his needs into the existing catalogue of psychic beings. This is like buying a suit off the rack—usually it fits well enough to serve, but it is never ideal. But the greatest fault with this method is that it starts with the name and goes on to work backwards to extract the qualities of the spirit.

---

*The Hebrew letter Aleph—represented by an *A* in the table—is often represented by an *E* for ease in pronunciation.

Here is a more rational system that will serve for the creation of all telesmatic images.

Begin with the purpose you wish the spirit to serve. Using its eventual function as a guide, list all those qualities you will require in your creation. These should include the physical, emotional, and mental features of the spirit. Narrow these down to the most essential. For example, suppose you wanted to create a protective spirit to watch over a friend. Some of the features you might desire in such a being are strength, fierceness, a terrifying aspect, a loud voice, great size, and the like.

From the list of qualities, extract a list of corresponding symbols. These might include the color red, the metal iron, thunder and lightning, screaming wind, the ax of war, flaming eyes, the lion, the bear, and the eagle. These symbols can be varied and multiplied until they can be made to fit together into a symmetrical figure. The result might be a great creature with the head of a lion, a flaming red mane, fiery eyes, the roaring voice of a storm, the wings of an eagle shining with flashing colors, the black skin of a bear, and an ax in its hands.

A fearsome creature indeed! Usually, in magic more is less, and it is no crime to be subtle. Such a roaring monster would be more likely to dismember the person it guarded than protect him from foes. At the very least it would scare the living daylights out of him should he chance to see it. However, it illustrates the method.

The next step, when the form has been arrived at, is to extract from it the name of the spirit. A short phrase descriptive of the qualities of the spirit is composed. The example might yield something like: "Great roaring angel with flaming wings." Each of the main words in the description must name one of the primary characteristics of the spirit. The number of words should be significant. Great-roaring-angel-flaming-wings is five words—the number of Mars and Geburah.

The Magus takes the first letter from each word and combines them to make a name. This process is Kabbalistic and is called Notariqon. The name AGLA, which is a name of God, is assembled by Notariqon from the Hebrew phrase "Thou art mighty forever, O Lord." However, it is totally unnecessary to involve a foreign language. A letter is a letter. The powers of the English alphabet are as great as the Hebrew, Chaldean, Arabic, or whatever.

The name of the spirit in the example becomes GRAFW. To pronounce the name may necessitate minor accommodations, perhaps the addition of vowels or the juxtaposition of letters. No addition should be completely arbitrary. All elements in the name must relate directly to the spirit. The name GRAFW can be made pronounceable by stretching the fourth letter into the first part of the word it represents: GRAFlaW.

Since the name comes from the essence of the spirit, it is charged with power over the spirit. In fact, the name is the spirit in another, more compressed form. By speaking the name rightly, the Magus can bring the spirit into being. By destroying the name—by reading it backwards for instance, or by ritually burning it—the Magus can destroy the spirit. The name can be used as a focus for physically containing the spirit when it is not being employed; when the name is written on a pentacle or figurine, the spirit can be made to reside within the object until called upon.

From the name of the telesmatic spirit is derived, by various means, its sigil. Also called the character or seal, the sigil is a geometric design that represents the spirit and acts as a visual avenue of communication and command. Because it is visual, the sigil can be more easily held in the mind during the exaltation of ritual than can the letters of the name. The sigil is another form of the name, or identity, of the spirit. Its making is described in the next chaper.

There is no essential difference between summoning a spirit and creating a telesmatic image. In the first case, the Magus uses elements derived from tradition, and in the second case, he himself chooses all the elements, guided by his purpose. The method of forming telesmatic images can easily be applied to existing spirits which are usually so poorly described in the literature that calling them forth necessitates creating their images in the mind. Starting with what is known about the nature of a given spirit, a shape can be built up and a magical esoteric name extracted from that form. Then a sigil can be constructed, based on the esoteric name.

After the form of a spirit has been conceived, it must still be brought to life. Until its birth it is like the conception of a work of art: it has no tangible reality. Spirits are made real through the rituals of invocation and evocation, already given. As a separate act, the Magus may wish to symbolically infuse vitality into his telesmatic image, but this is not required. The vitality of a spirit comes from the same place as the vitality of the Magus himself—the Unmanifest. By simply drawing the spirit forth until he can experience it, the Magus has caused its birth.

A telesmatic spirit can be prevented from running amuck if it is given a finite life span that ends with its usefulness. Its death can be automatically preset or consciously brought about by the Magus when he deems it prudent. Often both limiting factors are built into the telesmatic image as a fail-safe, the automatic destruct set to operate after a given length of time should the Magus be incapacitated.

Keeping to the example already used, the Magus might give the fearsome guardian he created the life span of a single cycle of the Moon, causing its power to increase as the Moon waxed and decrease with the Moon's waning. In addition, he might symbolically imprison the heart of the spirit in a small ball of wax to insure its instant obedience. He would guard this ball with signs and words of power to keep it safe from the spirit. The moment the spirit outlived its usefulness, the Magus would cast the wax ball into a fire, speaking an incantation for the complete destruction of the spirit.

A competent Magus will suffer no threat from his telesmatic images. The danger lies in his becoming fond of such beings, or even growing to love them. If this happens he may lack the Will to kill them, and then his danger becomes great. At first subservient and fawning, the spirits will draw on the hidden powers of the Self of the Magus and grow stronger day by day, until at last they are too powerful to command; for spirits grow stronger at the expense of the Magus, who correspondingly weakens. The liberated spirits will work all manner of mischief, from malice or exuberance, and will torment the Magus unmercifully unto death.

The Jewish folktale of the Golem should be taken as a warning. The Golem was a telesmatic image that has been infused into a likeness of clay to give it power over the material world.[18] In one version of the story, its creator, Rabbi Loew, allows it to keep its form longer than necessary because it is obedient and subservient to him. But all the while, the Golem grows in power, until at last it is destroyed only with the greatest risk and difficulty.

SIGILS

A SIGIL IS a symbol derived by one of various systems from the name of a spirit. By concentrating his creative Will on the sigil the Magus is able to call forth the spirit into his awareness. Since it is a graphic representation of the name, the sigil is more amenable to mental retention and handling than the name itself.

Ideally the lines and angles of the sigil reflect the nature of the spirit it designates. Placid spirits should have sigils made up of horizontal lines, gentle curves, and rounded shapes. Fiery spirits should be represented by sharp zigzags, pointed angles, and prickly shapes. Evil spirits might have sexual imagery worked into their sigils. However, in practice the designs are too often arbitrarily derived from a mechanical system of sigil making and have no aesthetic relationship to the spirits they represent.

Notice the insectlike quality of the seal of Bifrons, on the following page, left. It suggests the nature of this evil demon. By comparison the more modern sigil of the angel Michael, on the right, seems almost antiseptic.

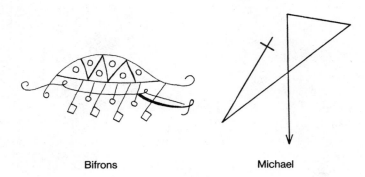

Bifrons   Michael

In magic the sigil is used as the physical focus through which an entity of the subconscious can funnel itself and give itself a tangible presence. To put it another way, it is the template placed over the aperture at the opened point of Self to insure that the potency called across the Veil from the Unmanifest takes on the desired form and no other. Through the sigil the power of a spirit is actualized. All types of magic depend on sigils of one form or another. These may be highly refined—number constants, or rather crude—clay idols. The term "sigil" is more narrowly applied to a two-dimensional design that may be drawn, painted, or engraved.

Many occultists have the notion that traditional sigils possess a dread potency all their own, akin to a loaded gun that even a child may inadvertently set off. They solemnly warn the novice not to dabble in matters he does not understand. Naturally, like the sorcerer's apprentice, the novice dabbles away eagerly at the first opportunity, but is usually disappointed with the results. He has yet to comprehend that the only power of magic lies within him.

Spirits take on form and identity only through the Magus. No sigil, however intelligently drawn, will conjure up a spirit by itself, anymore than a hammer will unaided drive a nail. A sigil is a tool of the human mind. It has no will, no desire, no intention. It is a key that may unlock a particular door into the subconscious, but only if it is well made and the Magus learns how to insert it.

Sigils are similar to words—if their meaning is not understood they remain so many squiggles of ink on paper, utterly impotent. Psychic entities respond only to the mind-states of the Magus. The term "mind-state" is here used to describe the total gestalt of thoughts, emotions, urges and sensations that exist within the personal universe of the individual at a given instant. Mind-states may change totally from one moment to another; or they may be reborn continuously, like the flame of a candle, and so sustained for extended periods.

Particular mind-states resonate in harmony with particular psychic beings. For each spirit there is a unique mind-state that it interprets as a summons to manifest on the circle of consciousness. When the polarity of this mind-state is inverted, the spirit interprets the change as a dismissal. No spirit can defy the directive of its mind-state. It is bound to react in certain ways by its very nature, as one string of a musical instrument will vibrate harmonically with another tuned to exactly the right pitch.

A sigil has power only when it invokes its key mind-state. Through meditation and determination the Magus will be able to infuse any sigil with some potency so that when visualized, it will resonate in his subconscious. The best sigils are those that by their lines and colors, encourage the necessary mind-state. The poorer sigils actually hinder the proper mental climate through their disharmonious elements. However, any sigil visualized before it is understood to link with a particular entity will invoke only boredom.

This differentiates sigils from the universal symbols of the Art, such as the pentagram and the triangle. By its makeup a universal symbol induces in all people who look upon it a similar understanding of some general principle. A sigil must be linked to a specific set of ideas before it can be understood. If sigils are letters, the symbols are numbers; if sigils are melodies, the symbols are rhythms. An uneducated man shipwrecked on an island could look at the universal symbols and draw meaning from them, although this meaning would likely be below the level of verbalization. If he studied the sigils, on the other hand, he would reap only confusion. Sigils appear arbitrary except to the individual who inwardly relates them to a specific mind-state.

Traditional sigils are often based on formal and abstract systems that have little vital meaning to the subconscious. They are technical patterns that fit admirably into an intellectual classification, but are dry and unresponsive in practice. Large amounts of energy must be poured into such sigils before any good can be got out of them. The traditional means of making sigils often achieves no better results than would cutting a variety of shapes from paper and putting them into a hat, then drawing them out randomly and affixing them to particular spirits. The necessary mind-states are not encouraged.

The perfect sigil would be able to call forth the desired mind-state in anyone who looked upon it. Almost certainly no such sigils have been discovered. This is not to say they are theoretically impossible—all human minds work along the same lines, and there may exist unfound signs of the most awesome power able to instantly evoke forces from the subtle spheres. In effect these hypothetical sigils would be universal symbols with a highly specialized function. But these ideal sigils will not be found among the traditional systems.

In the ancient texts two points are repeatedly made. The first is that all sigils are given only as examples since any individual can gain his own system of sigils through personal contact with the spirits. The second point is that sigils have a limited life span, and those effective in one age will not work in a later era; usually the period of potency is said to be only a few generations, sometimes only a single generation. From these cryptic hints the Magus should glean that sigils work by living associations and are most effective when used personally, less potent when used fraternally, still less potent when diffused throughout the culture in which they were created, and of no practical use outside that culture.

Sigils may be derived mechanically, intuitively, or through a combination of the two. Mechanical sigils can be swiftly turned out once the system of their making is established, but by their nature they are unresponsive and must be empowered, or loaded with meaning, by the Magus. Intuitive sigils have the greater potency because their inspiration comes from the depths of the subconscious, but they are difficult and time-consuming to make as each is a separate act of creation.

The difference between mechanical and intuitive sigil making is that in the first the sigil is related to the name mechanically, and in the second the sigil is related to the name intuitively. The two sigils given at the start of this chapter illustrate this distinction. The sigil of Bifrons is intuitive; the sigil of Michael, mechanical.

No sigil can stand alone. Each is only the visual representation of the name of the spirit. For the sigil to be significant, the name must have significance. For the name to be significant, the image it invokes within the Magus must be meaningful. And for the image of the spirit to possess meaning, it must accurately reflect the functions of the spirit.

Sigils may be mechanically derived by means of a radial arrangement of letters called the Sigil Wheel. The letters of the English alphabet are reduced to twenty-four by combining the *I* and *J* and the

U and *V*. Then they are written in three circles of twelve, seven, and five around a center in a clockwise inward spiral:

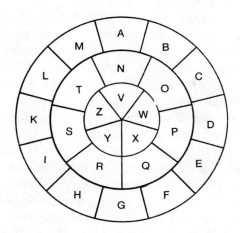

A piece of paper is placed over the Wheel and a continuous line traced from letter to letter in the spirit name. Double letters are indicated by a slight kink in the line (⇒); a letter directly between two other letters can be shown by a loop (⟋); the beginning of the sigil is marked by a cross (+); and the end by an arrow point (→).

With the Sigil Wheel any name can be converted into a graphic design by any person. If the name is meaningless the resulting sigil will also be without significance and therefore ineffectual. If the name is significant the sigil will be intellectually bound to it, but may be cold emotionally. It may be somewhat awkward to handle because of its abstractness.

Sigils may be intuitively derived by communion with the Light. First the Magus should strive to know the spirit intimately, meditating on the form and personality of the spirit until it becomes a living being in his imagination. Then he should pray to the Light, asking it to provide him with a dependable sigil, either through his Guardian or directly, by which the spirit may be summoned and directed.

The sigil will be given quietly, often at an unexpected time. Usually it will take the form of a persistent image, and the Magus may not realize for some time that he has been given the sigil he sought. It may be that the sigil will be given before the Magus asks for it, since time is a human concept and is no barrier to the Light. The Magus must learn to make himself a sensitive, finely tuned instrument if he is to succeed in obtaining sigils intuitively.

An ancient technique of focusing the attention is to place a small plate of silver on the altar and ask the Guardian to inscribe the sigil upon its polished surface. Sigils sent in this way were said to appear in tiny beads of dew that looked like the filaments of a spiderweb. No doubt the formation of those dew drops was helped by the fact that the windows of the ritual chamber were open and the ritual took place in the very early morning. The sigil image was hurriedly copied by the Magus before it faded away. Any hard shiny surface will serve, such as a plate of brass, gold, or even glass.

Crystals can also be used for intuiting sigils, as can automatic drawing. Smoke and water vapor offer good mediums in which images can form themselves. By gazing fixedly in a receptive mental state at an abstract pattern, the Magus can make certain of the lines come forward while the rest recede into the background. A black mirror can be made by coating a piece of plate glass on the back with several layers of black enamel and mounting it in a frame. This should be scryed in almost total darkness, with no reflections on the surface of the mirror.

Once the sigil is received, it must be tested by applying it to the symbols and words of power to insure that it is what it seems to be. If the sigil has been planted in the mind of the Magus by chaotic forces—unlikely if his intentions are pure—it will create discordance when tried against the Light. Like a poorly cast bell it will yield an ugly sound and must be discarded, and a more acceptable form sought.

Neither of the above ways of deriving sigils is completely satisfactory. The intuitive method is too dependent on whim, while the Sigil Wheel is overly rigid. A compromise that will be both effective and practical is needed between freedom and formalism. Here is a method of deriving sigils that combines the intuitive and mechanical.

The esoteric name of a spirit is first turned into a sigil by applying it to the Sigil Wheel. This part of the process is mechanical. The Magus then studies the rough sigil with his intuition, seeking those aspects that must be changed or eliminated. The changes must never be arbitrary, but they can be achieved by a variety of devices. The Magus can alter the words in the descriptive phrase of the spirit name to produce a more appropriate sigil, or change the order of the letters in the name.

He can also make use of the English version of the Kabbalah of Nine Chambers, the Aiq Bekar, which has been filled with the twenty-six letters of the English alphabet:

A = 1 J = 10 S = 100	B = 2 K = 20 T = 200	C = 3 L = 30 U = 300
D = 4 M = 40 V = 400	E = 5 N = 50 W = 500	F = 6 O = 60 X = 600
G = 7 P = 70 Y = 700	H = 8 Q = 80 Z = 800	I = 9 R = 90

This is the same grid used in the children's game of tick-tack-toe; and children often use it to make up secret codes, a letter being represented by an angle of the grid. *A* would be represented by the angle ⌐˙ , the single dot signifying that it is the first letter in the compartment. This code is centuries old and has its origins in ancient thaumaturgy. It is interesting to note that it survived down to the present as the plaything of children.

By using the Aiq Bekar the Magus can convert one letter into another through their numerical equivalents. Letters in the same compartment are considered to be magically related. For example, *A* can be interchanged with *S* because both letters fall into the first box of the grid. *A* is assigned a value of 1, and *S* a value of 100, which by magical addition is: 100 = 1 + 0 + 0 = 1. These new letters will yield a different sigil on the Sigil Wheel.

The emerging sigil can also be stylized to disguise its origin and to lend it a character of its own that agrees with the nature of the spirit. Straight lines can be curved. Ornamentation can be added where appropriate, and lines textured. Different colors that relate to the spirit can be used.

To use the hypothetical telesmatic guardian spirit named GRAFlaW as an example, a strict application of the Sigil Wheel would produce the sigil on the left, which could then be stylized and altered by Aiq Bekar into the sigil on the right:

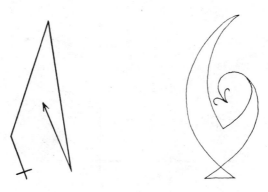

The Magus should always use his own language in magic, even though it is traditional to use Latin, Hebrew, Greek, and even Arabic. A native language is learned by the child in the cradle. It will always have deeper associations than any other. Also the Magus must know at all times exactly what he is saying without the least ambiguity. The use of Hebrew in sigil making is for the most part a superstition. It is true that Hebrew has many magical associations with a long tradition; however, the native tongue of the Magus is given to him by God and he should use no other in the majority of his workings.

The magical, or secret, name of a spirit should be thought of as its true name, or even as its soul, and will be different for each adept who derives it. The common name of a spirit, such as Baal or Michael, is the name of a collective ruling being—a poorly defined god-form—while the many different secret names apply to the numberless spirits under its rule. These are the armies said to be under the princes and dukes of hell; these are the servants of the archangels, not lesser individual spirits, but particular aspects of the one collective spirit that bears the exoteric name.

When the Magus calls forth one of the traditional spirits he will view it uniquely and call it by a unique name. Another adept will see the spirit that bears the same common name in a different way, and his esoteric name for that spirit will differ from that of the Magus. The spirits will be separate yet bound together by their traditional name and characteristics. Remember the answer given to Christ by the possessing demon: "My name is Legion; for we are many" (Mark 5:9).

However the Magus finally chooses to arrive at the sigils of his personal system of magic, he should form them after a single style so that they harmonize with each other, even though each is totally unique. This will involve limiting the materials, instruments, and colors with which the sigils are made. In unity is strength—confusion yields only weakness.

An excellent material for sigils is wax. It is pure and inert magically. It can be colored as desired and is easy to mold and engrave. If not physically destroyed by pressure or heat it will last forever. Wax sigils can be set under glass to protect their surfaces. New paper and colored inks are also excellent, and make durable and inexpensive sigils that can be readily carried and hidden. All instruments and materials must be purified and consecrated before use. This is a general rule in magic.

It may happen that the associations of a particular sigil are lost over a period of time and the sigil becomes a dead thing to its maker, no longer able to invoke a resonance in his subconscious. This means that the mind of the Magus has evolved and the mind-state he once associated with a particular spirit no longer seems apt. In this case the sigil must be discarded and the Magus should make a new one for the same spirit, guided by his expanded understanding. This will involve deriving a new esoteric name from the qualities of the spirit.

Strictly speaking, a sigil is not necessary to contact a psychic entity. Only the mind-state is essential, and this can be attained through a variety of focuses not regarded as sigils by Western Hermetic magic. This explains why the magic of an African shaman can be as potent as that of a Western adept; although the witch doctor uses dance and drugs and blood in his workings, he arrives at a mind-state as potent as that invoked through symbols, poetry and numbers.

COLORS

IN MODERN MAGIC the attribution of color to the major symbols seems determined by a mixture of dogmatism and caprice. A new system is presented here, based on the distribution of colors around a circle. Fourteen colors are used, and they may be subdivided into five categories:

1. *White*
2. *Primaries*—Red, Blue, Yellow
3. *Secondaries*—Orange, Purple, Green
4. *Tertiaries*—Yellow-Orange, Red-Orange, Red-Purple, Blue-Purple, Blue-Green, Yellow-Green
5. *Black*

These colors are produced by splitting white light into three parts, then combining these primaries into pairs to make three secondaries, which are further combined with the primaries to yield six tertiaries. Black is the absence of light.

A good color wheel should be consulted to understand how the colors relate to each other. Color wheels are sold in art supply stores. They show a radial spreading of the colors of the spectrum around a circle with the primaries set at 120 degrees to one another. It will also prove useful for the Magus to paint his own color wheel so that he develops a feel for the separate colors.

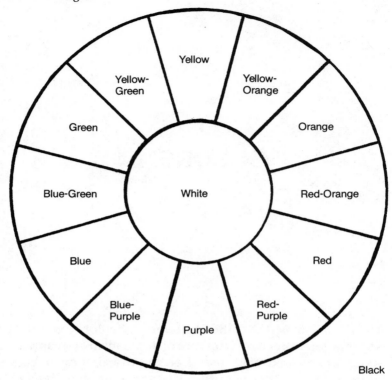

Yellow

Yellow-Green

Yellow-Orange

Green

Orange

Blue-Green

White

Red-Orange

Blue

Red

Blue-Purple

Red-Purple

Purple

Black

1. White

The color of spiritual radiance that shines forth from the center of Self and from the face of the All-Father.

Newton showed with glass prisms that white light is an amalgam of all the colors of the spectrum. The ancients did not know that white is a composite. To them it appeared the most rarefied and pure of colors. It is transparent, and cannot be fixed by a particularly quality—like pure water it has no flavor—yet it illuminates and pervades the entire world. For this reason the philosophers assigned to white the Spirit of the Unmanifest that is everywhere and nowhere, that promotes seeing but is itself unseen. In alchemical plates this understanding is best presented as a snow white dove that circles the mists of Chaos, with radiance streaming behind it, to form the world.

The modern awareness that white is a composite only reinforces the attribution of white to Spirit. Just as whiteness holds all other colors within itself, so does Spirit embody all form and substance. As colors are subjective elements of light existing only in the mind of the observer, so are forms subjective elements of Spirit.

2. Primaries

The three colors from which all others may be derived. There are two kinds of primaries—those reflected from paint and other colored surfaces and those of pure wavelengths of light. The pigment primaries are red, blue, and yellow. Light primaries are red, blue, and green.

For years it was thought that yellow was a legitimate primary. Then when science became capable of producing pure beams of color, it was found that no two colors could be combined to form green; therefore, green was a primary. However, yellow could be made by combining beams of green and red; it was not a primary.

The confusion resulted from the fact that pigments reflect not one but several colors with one predominating. When yellow paint is mixed with blue, green results because of the interaction of the other colors involved, not just from the action of blue on yellow.

Here pigment primaries are used because practical magic deals with them almost exclusively, and for the lesser reason that they are traditional.

It is easy to relate the primaries to the three principles in the first trinity of emanation:

Red is the masculine color, of the Father, the color of Will, of action, of command, of outward streaming. It is fiery and explosive by nature.

Blue is feminine, of the Mother, the color of reflection and inner feeling, secrecy, nurture and formation, the color of lakes and oceans, and of the sky. It is passive and accepting by nature.

Yellow is androgynous, of the Child, the color of the intellect and learning, of meditation. It can both give and take, can act or wait according to circumstance. It is the color of art. Its nature is best represented by the pathway of golden light reflected from the rising Sun on the surface of the sea.

3. Secondaries

The three secondaries result from combining the primaries in pairs. Each shares the qualities of its parents yet is an individual in its own right.

Orange is opposite blue and is the combination of yellow with red. It is a bold color of material success and worldly triumph. Energetic but not impetuous, it is pervaded with positive feelings and good cheer.

Purple is opposite yellow and is formed by combining blue and red. The least favorable of all the colors, purple has a sickly quality pertaining to disease, putrefaction and corruption. It is the color of futility and impotent rage.

Green is the opposite of red on the color wheel and partakes of yellow and blue. It is the color of love, sharing, and accepting. Also it is the color of natural magic of the Pan variety. Green is linked with the wood spirits and the joyful abandonment of spring.

4. Tertiaries

The six tertiaries result from combining the secondaries with the primaries. They are one more level removed from the Light and therefore are magically less potent.

Yellow-Orange is opposite blue-purple. It is the color of mild cheese. It represents calculation combined with a drive to achieve desired ends. It is diplomatic and capable of putting on a smiling face, yet always the element of mind is paramount in this color.

Red-Orange is opposite blue-green on the color wheel. It is the color of amber, of playfulness and mischief. It possesses the energy of boyish spirits too wild to be directed but without malice.

Red-Purple is opposite yellow-green. It is the color of port wine, of strength submerged in brutishness or stupidity, and of energy and potential allowed to lie dormant and decay.

Blue-Purple, opposite of yellow-orange, is the color of the sky at late twilight. It represents inaction and coldness, poisons of the physical, social, and mental kind, and the sucking up and harboring of corruption.

Blue-Green, opposite of red-orange, is the color of the mysterious ocean depths. A clean color and alive, it withholds itself and conceals its inner wit and warmth. Yet it can be nurturing and strengthening.

Yellow-Green is opposite red-purple and is the color of new grass in spring. It symbolizes a lethal combination of life energies and adaptability that is not necessarily hostile but is extremely potent. If opposed it can take on the aspect of the green-eyed monster and pitilessly seek its inevitable revenge.

5. Black

Black is not a real color but is the quality that results when light is withdrawn. It represents the antithesis of Spirit. By understanding black a truer understanding may be gained of Evil.

Black is the shadow where light is not. It can only be recognized because light does exist beside it, thereby defining the shadow and giving it a hollow shape. In the physical world there is no such thing as utter darkness, since radiation of some kind is always present in any enclosed space. Darkness, like every other thing, takes its form from the Light.

Evil represents a place where Spirit is weaker. An evil soul is one that has defiled itself before the Light. Like cancer, evil grows by eating at the edges of the Light and enlarging a space for itself. One spark of the Light banishes it, but it can never be destroyed because it never truly exists. Always it is ready to return the instant the lamp of Spirit flickers.

Due to the fall of mankind from grace, the illusory qualities of blackness appear real to human perception. They take the form of cruelty, indifference, hatred, and silence—but the one characteristic that binds them all is emptiness.

It is useful in practical magic to assign these fourteen colors to the major symbols. When the symbols are drawn and used in a working, the appropriate colors give them a greater impact on the psyche. The great symbols in magic are the one wheel of Spirit, the trinity of motions, the five elements, the seven planets, and the twelve Zodiac signs.

1. Wheel of Spirit

The wheel of Spirit receives white because it is the center and embodies all qualities within it. The symbol should be drawn with six spokes, rather than the traditional eight, to suggest the color wheel with its three primaries and three secondaries:

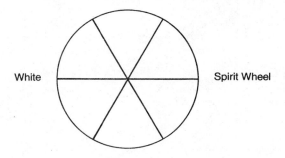

2. Three Motions

The three motions are assigned the primary colors and can be graphically presented by a circle divided into three wedges of 120 degrees each. Cardinal or linear motion is red by nature. Fixed or rotary motion is blue. Mutable or vibratory motion is yellow. Because yellow is the mediating color, it is placed at the top of the circle:

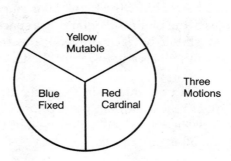

3. Five Elements

The assignment of the colors to the five elements is also based on the primaries, but with white and black added. The elements Fire, Water, and Air are very similar in action to the linear, fixed, and vibratory motions except that the motions act as verbs, so to speak, while the elements act as nouns. The colors assigned are the same. Elemental Spirit is the Light considered as an individual quality rather than as the force that pervades all qualities. Its color remains white. Earth is symbolic of all matter, and on a higher level, of all form. Matter viewed apart from Spirit is hollow and lifeless; therefore, Earth is assigned the color black, the color of shadows:

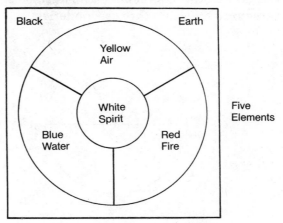

4. Seven Planets

Color correspondences with the seven planets have been integrated with the new positioning of the planets on the points of the hexagram. The changes in position of Mercury, the Sun, and Saturn from the traditional placements results in the most appropriate color assignment to each planet:

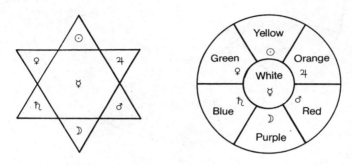

Seven Planets

5. Twelve Zodiac Signs

·Finally, the colors of the Zodiac are derived from the Cardinal, Fixed, and Mutable divisions of signs. Since neither the Zodiac nor the color wheel are subject to alteration, assigning the proper colors to the signs is simply a matter of rotating the twelve colors of the wheel over the twelve signs of the Zodiac until the best match occurs, while bearing in mind that the primary colors must fall on appropriate signs of motion.

It is necessary to reflect the Zodiac and view it from the back, just as it was in assigning it to the four emblematic beasts—the Lion, Eagle, Angel, and Bull. This act brings the Zodiac to Earth, where it may be integrated with earthly systems. It does not affect the relative order of the signs or the colors.

Considering the first sign, Aries, as the most strongly red and placing it on the color wheel in the red panel, blue will fall on Leo and yellow on Sagittarius. (See diagram on p. 294.)

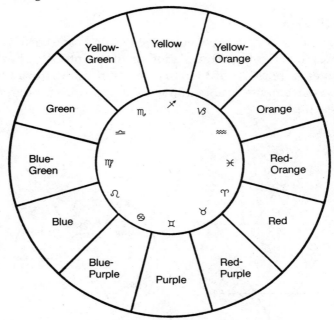

Twelve Zodiac Signs

The entire system of colors can be displayed through a single three-dimensional symbol composed of four pyramids, each made up of four equilateral triangles. The resulting model has twelve facets. One facet is assigned to each color. White, Mercury, and Spirit are not visible in the model because they are at its center and so concealed from sight. Black and Earth exist beyond the limits of the model.

On the following page is an exploded view of the grand symbol of colors. It should be studied closely as it presents a useful set of relationships.

The three primaries are located on the visible sides of the central pyramid. The secondaries are on the next outermost circle of triangles. Notice that the triangles of colors opposite on the color wheel are joined at the bases—for example, the triangle of red is joined at the base to the triangle of green, and these colors are at opposite extremes of the color wheel.

The outermost circle of triangles contains the tertiary colors. The visible facets of each outer pyramid are made up of one of the secondaries plus its two related tertiaries—for example, the pyramid on the right is assigned green and its two related tertiaries, yellow-green and blue-green.

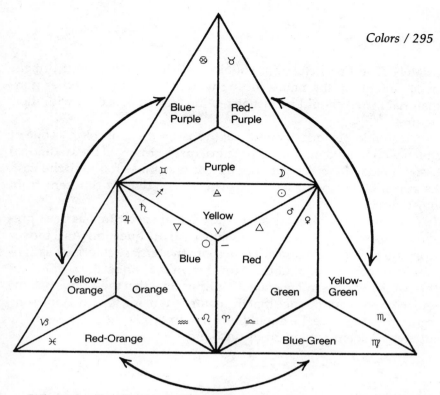

When the flat display is folded together into a model, the edges indicated by the arrows join each other. The base of the yellow-green triangle, for instance, joins the base of the red-purple triangle. Notice that these colors are opposites on the color wheel.

Each division of motion among the Zodiac signs forms a cross on the model. The Cardinal signs Aries and Libra, colored red and green, describe one line with their joined bases, and on the opposite side of the model, the other Cardinal signs, which are Capricorn and Cancer— yellow-orange and blue-purple—define a baseline that crosses the baseline of Aries and Libra at right angles. The model is an accurate three-dimensional representation of the Zodiac and the color wheel.

When the Magus constructs the model, the signs for the motions, planets, and Zodiac should be painted on the triangles in the opposite, or flashing, colors. Opposite colors are called "flashing" because when brought together they appear to flicker and pulse due to retinal fatigue.

Color is used in magic in the same way all other symbols are used—to provide a foundation for a particular set of desires and thoughts and feelings the Magus wishes to call up and maintain within his psyche. All visual symbols should be colored appropriately. The ritual chamber should be bathed in the color of light most suitable to the nature of the working. Spirits and other nonmaterial forms should be visualized in colors that accord with their natures.

It should be born in mind that the assignment of colors is one of the most disputed matters in practical magic. Many of the traditional assignments in the West are not the same as those found in the East. Each school seems to have its own system, wildly different from most others.

A system of colors based on the circular spectrum has been presented that attempts to deal rationally with the question. As it moves from the primaries and secondaries into the tertiary colors, its assignments become more doubtful. However, it is a connected whole, and this itself is very useful in magic. It is important that the Magus believe with complete confidence that the color he is using for a symbol is the right one; therefore, he should feel free to disregard any system the moment it seems awkward or unsound.

DREAM MAKING

PSYCHIC IMAGERY IS sometimes dismissed with the asser-
tion that it is no more than self-deception, a kind of hypnosis that can
take on a druglike attraction for weak, hysterical minds. Critics observe that when adepts claim to visit the psychic, or astral, realm, outwardly they close their eyes and slip into a kind of trance, their
physical bodies traveling nowhere. From this they conclude that psychic travel is the same as daydreaming.

This account given by Abraham the Jew in the *Book of Abramelin* of
his experience with an Austrian Witch is typical:

> She rubbed herself with the same unguent, and I was very expec-
> tant to see her fly away; but she fell to the ground and remained
> there about three hours as if she were dead, so that I began to
> think that she really was dead. At last she began to stir like a per-
> son who is waking, then she rose to an upright position, and with
> much pleasure began to give me the account of her expedition,
> saying that she had been in the place where my friend was, and all
> that he was doing; the which was entirely contrary to his profes-
> sion. Whence I concluded that what she had just told me was a
> dream, and that the unguent was a causer of a phantastic sleep;
> whereon she confessed to me that this unguent had been given to
> her by the Devil.[19]

The disgust of Abraham is understandable inasmuch as he
expected to see the Witch born physically away on the air. However,

behind his words is the automatic, unquestioned assumption shared by the skeptics of modern times—that dreams and other illusions are of no importance, therefore psychic travel is of no practical value, at best an amusement, at worst a dangerous fascination.

It is true that some psychic travelers have become blinded by the dazzling pageantry of their inner landscapes and have been caught up in them on an emotional and sensual level against their better judgment. However, the dangers of the psychic sphere in no way diminish its importance. Dreams, hallucinations, and astral travel are at root similar phenomena, but far from being frivolous they represent the Middle Temple of the Magus and form a vital connecting link between the mundane world and the Light. They are invaluable tools in magical working.

In dreams the raw potencies of the subconscious put on symbolic bodies, focusing themselves into compact beings that can react to and manipulate their surroundings. Since they have no power to create forms on their own, they play upon the vulnerability of the sleeping or daydreaming person, causing him to unwittingly shape bodies for them to inhabit.

The creatures of the subconscious take on these forms to gain power over the dreamer, who is by natural right their master, but who, through his ignorance and weakness, they hope to transform into their slave. But in taking on forms dream spirits render themselves vulnerable. It is an ancient tenet in magic that a spirit cannot be harmed by physical means unless it puts on a physical body to better work its purposes. To kill a man a demon must take on material form, but once it does so it can itself be killed with cold steel or fire.

The meaning behind this folklore is that so long as entities are without form they remain unperceived and thus are impotent. When they take on a visible shape they can attract the notice of the Magus and use his own powers against him. But when the Magus becomes aware of their purpose and of his own hidden strengths, he can turn that power away from himself and focus it on his tormentors.

The real vulnerability of spirits is that of form to Will, not flesh to steel. The power of all spirits is only apparent. In reality it comes from the Unmanifest, the source of all power, through the point of Self of the Magus. The spirits only act as mediators. In themselves they are utterly ineffectual. That is why they are attracted to human beings. Human beings are the source of power but do not know how to direct it. Spirits know how to direct the power but cannot bring it across the

Veil on their own.

Know that in the dream the dreamer is god. The sleeper creates the universe of the dream in a manner analogous to the way divine Spirit creates the physical universe of time and space. According to Hindu faith, all men are dreams of Brahma. By Hermetic doctrine, that which is below is like to that which is above.

Dreamers are sleeping gods unaware of the extent of their powers. They show no sign of free Will during the dream but merely act out a role; however, even the lowest actor knows why he is in a play; the dreamer knows neither why he is present in the dream nor what will happen next. He is a plaything for the dream entities, tossed this way and that by desires other than his own.

This passivity during the dream-state continues throughout the entire lives of the greater mass of humanity. Most men and women remain mere pawns in their psychic worlds until the day they die. They neither write the script for their dream plays nor take an active part in their direction.

It need not be so. The dreamer has the power to rule his dreams and visions. Like the awakened kraken he can rise into awareness and with a single word bring the entire dreamworld crashing down, because the dream is his to make or destroy. Just as the conscious can learn to rule the subconscious elements of the mind during waking, so also can it rule them during sleep.

In waking life the subconscious often controls the actions of a person because his awareness is not sensitive enough to observe the invisible entities of the subconscious at work. These forces can only be noticed by their effects. During sleep, however, the elements of the subconscious are visible to the awareness in symbolic bodies that express their desires. This renders them vulnerable. In the dream, wish becomes reality. The dream landscape is a battleground upon which the war between the subconscious drives and the self-aware ego is played. When the dream is over both sides return to their respective worlds; but they carry the scars of battle with them.

For most people the outcome of each skirmish is decided before it begins. Indeed, with a kind of sadistic delight the demons of the subconscious can force the perceived self to experience the same dream over and over, perhaps hundreds of times, always with the same outcome and no hope to change it. By compelling the dreamer to reaffirm their identities the spirits grow more concrete, for the subconscious conviction of the dreamer is their life force.

300 / New Magus

The Magus will not long endure this humiliating subjugation. He knows full well the difficulty of reaching the subconscious entities during waking. They hide in the darkness of his mind beyond the limits of his perceptions and bide their time, waiting for him to relax his vigilance. But during sleep they reveal themselves freely, confident of the impotence of his consciousness. Thus the Magus can best come to grips with these entities and affect them for his purposes during the dream.

Taking control of the dreamworld involves four stages of development:

1. *The first is becoming aware inside the dream.*

So long as the dreamer remains a passive observer of events, he can do nothing. He must become aware of his identity, that he is asleep, that he is dreaming. He must observe with critical judgment and must detach himself emotionally from the events transpiring around him. In this way the dreamer can learn to view the horrors of his nightmares with quiet interest, or perhaps mild amusement, as if he were watching a badly made film.

Achievement of this first stage is not uncommon among those who claim to know the Art, and even among the ignorant. Occasionally someone will realize that he is dreaming without immediately waking up, and experience a mild sense of surprise. Among the uninitiated this advantage is never followed up by any positive action, and so it is wasted, perhaps never to come again.

Attainment of the first stage will begin with the Magus gaining awareness occasionally, usually toward the end of the dream. At first his mind will be in a sluggish stupor, as though he were drugged, and his thinking irrational. Eventually he will reach the point where he can observe a dream from the start with alertness.

Certainly the subconscious entities will fight his growing power by obliterating the dreams from his memory so that upon waking, the Magus will not know if he was aware during his dreams or not. This matters little in the long run. Once awareness is achieved the Magus may rest assured that he will never lose this power, whether or not he recollects exercising it. By a sustained act of Will the Magus can train himself to gradually retain more and more of the dreams upon waking, as he probably will wish to do in order to keep track of his progress.

2. *The second stage is intervention in the dream.*

Instead of merely watching it unfold, the Magus acts to frustrate the outcome of his dream. In a nightmare where he is falling he will cause himself to grow wings and fly to safety. In dreams Will becomes reality. If attacked by foes the Magus will project a pentagram and consume them. These acts of resistance will greatly reduce the incidence of nightmares. Malefic spirits will see the Magus coming, as it were, and give him a wide berth.

There is no limit to the power of the Magus inside his dreams. He can shatter mountains and turn deserts to gardens. He can create life from clay and destroy it. The wise Magus will use his power with discretion lest he upset his inner psychic balance and drive himself mad. For he should be aware that not all dreams are intended to harm him. Many are profoundly beautiful and designed to teach. As all dreams are not bad, neither are all dreams good. The Magus must not commit the error of psychology, which supposes every dream to take place for the health of the dreamer. He must learn to distinguish his friends from his foes in the astral landscape.

At first the dream demons will be easily routed, because the newly awakened Magus will possess the element of surprise. Indeed the shock on the faces of his tormentors when he first opposes them will afford the Magus some amusement. The spirits will react to his first independent actions with utter amazement and will literally be frozen with confusion. Later, however, they will resist his attacks more cunningly and try to challenge his supremacy. One trick they use is to terminate the dream before the Magus has a chance to bring his full Will to bear upon them. In this way they attempt to deprive him of the savour of his victory and to sow doubt in his mind. Another way is to paralyze his resistance through continuous fear, especially through some weakness such as a phobia. But be assured and persevere.

It is a curious feeling to first confront the entities of the subconscious and do battle with them. The Magus is made to realize that his psyche, which he was in the habit of regarding as his own backyard, is part of a larger universe that is filled with other inhabitants; some good, some evil, but most merely indifferent to him; yet all with their own purposes and functions.

3. *The third stage is the creation of dreams with the conscious Will.*

This is a stage most adepts never reach. Those who commonly

scry in the spirit vision or do path working practice the second stage of control: they observe their dreams and react to them actively. To create dreams entails carving them from the stuff of the psyche. As a sculptor cuts stone to suit his designs, the Magus composes the dream to suit his purposes, rather than attempting to make a dream that has been forced upon him serve his ends.

Dream making is possible during wakefulness. The case of the Bronte sisters comes immediately to mind. These three women, who produced such literary masterpieces as *Jane Eyre* and *Wuthering Heights*, developed with their precocious brother a mental game they called "making out," in which they created their own psychic world of kingdoms and wars and heroes. This is not so very unusual among children, but the Brontes, who lived isolated lives before the age of radio or television, carried it to a high degree of perfection.

Charlotte Bronte later confessed to a friend that she could at any time sit down in a quiet place and call up a pageant of fantastic images to dance before her eyes that seemed as real as the solid furniture around her. As an adult she became frightened of her power, which had a seductive compelling allure and threatened to get out of control, and she forced herself to stop the practice, even though she admitted it still gave her great pleasure.[20]

Beyond question it was this early undirected training that enabled these uneducated and simple women from an unremarkable family to each produce works of literary genius. Because they did not clearly know that they were in command of their visions, they allowed themselves to slip into the role of passive observers and risked certain dangers from the entities they called up before them. Charlotte was right in following her instinct that made her give up her unintentional psychic scrying.

There have been many cases of trained adepts, who should have known better, becoming so deeply involved in visions that they gave up their primary concern with the physical world and became like opium addicts caught up in drug-induced illusions. The case of Florance Farr, the Victorian actress and magician, is one well-known example.

Sometimes those of lesser attainment mistake their wishful imaginings for true psychic visions. The only test is the quality of the experience. If it is as real as life and substantial enough to touch and if it exhibits minor details that were not preconceived, it may be a true psychic experience. It is no good hoping for verification of the visions by events in the physical world—the two do not always correspond.

The burning question of the Magus will be "How can I gain this control over my psychic sphere?"

Unfortunately this cannot be simply answered. There is no exercise that will guarantee success because control over the dreams and visions only comes when a certain level of self-awakening has been reached. The Magus must persevere on his path of becoming, pray for enlightenment, make himself a pure vessel for the Light, and actively court his Guardian. He must meditate often on inner silence and hone his Will into a fine cutting instrument. He must become familiar with the tools of the Art and must practice visualization exercises until he can see the primary symbols with his open eyes in daylight.

Then if he decides on a problem he needs to solve and on the form of the solution, and upon sleeping he dreams the dramatized solution of that problem, he may congratulate himself on his level of attainment.

Most of all it will help if the Magus is aware that conscious control of his dreams is possible. If he anticipates his growing power it will surely come, first in fits and starts, then more evenly as he progresses in the Art. But if the Magus is convinced that such control can never be his, that it is impossible to make and shape dreams, it will considerably hinder his advancement.

The power of dream making is immense. The Magus is enabled to translate a difficulty in his life into dream symbols over which he can exercise total command, and by symbolically vanquishing the problem in the dream he causes a reaction of forces that will extend into his waking material world.

The danger is that the Magus will use his power unwisely and interfere with the subtle necessary functionings of his subconscious. Here the golden rule must be: Act only where necessary; act only for the Light. Consideration of this rule will help remove some of the temptations the Magus will experience and will free him from most of the potential dangers of dream making.

4. *The final and highest stage of control is dreamlessness.*

This stage is attained by certain Tibetan monks, who subsist in a totally dreamless state in constant awareness of the Light. These masters have reached the Inner Temple and have no reason to play with the symbols of the Middle Temple. As long as the Magus is acting upon and reacting to his dreams he is still a prisoner of karma, as the adepts of the East would say—that is, still bound to the wheel of action

304 / New Magus

and reaction. Only by utterly annihilating the illusions of dreams and also the illusions of waking life can the fixed axis of the wheel of Spirit be attained.

This fourth and final stage is not for the Magus because it precludes magic. By its nature magic is part of cause and effect. The dreamless state has nothing to do with the world of forms. The Magus is always one who wishes to change and create—the mystic desires only to be.

However, magic must never be thought of as a lower study than mysticism. The true Magus transcends the mystic. Like the master of magic, Christ, he attains oneness with the Light, then voluntarily renounces it to return to the world of illusion to reform and elevate humanity. The very highest level of attainment is always that of the Magus. All the great prophets were magical adepts who transformed their mystical insight into manifest terms that could in part be assimilated by the unenlightened. It is the destiny of the Magus to be involved in mankind.

THREE WEAPONS

MORE OFTEN THAN not magic is used for evil. This is not so much the result of deliberate planning as it is a temporary falling away from the strict moral standard necessary to work the Art without defiling it. The adept, who is usually intelligent and sensitive, gains along with his power the increasing ire of dark forces, who are ever eager to bring him down to their level should he give them the slightest opportunity.

The Magus will find himself often tempted to use his magic for material ends that have nothing to do with the Light. He may make enemies and be threatened by physical or social violence. What could seem more natural than to use his hard-won skill in self-defense? Or he may see the chance to better his lot by manipulating other people, perhaps to gain love or to rise in a chosen profession.

When the Art is used for purposes not directly in the service of the Light, a door is opened that allows the forces of Darkness to enter. So long as the Magus dedicates himself to cosmic law, evil cannot touch him. But if he plays the hypocrite and deludes himself that he is working for the All when, in reality, he is only working for the material interests of his ego, God will grind him down like Job until he either recognizes his foolishness or is consumed by it.

This is the meaning of Lucifer's temptation of Christ. Lucifer urged Christ to prove his power by throwing himself off a mountain.

Christ declined because he realized that to use the Light in such a trivial and vain display would make him unworthy to receive it. It is by no means certain that Christ would have risen from the rocks below. Christ knew this. Lucifer knew it also. There was a good chance that the Unmanifest would turn its eye away from Christ in sorrow and disappointment at the instant he chose to leap from the mountain, allowing Christ to fall to his death.

There are contemporary examples of the chastening hand of the All. The bands of lunatics who periodically gather in the desert to greet the landing of giant spaceships—spaceships that never come— is the seduction of Lucifer in the modern world. So are the demonstrations of levitation by Eastern fakirs that fail before thousands of spectators and invite the scorn of humanity. Evil continues to scourge those who presume to use the Art for personal gain in defiance of cosmic law. He who tries to get something for nothing will get more than he bargains for.

Having issued this warning it can be stated that it is lawful to use the Art in defense against unprovoked attack. This applies on the physical, astral, and mental circles and can be extended to include the defense of other innocent beings. Attacks can take the form of bodily assault, intimidation, lies, slanders, double dealing, and psychic harassment for the purpose of inducing madness or breaking the Will. Attackers can be animals, humans, spirits, or blind yet malignant potentials such as those that may infect certain localities.

Defenses against these attackers can be divided into active and passive. An active defense exists when the Magus recognizes a threat and acts before it can be realized—a preemptive strike, to use a military term—or when the Magus reacts to an attack by attempting to destroy it at its source. A passive defense is one that can be continuously maintained for long periods without conscious intervention, or one which is called into being at the onset of attack to deflect the hostile force harmlessly away.

Of the forms of attack the most dangerous potentially is the psychic type that comes in the guise of nightmares, hallucinations, headaches, fatigue, persistent clumsiness or absentmindedness, obsessive thoughts, or a pervasive sense of fear or hopelessness. The victim seldom knows he or she is under attack and so takes no defensive measures.

Of the attackers the most dangerous are the conscious psychic entitites, for a similar reason: the victim seldom knows he is under attack. He usually does not even believe in the possibility of spirits on the conscious level. First he will see a doctor, then a specialist, then a psychiatrist, and finally end his miserable days pumped full of drugs and locked away in one of the little padded rooms where society keeps its enigmas.

Medical science would describe psychic entities as figments of the imagination, or as aspects of deranged personalities; both descriptions are true in their way, but of little practical value. If, on the other hand, they are called demons and conceptualized as discrete beings with bodies and names, they can be fought with psychic weapons on the battlefield of the imagination.

Of the two modes of psychic defense the active is fraught with more peril because it can, through ignorance or malice, be used to harm innocents. The Magus may think he is under attack from another person when really he is being manipulated by a spirit to unwittingly commit an evil act. He should bear in mind that he is fallible and rely solely on passive defenses wherever possible.

The potential variety of magical weapons is infinite, limited only by the imagination and skill of the adept. However, in essence all derive from three symbolic types. These three forms alone will render the Magus invulnerable to attack and will give him an offensive capability should this prove necessary. The weapons are:

1. *Sword of Will*
2. *Shield of Faith*
3. *Armor of Tranquility*

1. Sword of Will

The Sword is conceived by the Magus as a flaming beam of ruby light extending from the index finger of the right hand into space for an unlimited distance. It has the power to blast at all levels and to wither life, and can cut like a laser through deceit and confusion. When powerfully extended to the beating heart or the brain of an enemy, it can kill. It is not bound by time or space and can strike across seas or into the future. Since the past is accepted by the mind of the Magus, the Sword cannot easily be used to alter past events. It extends and retracts instantly at will when the right hand is raised or relaxed. Its color is red, its element Fire, and its motion linear.

2. Shield of Faith

The Shield is the opposite and complement of the Sword. It is conceived by the Magus as a disk of light that extends from the left palm when it is held outward—the traditional sign of warding off evil. It is formed of a clockwise whirling cross that is usually pictured as about six feet in diameter, but its size can be increased or decreased at will; and the Shield can be sent forward to any distance to form a psychic barrier between the Magus and his foe. No evil intention can break the plane of the Shield. When powerfully projected the Shield will stop a charging beast in its tracks. Like the Sword it must be consciously extended, but can be formed or retracted at a moment's notice. Its color is yellow, its element Air, and its motion vibratory.

3. Armor of Tranquility

The Armor is formed around the entire body from the limit of the perceived self, which is usually called the aura. The mystical aura is an imaginary sphere that extends around the body at approximately arm's length and defines what the individual regards as his space. A person is uncomfortable when this space is violated by someone he has not invited in. To create the Armor the Magus contracts his aura and hardens it until it is a gently glowing second skin that floats about an inch over his body. The Armor acts like a prism, refracting the force of evil intention around the Magus. In effect it renders the Magus transparent so that the evil can pass through him without causing any effect. The length of time the Armor can be maintained depends upon the strength of the Magus, as it will eventually sap his vitality. It should never be formed without strong reason as the Magus may grow to depend on it. Its color is blue, its element Water, and its motion circular.

Energizing these three weapons is the Earth center, which is traditionally conceived as a sphere located about two inches below the navel on the spinal column. No physical body exists here; the point is only a workable focus through which the true Earth center may be contacted.

Earth is a mixture of the three higher elements, or more precisely is their precipitate in the physical world. The elemental Earth principle is used to empower the three higher elements. It is significant that in the myth of Hercules where the god wrestles the giant named Antaeus, the giant gains his immense physical power from his repeated contacts with his mother, the Earth. Hercules only defeats

Antaeus by holding him aloft and crushing him. Here is a lesson for the Magus, who will take care that his Earth center is never cut off when he is employing the weapons as this will deprive them of all their power.

This is an exercise designed to invoke the Earth center. Sit comfortably and concentrate the mind on the point inside the spine on level with the lower intestine approximately between the kidneys. Attempt to feel there a small gray or black sphere the size of a marble, hard and heavy as clay. Then picture it as a whirling vortex drawing up energies from the center of the Earth. Visualize the body growing more massive, and ultimately turning to stone and sinking to the center of the Earth, where the Earth center and the center of the Earth unite.

When this has been accomplished, move the point of Self into the Earth center. This cannot be done by shifting the point of Self, which is eternally fixed in the center of the universe; rather the Magus should visualize the entire manifest universe moving upward while the point of Self stays where it is, until the Self unites with the Earth center.

The Magus should devise meditations of his own built on a similar structure. If used effectively, these will awaken his Earth center. Waves of pure force will flow through his body, where they can be directed into the magical weapons. Once the Earth center is truly awakened it can be invoked in a moment and will become an automatic welling out of power along the ray of Will of the Magus.

The weapons should be keyed to certain words of power and specific gestures. To evoke the weapons the divine names of the seventh, eighth, and ninth Sephiroth might be used, and the gestures of the extended right index finger, the palm of the left hand, and the two hands clasped over the heart. Any words or gestures will serve provided they are in harmony with the nature of the weapons. Similar signs are used to signify the withdrawing of the weapons. They need not be noticeable to others, but they must be absolutely clear to the Magus himself. Once established these keys will instantly put the Magus in the proper mind-state to use the weapons.

The Magus may wonder how effective the weapons will be against a physical attack. The answer depends on the Magus. If he has formed them correctly the weapons will be visible at times to the untrained physical eye—at least, this will be the impression of the observer. Actually they are seen with the mental eye and projected onto the senses. In a similar manner they will be physically felt—the Sword as a piercing blow, the Shield as a barrier, and the Armor as a slipping away of purpose.

Most dangers exist in the imagination. The Magus should clearly grasp the truth that his greatest enemy is himself. Merely by mastering himself the Magus will overcome all obstacles in his life. For a man at peace with himself, confident, healthy, fearing nothing and desiring nothing, loved and loving, is virtually invulnerable. What can harm him so badly that he cannot overcome the hurt? Even death will not find him unprepared.

FINGER MAGIC

AS WAS POINTED out in the chapter on the decagram, the standard glyph of the ten divine emanations, which is called the Tree of Life, was undoubtedly derived from the structure of the human hand. For this reason the logical and practical attributions of the Kabbalah can be related to the fingers in such a way that a complete system of magic can be formed based on the movements and positions of the hands alone.

This is not a novel idea. Hand positions have always played an important part in Eastern religions. The Buddhist priests tend to guard the esoteric meaning of their intricate hand positions jealously, and it is questionable if the true meaning of the Buddhist finger magic has ever been revealed, although books have been written on the subject.[21]

Fortunately the Westerner need not depend on the whims of Buddhist monks. He can formulate his own system of finger magic that will be every bit as powerful as any coined in the East.

The fingers of the right hand correspond to the upper five Sephiroth. When the right hand is viewed from the back by its possessor, the zigzag pattern of the Lightning Stroke is at once apparent, indicating the proper ordering of the fingers.

The middle finger belongs to Kether.
The ring finger is to Chokmah.

The index finger is to Binah.
The small finger is to Chesed.
The thumb is to Geburah.

Like the glyph of the Tree, the hand is properly viewed from the back. Its reflection in the mirror surface of a pool makes up the lower five Sephiroth. Being a reverse of the upper five, this is viewed from the palm. However, the true order is inverted if the Magus tries to look directly at the palm of his right hand. Therefore either the right palm must be viewed in a mirror or the left palm, which is the mirror image of the right, must serve for the lower five Sephiroth.

If the left palm is considered, the true descending order of the lower five Sephiroth will be seen in the continued zigzag course of the Lightning Stroke.

The left middle finger belongs to Tiphareth.
The left ring finger is to Netzach.
The left index finger is to Hod.
The left small finger is to Yesod.
The left thumb is to Malkuth.

By crossing the small finger over the thumb of the left hand and regarding the palm, the familiar pattern of the lower half of the Tree will be discerned.

Pressing the hands flat together palm to palm symbolizes the joining of the higher and lower natures of humanity. This is one common prayer gesture. Clasping the hands so that the fingers interlock symbolizes a more profound merging of the two aspects and a shattering of the mirror plane of illusion that separates the halves. This is also a common prayer gesture, but more intense.

Touching any two fingers together forms a path on the Tree, and when this is done by someone aware of the secret meaning of the gesture, it invokes the powers that relate to the path.

Right middle to right ring invokes the 11th path between Kether and Chokmah.
Right middle to right index invokes the 12th path between Kether and Binah.
Right middle to left middle invokes the 13th path between Kether and Tiphareth.
Right ring to right index invokes the 14th path between Chokmah

and Binah.

Right ring to left middle invokes the 15th path between Chokmah and Tiphareth.

Right ring to right small invokes the 16th path between Chokmah and Chesed.

Right index to left middle invokes the 17th path between Binah and Tiphareth.

Right index to right thumb invokes the 18th path between Binah and Geburah.

Right small to right thumb invokes the 19th path between Chesed and Geburah.

Right small to left middle invokes the 20th path between Chesed and Tiphareth.

Right small to left ring invokes the 21st path between Chesed and Netzach.

Right thumb to left middle invokes the 22nd path between Geburah and Tiphareth.

Right thumb to left index invokes the 23rd path between Geburah and Hod.

Left middle to left ring invokes the 24th path between Tiphareth and Netzach.

Left middle to left index invokes the 25th path (which is usually numbered the 26th) between Tiphareth and Hod.

Left middle to left small invokes the 26th path (which is usually numbered the 25th) between Tiphareth and Yesod.

Left ring to left index invokes the 27th path between Netzach and Hod.

Left ring to left small invokes the 28th path between Netzach and Yesod.

Left ring to left thumb invokes the 29th path between Netzach and Malkuth.

Left index to left small invokes the 30th path between Hod and Yesod.

Left index to left thumb invokes the 31st path between Hod and Malkuth.

Left small to left thumb invokes the 32nd path between Yesod and Malkuth.

Any of these conjunctions of the fingers can be made without undue straining of the hands. It will be observed that other conjunctions are possible besides the traditional twenty-two paths. These are entirely permissible. Their meanings will be derived by considering the combined meaning of the two Sephiroth involved.

Every path formed makes a trinity of mover-moving-moved or subject-verb-object. In the same manner as the third point of a trinity, the path cannot be considered alone but must not be thought of as simply the addition of two principles. The path is a thing in itself, made up of the combination of qualities yet unique as the child is unique from its father and mother.

The direction of force along the path will be from higher to lower if form is being called from the Unmanifest, and lower to higher if energy is being projected through the Veil toward some object of desire. This perception of movement of force is relative. If the Light appears to be coming toward the Magus the direction of travel will be perceived as downward; but if the Magus appears to be traveling toward the source of the Light, the direction of motion will seem to be upward.

The common gesture of the thumb and index finger of the right hand formed into an O is a sign of attainment, the Path of the Chariot. The middle, ring, and index fingers of the right hand held up united form a powerful sign of the trinity and are consciously used this way in religions, though not related back to the Tree. The right thumb inserted through the curved middle and index fingers of the right hand is an intrusion of the warlike vigor of Geburah into the perfect harmony of the highest trinity, where it displaces Kether; thus it is a perverse symbol of rulership by the lower forces.

The right index and middle fingers upraised in a V symbolize the convergence of Kether and Binah, which is Light and understanding, or inspiration and intellection. The right middle finger upraised with the hand inverted back to front is a sign of exaltation of the primal Darkness to the highest throne of Light. It is akin to kissing the devil under the tail.

Any two fingers crossed signify the dynamic balance between their respective forces. With practice the Magus will find that he is able to cross any two fingers on either hand unaided by the other hand, the most difficult pair being the index and ring.

A finger pointed signifies a ray of force sent from the Sephirah which that finger represents. For example, the most common form is the extended right index, which sends a ray from Binah and causes its object to "get the point" of an argument or a statement. It is often unconsciously used in heated debate. However, any of the five fingers of either hand may be employed to extend rays of force from the Sephiroth.

The traditional washing of the hands before undertaking a ritual becomes the symbolic cleansing of the entire universe of manifestation from the highest expression of the Light to the forms of the material world. Once this is understood a full body cleansing before ritual becomes unnecessary: the Magus will have already cleaned his body in washing his hands. Before any ritual involving finger magic is worked, the hands should always be washed to clear away evil and discordant influences. The state of cleanliness is not as important as the deliberate act of washing away corruption.

For serious finger magic a set of ten rings should be made, each tailored to fit one of the ten fingers and inscribed with the symbols and names appropriate to that Sephirah. The correspondences can be found in the table on the Tree of Life.

The donning of a particular ring will focus the mind on its purpose and provide a physical point of sensation that the Magus can be conscious of even with his eyes closed or in total darkness. These rings need not be elaborate or expensive but should be handcrafted by the Magus so that the maximum of meaning is infused into their substance. The finger through the circle of the ring is akin to the axis of a dynamo. It stands for the opening through the Veil into the Unmanifest through which the Will of the Magus passes.

In emergencies a loop of colored embroidery thread or ribbon may be used in place of a ring. The old trick of tying a string around the finger to spark the memory is not without its foundation. The pressure of the thread will keep the subconscious mind bound to its purpose even if the conscious awareness wanders.

In a like fashion two fingers can be bound together or linked by a ring to evoke the power of a particular path. This is useful if two fingers are hard to hold in contact for long periods of time.

Women may be inclined to color their nails the appropriate colors of the Sephiroth. Such colors, tastefully shaded, might be worn regularly as a reminder of the distinctions between the fingers. Men would more likely use a scribe and scratch a small symbol of the appropriate Sephirah in each nail. In past ages this was done by the Vikings to call forth the power of particular runes.

In magic of the most material kind blood is sometimes used in bringing about a tangible manifestation of forces. Blood should never be used unless absolutely necessary because it excites the lower entities and can send them like sharks into uncontrolled madness. However, where a physical effect of a grossly material kind is needed the spilling of blood can create the necessary vitality. It must always be the blood of the Magus that is spilled. Black magicians think to spare themselves some pain by sacrificing and bleeding animals or even other men, but they delude themselves. As always they think they can cheat God. Only the blood of the Magus himself, shed in voluntary sacrifice as a symbol of his sincerity and sacrifice of soul, is effective in his workings.

When the correspondences of the fingers have been learned and have become second nature, the blood from a particular finger will partake of its magical properties. Physically the blood will be no different from the blood in the rest of the body, but psychically it will have the energies of the particular Sephirah that relates to the finger from which it was drawn.

Each finger is different from the rest on the hand and different from all others on Earth. This uniqueness shows up in the fingerprint. Sometimes the differences are very slight, but no two fingerprints are identical. The fingerprint is an externalization by the Spirit of the unique relationship between a particular individual and the ten Sephiroth.

The fingerprint can be used as a potent sigil for the powers and spirits of a Sephirah. Impressed upon a paper seal or wax tablet, it embodies both the Sephirah and the Magus who is using the power of the Sephirah in his Art. If the paper or wax seal is further inscribed with the name and sign of a particular spirit, it becomes a specific and powerful magical instrument, the physical record of an act of the magical Will.

In an emergency—for example, if the Magus should find himself imprisoned with nothing other than the clothing he is wearing—a temple in the astral may be built upon the foundation of the hands. The flat palm serves as the Disk; the cupped palm as the Cup; the clenched fist as the end of the Rod; and the spear-shaped hand as the Dagger. The elements are related to the four lower Sephiroth— Netzach, Hod, Yesod, and Malkuth—corresponding to the ring, index, small, and thumb of the left hand. The middle finger of the left hand stands for Tiphareth and the quintessence, or fifth element, of Spirit. The fingers of the right hand are higher reflections of these qualities.

A magic circle can be formed by joining the hands together, and inserting one of the fingers into the center. Any of the ten Sephiroth can be made the focus of a ritual working in this way even if larger physical movement is no longer possible. Of course, each of the fingers can be used to draw the magic symbols in the air so that they can be better visualized in the imagination.

Thus the Magus is never deprived of his Art once he has mastered it. Even if no motion at all is possible, he may continue to work on the astral level and through the use of voice keys. Finger magic is ideal in situations where a larger gesture would be theatrical or difficult to execute. Remember, it is the mind that makes magic, not the body. Both are one, but the mind is closer to the point of Self, from which all power emanates.

RUNES

RUNES ARE THE magical symbols used by the Germanic tribes before the coming of Christianity. Their beginnings are lost in time. Petroglyphs have been found with runelike inscriptions that date back to the Stone Age. Around the first century these magical signs were merged with the Roman alphabet by barbarians living in northern Italy, and the runic script came into being. At times fiercely persecuted by the Church, the use of runes continued down into the 17th century in Iceland and other northern outposts.

The runic alphabet is a complete magical system that joins symbolic meaning with writing and, in this sense, is strikingly similar to the alphabet of the ancient Hebrews. Each rune is both a letter and a symbol of power. By combining the runes and forming them into words, complex magical effects can be achieved.

The number of letters in the different rune alphabets varies from thirty-three in the Old English to sixteen in the northern Scandinavian. For modern magic the twenty-four character German Futhark is the most serviceable. The name is taken from the first six letters, which are translated as F-U-Th-A-R-K.*

---

* Although the German rune alphabet is given here, the Old English names for each symbol have been used because they are more pronounceable and familiar. However, this German alphabet should not be confused with the later and larger Old English alphabet.

319

1. FEOH: ᚠ or ᚡ English: F

Literally "cattle"—by association, that which is domesticated and mild. Of a broken spirit. Slavish, stupid, slow. To be used and owned by free men. Impotent. Weak or cowardly. Also, movable possessions.

This rune can be used magically to break the spirit of a foe and weaken him until he is incapable of effective action. When cast it creates indecision, dullness or fear, depending on how it is emphasized.

2. UR: ᚢ or ᚢ or ᚣ English: U, V

Literally "aurochs"—a fierce wild beast feared and respected by hunters. Courage, boldness, strength, virility, speed, and agility. Freedom. That which can never be dominated or enslaved. The triumphant soul of nature.

Can be used to inspire resolve and courage. To cause to act quickly. To gift with male prowess. To shatter the bonds of enslavement. When cast maliciously it can make a man rash.

3. THORN: ᚦ English: Th

Literally "demon"—a spirit of destruction and pain. Evil, murderous, malicious. Sower of storms and tempests. Annihilator.

Used to physically destroy an enemy or to cause a disaster. Cast, it brings ill fortune, accident, sickness, and death.

4. OS: ᚨ or ᚫ English: A

Literally "god"—an angel of reason and order. Good, kind, benevolent. Stern but just. The source of luck and happiness.

Magically it is used as a sign of fortune. It opens the way in a just cause. Cast, it brings justice and reason.

5. RAD: ᚱ English: R

Literally "journey by horse"—physical travel. By extension, a journey in search of fulfillment. A quest. The seeking of enlightenment. A test of courage and Will.

Magically it is used to seek into the unknown. Cast, it causes a major change.

6. KEN: ᚲ or ᚳ or ᚴ English: K, C, Q

Literally "torch"—a flame that guides. Thus stability, comfort, direction, aid. It lights the way out of difficulty.

Magically it is used for guidance in times of confusion. Cast, it can save a person from losing a grip on life.

7. GYFU: X   English: G

Literally "gift"—sacrifice to the gods. Something given up freely that is of personal value. Can be a ritual sacrifice or a life sacrifice such as forsaking present happiness for future success.

Magically it represents what must be given to gain knowledge. No advance is possible without pain and loss. Sometimes sacrifice is made to end ill fortune. It is good to sacrifice the lower for the higher and evil to sacrifice the higher for the lower. When cast it makes another the unknowing sacrifice, like Job.

8. WYN: P   English: W

Literally "joy" or perhaps "glory"—the blessing of the gods. Exaltation, ecstasy, illumination. Perfect knowledge. The merging into the Light.

Magically this stage follows trial and carries wisdom and power. Cast, it can give insight into difficulty and triumph over adversity.

9. HAEGL: H or N or ⵟ English: H

Literally "hail"—hardship and the winter of the soul. Involuntary suffering without purpose. Loss. Death of a loved one or personal sickness. Any injustice cast down by the fates.

Magically this rune can be used to call forth ill fortune that does not redeem. Cast, it carries remorseless pain and loss.

10. NYD: Y   English: N

Literally "need"—the necessity to survive that drives men onward. Defiance of the human spirit against the fates. In mankind that which refuses to be broken. Stubborn will to endure.

Magically it gives fortitude and defiance when all hope is lost. Fearlessness in the face of certain death. Cast, it lends courage and causes inner strengthening.

11. IS: | English: I, Y

Literally "ice"—changelessness and the stilling of life. Sapping of determination. Motionlessness. Silence.

Magically it is used to stop an event from taking place or to freeze an intention or emotion before it is fully born. To preserve or fix. When cast it stills all change, physical, emotional, or mental.

12. GER: ⟨⟩ or ♦   English: J

Literally "year" and more narrowly "harvest season"—complete cycle. Turning of the seasons, of the Sun, and stars. By extension all whirling energies. The tourbillion.

Magically it causes inversion: it makes the high low and the low high. Turning of the wheel of fortune. It is also used to actualize desire. When cast it brings events full circle and can change luck.

13. EOH: ⌁   English: E

Literally "yew"—source of strength. Yew wood was used magically for the making of wands and militarily for the making of weapons. By association it stands for service, dependability, honest virtue. To be relied on in times of need.

Magically it lends strength to an operation. It provides a firm foundation. Cast, it calms hysterics and can make a frivolous person serious.

14. PEORD: ⌶   English: P

Literal meaning unknown—but perhaps "apple" in the sense of fruit-bearing tree, thus cornucopia. Abundance, luxury, opulence, indulgence, pleasure.

Magically it brings abundance, which may or may not be abused. Cast with evil intent it can cause drunkenness, lust, gluttony, and other sins. Cast with good intention it can satisfy material wants. To a rich man an evil, to a poor man a good.

15. EOLH: Y   English Z

Literally "defense"—protection from evil. Sign of the splayed hand. A shield against attack. Sign of peace. A command to stop.

Magically a barrier against attack or misfortune. Cast, it protects a person or prevents him from harming another.

16. SIGEL: ⟨ or ⨆   English: S

Literally "Sun"—the shape of the rune is a lightning bolt or ray from the Sun. Thus an instrument of destruction. A weapon of the gods. Equivalent to the sword of justice.

Magically it is used to destroy enemies, especially in a holy cause. Can be used to punish disobedient spirits. Cast, it can strike a foe dead, apparently from heart attack or stroke.

17. TIR: ↑   English: T

Literally the name of a war god, also called Tew. His name was invoked to gain victory in battle. Guards soldiers from hurt or death by the weapons of the foe. Marked on a weapon, helps it to strike true and keeps it from breaking.

Magically it is used as a charm against attack and to give fortitude in psychic combat. Cast, it can cause strife and discord.

18. BEORC: ᛒ   English: B

Literally "birch twig"—symbol of fertility. The bark of the birch has healing virtues. The scent of the burning wood is aromatic. Women were lashed with birch twigs to make them fertile. Generally it represents healing, health, love, growth, beauty. The powers of Spring.

Magically it can be used to encourage growth on all levels. Also used to cause love. Cast, it can cause lovesickness, and also the conceiving of children.

19. EH: ᛗ   English: E

Literally "horse"—means to an end. The method. The medium. The horse was sacred, closely related to the Sun. Grace, speed, strength. The virtues of the physical body.

Magically the instrument needed to accomplish a task or attain a goal. Cast, it can provide the means to solve a problem, but can also be used to make a person an instrument for a given end.

20. MAN: ᛗ or ᛘ   English: M

Literally "mankind"—Adam, the father of the race. The will to an end. Intellect and imagination. The mental virtues. The soul. Cunning, purpose, mind over matter.

Magically the force that overcomes obstacles. The impetus to solve a problem. Cast, it can be used to exalt the intellect or to dominate the mind of another. It is the spirit of the trickster, blind nature defeated by guile.

21. LAGU: ↑ English: L

Literally "water"—the rune is in the shape of a bent reed. May mean water as a source of generation, or the dark waters of the underworld and the ocean of dreams. Akin to the symbol of the Cup or Grail. Thus spiritual love, friendship, kindness, sharing, yielding. Life-giving power. But also secrets and mysteries.

Magically a force that cleanses, revives, and refreshes. Adaptability. Acceptance. Love can be drawn from or sent through this sign. Cast, it gives spiritual love and peace of heart, a gathering of massive strength. But cast with evil intention, nightmares and hallucinations. Madness.

22. ING: ◇ or ⊗ English: Ng

Literally the name of a fertility god from which the Ingwine (Danes) took their name. Carnal or physical love. Procreation. Sign of the family, of pregnancy. God of the hearth.

Magically it is used to bring a project to full term. To realize an end. Cast, it can cause desire in men and women.

23. DAEG: ⋈ or ⋈ English: D

Literally "day"—the ascendancy of good forces. The light of day that drives away the darkness. Safety, prosperity, happiness. The valued things of the Spirit.

Magically the dispersal of evil forces. Its action is gentle, like the coming of dawn. Cast, it can clear away obsessing influences.

24. ETHEL: ◇ English: O

Literally "inherited property"—native land. Specifically house, land, possessions. Material goods. Stability and continuity. That which can be passed down to posterity.

Magically this sign can be used to represent a material or mental possession. What is done to it will then befall the thing it represents. Cast, it can signify the coming into an inheritance or the loss of property, depending on what other runes accompany it.

To understand the relationships between the runes they must be written down in their traditional order in three groups of eight runes each, called *aettir*. The rectangular enclosures display the various ways the runes may be grouped:

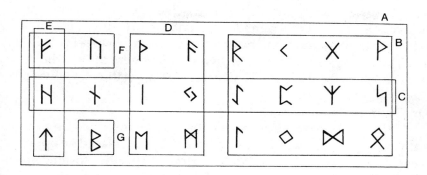

A: One group of twenty-four

An integrated whole that exhibits all the major forces in human life. There are the gods of justice and retribution, of war, of the family. There are the blind forces of nature. And there are the many facets of human personality. The rune alphabet may be assigned to the twenty-four hours of the day and to the letters of the English alphabet when it is reduced by combining the *J* and *I* and the *U* and *V*. Each rune may also be given its own color by combining the twelve colors of the color wheel into twenty-four.

The ordering of the runes should not be carelessly tampered with in making these assignments as it has been more or less fixed from several important archeological discoveries. However, there are minor discrepancies—Daeg is sometimes given as the last rune, for example.*

B: Two groups of twelve

The runes may be divided in half, one portion signifying the hours of the day and the other the hours of the night. Assigning each rune a specific hour on the clock may be useful in helping to focus the mind on the power of the rune. The signs of the Zodiac can be given to each half of the alphabet, one side the Zodiac of Light and the other the Zodiac of Darkness.

---

* In most German rune alphabets ETHEL is the last rune. It has been observed that this neatly brackets the alphabet with two symbols for property—FEOH for "cattle" and ETHEL for "land." Exceptions are the Vadstena and Grumpan alphabets, derived from two 6th-century Swedish medallions, which invert DAEG and ETHEL. The order of these runes is also inverted in the Old English Rune Poem, leading scholars to speculate that it resulted from the influence of Christianity and was inspired by the desire that the third *aett* end on the spiritual symbol for "light" rather than on the material symbol for "land."

C: **Three groups of eight**

This is the traditional division of the runes. Even when the alphabet was later reduced to sixteen characters, the names of the octaves, or *aettir*, were retained to describe a three-fold division. The *aettir* take their names from the first rune in each group—Feoh, Haegl, Tir. The octaves should be assigned the members of the trinity, the three motions, the three levels of man, and similar threefold divisions.

D: **Four divisions of six**

If four cubes are made, each cube may be inscribed on its sides with the runes in each of these groups, pairs being placed on opposing faces. Also if the *aettir* were folded into four so that they formed a four-sided tube, each of these divisions would form one of its sides. They should be assigned the seasons, the quarters, the elements, the letters in the fourfold name of God, the four beasts, and the four angels.

E: **Eight groups of three**

Repetition of the runes in threes was a common magical practice. It signified totality and completion. Each group may be assigned one of the planets, one being given the Earth. The groups may also be associated with the Light or Dark natures of the four elements.

F: **Twelve groups of two**

This is the most useful and revealing of the divisions. Many of the others are arbitrary, but there seems to be a real significance to the way the runes are paired off. For example, cattle and wild ox, man and horse, demon and god—these and other correspondences are too plain to overlook. Each pair presents a duality. Is is frozenness; Ger is change. Rad is quest; Ken is guide. Haegl is hardship; Nyd is will to endure. And so on.

The above assignments are deliberately left vague so that the Magus will make them based on his own knowledge and intuition. Like any good magical machine, the runes are flexible and always contain more meaning than can be consciously grasped.

Magical use of the runes entails five operations that are integrated into the standard ritual format: Cutting, Reading, Staining, Evoking, and Sending.

1. **Cutting**

First the runes must be cut clearly and accurately with a consecrated knife, or marked with a consecrated pen, used for no other purpose and kept ritually pure. Each stroke of the rune must be cut or
marked in a single motion—two strokes for cutting—and no line ever
retraced or carved over. The main stems are marked first in a downward stroke. Cross bars are made to the right.

2. **Reading**

As the rune is cut or marked the Magus should speak its name
and visualize it strongly, so that it is marked not only on the physical
surface but also on the psychic circle. This entails a full familiarity and
knowledge of the runes, since no rune can be actualized mentally
unless it is known both rationally and below the level of cogitation.
The rune is a symbol name for something complex and subtle that
cannot be embodied in words—this meaning must be sensed by the
Magus at the time of the cutting.

3. **Staining**

The runes must be stained with the fresh blood of the Magus just
prior to their evoking. This is the feeding of the runes, the catalyst that
vitalizes them. The blood is the physical switch that activates their
potencies. It should be pointed out that blood magic is dangerous and
should seldom be resorted to. The Magus cuts his breast under his
heart, or the palm of his left hand, with a consecrated knife—the same
that has carved the runes, if they have been carved—and with his right
index finger he traces the runes over with his blood.

4. **Evoking**

As the runes are being stained the spirits of the runes are verbally
and psychically evoked and directed to enter the runes. The physical
shape of the runes becomes the dwelling place of the magical powers:
the blood their food. The Magus calls forth the spirits with a chant of
his own making, creating a whirl that opens a door through the Veil of
Unknowing. This is done by stirring the knife stained with blood over
the blood-stained runes nine times in a clockwise direction.

5. **Sending**

The runes are sent, or cast, onto the object of the ritual working.
This involves telling the spirits who they are to act upon and in what

circumstances. The runes must be physically and psychically linked with the person the magic is about. The Magus concentrates on that person, repeating his or her name; it is good to have a photograph and a signature to aid this visualization. If certain conditions are involved, such as a particular time and place, the person is visualized in that setting. Then the runes must be physically placed in the possession of that person—sent through the mail, hidden where they will be found, or delivered by hand.

The Magus will be in danger after he has stained and evoked the runes, but before he has cast them, especially if they are intended for some evil purpose. Runes are often used for evil since they are by nature violent and pitiless. The Magus protects himself with the rune Eolh Y , which should be made in the form of a pendant and hung on a leather thong around the neck. The pendant should be iron or oak. As the runes are stained with blood this protective amulet is also stained so that both become potent at the same time. The pendant is stained first, and a short chant of evocation spoken over it before the runes involved in the ritual are stained and evoked. Since the pendant is kept pure, wrapped in white linen and apart from all eyes except those of the Magus, it is in a constant state of readiness and requires only the staining to make it active.

As an added precaution it is well to set the time for the working of the runes at least several hours in the future so that the Magus may be nowhere near when they take effect. Of course if the runes are being used for some benevolent purpose, such extreme protection is not needed.

Remember, a gift demands a gift. The gift the Magus offers to the spirits of the runes is his own lifeblood. The service they perform is their gift in return. However, it often happens that their service is large and the sacrifice of the Magus small. Then will the spirits come looking for further payment, which will always be taken in blood, sweat, or tears.

If you receive an evil rune from another you must cast it back upon its maker before the time established for its working. This requires that the rune be purified and cleansed of the associations that bind it to you, then psychically and physically linked with its maker. You should wear the rune of protection while turning the serpent to bite its own tail. Give the rune back shortly before the time of its working so that its maker will have no time to defend himself.

The proper use of the runes depends on the understanding of the Magus. Every case is different. Only rarely are the runes employed singly. Usually they are combined and repeated in series. Sometimes they are formed into words of power. Using the Kabbalistic technique of Notariqon and the English letter correspondences, the Magus should be able to form his own words of power from phrases expressing his intent. Sigils based on these words can be combined with the runes, although they are unnecessary.

Suppose it was desirable that a man should produce a child. The Magus might write Man ᛗ three times to symbolize his three levels of being, then Ur ᚢ four times to actualize his potency, then Peord ᛈ nine times to suggest the nine months of gestation and the nine emanations, and finally Ing ◇ once to symbolize completion in the material sphere.

It is regrettable that the traditional methods for using the runes have been lost. All that remains are a few fragments of poetry and some folk rhymes, and a cryptic remark or two from ancient historians. Perhaps in time archeology will bridge this gulf of ignorance. However, a true Magus will never have trouble directing the runes to achieve his ends. He will draw the magic from within and create new chants and rituals to replace those that have been forgotten. Rune magic will never die as long as there are those willing to work it.

HEALING

MAGICAL HEALING IS based on a simple principle—that disease has not only a physical body but a soul upon which that body is patterned.

The soul is the coding that gives a thing its unique identity. It is below the level of matter; genetic keys are based on the pattern of the soul. Spirit, by contrast, is the force that impels matter to adapt itself to the soul. Matter is receptive and passive. Spirit is assertive and active. The soul is double polarized, passive to Spirit and active to matter.

The soul is what joins Spirit to matter. As such it has no real existence, any more than the present moment can be said to occupy time. The soul is an interface, a gridlike matrix half composed of force—Spirit—and half made up of inertia—matter. When the pattern of the soul is disrupted, the link between Spirit and matter is broken. Take away the soul and the body at once begins to deteriorate, as the Spirit has no lens through which to focus itself. Destroy the soul of a disease and the Spirit-force of the disease will harmlessly disperse, causing the body of the disease to quickly decay.

If the soul is thought of as a series of numbers that make up a modern digital recording—a very apt metaphor—destroying the soul is akin to mixing up the order of the numbers, which results in so much white noise. None of the individual numbers has actually been destroyed, but the music is gone. So at the point of death nothing is actually lost, spiritualist assertions to the contrary, yet a change occurs from order to chaos.

Take cancer. When a tumor appears it is a physiological response to a deeper, invisible process. The tumor has no reason for growing in the human body. It is not naturally a part of the human form. Yet it suddenly appears and starts to grow. Assuredly it cannot come from nowhere. Something commands it to grow and provides the pattern upon which it forms itself, and this directing force is below the level of the physical causes of the tumor. It is the soul of the cancer—an evil soul because it is out of its natural order.

The Magus does not attempt to attack the tumor itself. The tumor is only the effect, not the cause. It is the flower and not the root. The objects least amenable to magic are physical forms. Rather than trying to destroy the tumor the Magus directs his energies to the heart of the problem, the soul of the disease that is the dark identity driving it.

All patterns of being spring from the Unmanifest and all eventually return there. The task of the Magus is to send the soul of the disease back across the Veil a little earlier than might otherwise be the case. He does this by creating a vortex that pierces the Veil and opens an aperture in it. Then he encompasses the soul with his Will, drawing a circle around it, and sends it along a ray through the hole in the Veil with the aid of the physical mechanics of ritual, finally sealing the door to the Unmanifest with a counter vortex.

This annihilates the soul of the disease. In the example of cancer, the tumor will not go away at once, anymore than a human body instantly decays after death when its soul leaves. But the ego that gave form to the cancer no longer exists, and it at once ceases to grow. It no longer has purpose or direction since its reason for being has been destroyed. It is dumb, lifeless tissue that the natural processes of the body begin to remove and excrete. Eventually the tumor will disappear as the cells and fluids that compose it are broken down and carried away.

Magical healing can be applied to all diseases no matter what their physical basis. In an infectious disease the soul is carried by the virus or bacteria, which forms a collective oganism much like an army that mounts an attack on the healthy systems of the body. The soul of the disease is also collective; it exists in each microorganism and also in the colony at large that fights with a unified purpose to overcome the body's defenses.

The Magus conceptualizes the soul by fixing his mind on the

symptoms of the disease and on the shape and action of the micro-organisms. In conceiving the soul he uses all the information at his disposal. Understand that the conscious mind can never hope to grasp the soul of the disease in all its subtlety. It does not have to. The subconscious power of the Magus, activated by his Will, forms an encompassing view of the soul by tapping into the omniscience of the Self.

Once the soul is sent through the Veil into the nothingness of unlimited potential, the viral or bacterial colony dies, and the symptoms of the disease such as fever, vomiting, vertigo, and so on gradually clear up. The natural defenses of the body do the same thing when they overcome disease, but they destroy the soul by destroying the body of microorganisms upon which it is based. If either matter or Spirit is removed from the soul, it loses half its substance and ceases to be. Magical healing attacks the soul of the disease directly, snapping the link between Spirit and matter in the middle rather than unraveling the physical end.

This is the underlying rationale behind the well-known witching away of warts, which are in fact colonies of viruses. The Wise Woman uses her Will and the unconscious Will of the afflicted person to send the soul of the wart away, after which the body of the wart soon dissolves into nothingness. The reverse of this is the unconscious creation of the soul of a disease, such as hysterical pregnancy in women or the formation of stigmata in the religious.

All modern medicine is a treatment of symptoms. The disease is burned or cut out or poisoned, but always the effort is directed against the physical body of the disease, never at its soul. Even inoculation merely prepares the human body to resist the body of the micro-organism. Perhaps the closest science has come to attacking the soul of a disease is its battle against smallpox, where the goal was to destroy every smallpox organism in the world, thereby making future infections impossible. However, this is doing it the hard way, attempting to destroy the soul by taking away all the houses of flesh in which it could possibly find refuge.

By the way, there is an analogy to be drawn here with the legend of the vampire, which says that the vampire must always maintain a number of coffins filled with its native grave earth, for in this alone can it find rest during the light of day. One way to fight the vampire is to destroy all its resting places. But this is an uncertain method; it is impossible to be sure all the boxes of earth have been found.

334 / New Magus

The boxes of earth are analogous to the microorganisms. When a cancer is cut out the surgeon is never sure he has removed all its parts. If even one cell remains, the soul of the cancer, the vampire of the human body, can replace what it has lost. Even with the secrets of genetic coding within its grasp science is still only dealing with the body of disease, not the soul. It will always treat the symptom. For this reason its power over disease will always be limited.

There is often an abyss between theory and practice. If the magical banishing of disease were a simple matter people would be curing themselves left and right. Magical healing is a skill that requires natural talent, intelligence, knowledge, will power, imagination and faith. The last is in short supply in the West.

Yet throughout the world there are signs that this method of treating disease can be effective. The common cure of warts is one. The miraculous remission of otherwise fatal diseases is another. The faith healings that cannot wholly be dismissed as fraud is still another. The amputee who can feel his leg after it has been cut off points to the soul that lends a pattern to the flesh, even if it does so through the metaphor of aberrant nerve impulses.

Few people would dispute that the powerful willing of a thing can bring it to pass; the argument arises over the means by which the force of Will is realized. Science and medicine would say that Will must realize itself through commonly accepted natural laws. Magic— and at one time, religion—would maintain that the lowest order of being, the physical, can at certain times be bypassed by an active Will applied with true understanding.

One useful practical technique for curing disease is to picture the body glowing with perfect health, all organs and systems functioning at peak efficiency, the body radiating vitality. This allows the soul of the body to dominate the soul of the disease and force it out with the physical weapons of the natural defenses. This method is unconsciously used by those who pray for their own health or the well-being of another ill person. It can be effective but is indirect.

A more active variation on this method is used by the Spiritist religions of South America, where the spirit medium makes the motion of reaching through the aura of the sick person and physically tearing out the disease and casting it from him. In effect the medium takes the soul of the disease onto himself, then expels it before it can harm him.

The Spiritists believe themselves utterly without power, merely instruments for beings on higher planes that use them to cure the sick. As is so often the case, they are both correct and incorrect in their assumption. True, their conscious identity has no power, yet the spirits they perceive as entirely apart from them are born in their sub-conscious and are subject to their awakened magical Will, if the Spiritists only knew it.

The Magus will use a more forthright approach to destroy the soul of disease. A simple method is to mentally embody the disease, then hold the hands together and visualize a pulse of light in rotation expanding from a point, while opening an aperture in the hands. Project the soul of the disease through the hands, which are held outward at arm's length and pictured as defining the Veil of the Unmanifest. Finally close the hole between the hands and visualize the aperture through the Veil sealing after the soul of the disease with a reverse vortex. This can be done quickly under any conditions.

Often a healing ritual will have to be repeated several times, depending on the strength of Will of the Magus and the faith of the patient. However, it may happen that the first ritual has been success-ful and the succeeding ones are superfluous, as the symptoms of dis-ease need time to disappear after the soul is banished. On the other hand, the symptoms may appear to clear up immediately, having been psychically overcome by the confident expectation of the af-flicted person.

Faith does more than simply delude sick people into believing they are well. For an action to take effect in the subconscious, com-plete belief in its success is necessary. Doubt makes prisoners of all men. Doubt is like darkness, a negative quality without substance. Faith is akin to the light that dispels shadows before it. Doubt cannot exist in the presence of faith. When doubt is dispelled, desires can be realized, and not before.

Healing can be extremely dangerous to the Magus. By calling attention to himself he invites a host of disease souls to attach them-selves to his aura like leeches, where they wait for the least weakness. If he is tired when he performs the healing, the soul of the disease will fasten onto him, and he will find himself too weak to fight it. By choos-ing to destroy the soul of the disease the Magus insures that it will seek him out malignantly, for the natural reaction to a blow is to strike out. This is karma and applies on the lowest as well as the highest levels.

Even the Magus is not all-powerful. He must weigh the danger to himself against the good that he may be able to do for others. If his good intentions are greater than his talents as a healer, he would be foolish to attempt to force his powers into this channel. Healing is an art all its own. Some are born to it. Others never get the knack despite their many notable achievements.

THE WAY

HERE IS A parable. A man is born onto a sandy plane that extends limitlessly to the horizon. There is a narrow path on the plane, and when the man awakes he is standing at the beginning of the path. He is born blind and begins to walk without knowing why or where he is going, conscious only of his emptiness and seeking some unconceived fulfillment.

Because the man cannot see the path and at first does not know it exists, he readily wanders off. His feet make a confused and winding trail in the sand. There are apples to be picked merely by stepping into the plane, and he eats of them without question. Some are sour and some are sweet, but both equally poisonous, and cause him much suffering.

The path has a stone surface for walking. At first it seems cruel on his naked feet compared to the soft fine sands of the plane, but in the long term the flat stones are better for getting on because the sands tire and cling. The man gradually becomes aware of the difference in texture between the path and the sand. For a long time he pretends that one way is as good as any other. Only when he has wandered on and off the path many times is he forced to realize that the path is best for him, because to stay on the path is to progress, even though slowly and with many missteps, while to depart from it is to wander aimlessly.

He becomes conscious of countless paths other than his that crisscross the plane with other men and women walking on them. Each person cries dolorously for guidance, but no one heeds the cries of his neighbor. The man experiments, taking shortcuts along some of these other paths, but his path is straight and leads directly to his destination. Eventually he realizes that his own path is the shortest route to his ultimate goal.

The man continues year after year, ignoring the cries of others asking him to depart with them across the sands, not knowing what his destination will be but convinced that it is his alone. The very emptiness and endlessness of the dark way before him draw him onward.

At last, when he is aged and tired of wandering he reaches a tall doorway of shining gold and passes through. His eyes are opened, and he is bathed in a beautiful white radiance that washes away his cares and returns to him the heart of a newborn child. Then he knows the reason for his weary years of wandering alone in the desert. He is filled with quiet joy and great peace.

What does this parable signify?

The plane is eternity. The sands are the sands of time. Across them blow the winds of change, shifting and obscuring them. The blindness of the man is his ignorance. The path is his destiny, the one thread of circumstance extending through his life that will allow him to achieve the purpose for which he was created.

The winding and confused track left by his feet in the sand is his fate. Rarely will the track of fate overlap the path of destiny. The sweet and sour apples that grow off the path are the fruits of fortune. Even when they seem good they are bad because they lead away from destiny. On the path of destiny there is no luck—all happens according to plan and for the best.

The other wanderers in the desert are lost mankind, each person crying selfishly for comfort, never heeding the cries of despair all around. They seek to lure others across the shifting sands to share in their misery, in the vain hope that the lost can comfort the lost with lies.

At the end of the path is the door of death, which a man can only pass through with honor if he has been faithful to his destiny. The innumerable tracks of fate also have their doors, but these are low portals a man must stoop his head to pass through and there is no joy beyond them, only darkness and cold.

Destiny and fate are two terms that are often confused. There is only one destiny in the life of an individual, but many potential fates. The destiny is the most perfect possible realization of the talents and abilities a human being has received at conception—perfection as defined by the All. A perfect life in the eye of God may seem a wasted life in the eyes of society, while social success may be futile from the divine perspective. Fate is simply the actual use to which these potentials are put. If perfect destiny is realized, then fate and destiny overlap. Usually frail humankind falls short of perfection, and the actual fate of an individual diverges from his destiny.

At every moment in life numerous choices present themselves. Should one say yes or no? Go or stay? Laugh or cry? Fight or flee? Even a seemingly small decision can come to have great significance in later life. Consider life as an infinite series of overlapping cinematic films. Each time a choice is made the image splits into two or more alternatives. In a short while the screen of life is crowded with thousands of possibilities, all running about in different directions. One image goes to university and becomes a lawyer. Another quits school and drives a truck. One proposes and is happily married. Another stays single and lives alone.

The point to grasp is that only one of these many cinematic images is the true Self realizing its full potential through the individual ego. All others are greater or lesser approximations of the single perfect destiny. The series of images a person has actually followed up to the time of death becomes his fate, which can never be erased or altered.

The great task of life is to bring destiny and fate into harmony. Destiny can never be altered: it is fixed at the moment of conception. Fate cannot be changed in the past but can be directed in the future to accord more or less closely with destiny. Practically speaking, it is impossible for a human being to ever achieve his perfect destiny, but life is judged a success or failure by how nearly the destiny is approximated.

The Magus should know better than to oppose his destiny. He has been granted the option, but to do so is to willfully seek to be less than he might become. Because his destiny is the ideal realization of his being, he cannot help attaining happiness and fulfillment if he is able to follow it even to a degree. If he fights his destiny he is in effect battling himself. Therefore there is no element of glory in resisting, only futility and waste.

If he wantonly chooses to turn his back on his highest possibility, the Light will not oppose him. This is the true meaning of free will: everyone is free to ruin their lives if they choose to do so. God will watch in sorrow but will not act to stop them. However, if the Magus decides to seek his destiny and asks the Light for guidance with a sincere heart, he will be guided. The Light will give him the inner sense to know when he has lost his way and the strength of purpose to resist the lure of those who would distract him from his path.

Destiny is never easy but it is always appropriate. Only when the Magus has achieved this realization can he resist the impulse to depart from his path and take a short cut to happiness. Such short cuts lead nowhere. Attempts to cheat destiny end in shimmering mirages that tempt the foolish ever deeper into the wilderness. Only through self-knowledge—needs, desires, limitations, and abilities—and by being receptive to the guidance of the Light can the Magus hope with reasonable confidence to tread the single true Way of his life. This is the esoteric Tao of Chinese philosophy, always unique yet always perfectly suited to each individual.

The Way is not predestined, as this term is commonly understood. Rather it is the best response to conditions as they arise, given the existing resources. It can be visualized as water flowing downhill, which always seeks the easiest course to the sea. So does man always seek the easiest channel to God when he is right in his soul. To pursue destiny is to follow cosmic law. Denial of destiny is madness, akin to a river flowing backwards.

The nearer the Magus comes to achieving his personal destiny, the more fulfilled his life will be, not only on the spiritual level but very probably on the material level as well. To be the best you are is to achieve the best you can achieve. In business, love, health, and society—this is everywhere true. No average human being is so deprived of ability that he or she cannot attain wealth and happiness if that ability is well applied. It is not predestined by God that certain people should be poor. They make this choice for themselves. Destiny is always the best path through life because it leads directly to the Light, the source of all pleasures and victories that matter.

MAGUS

A MAGUS IS one who bears the primal fire from heaven to Earth.

The fire the Magus carries is the force of purpose that lends order and direction to all creation. It is the Spirit that animates and drives.

The heaven is the dimensionless body of the undifferentiated All, the Unmanifest, present in every timeless and spaceless point in the universe.

The Earth is the underlying locus upon which all forms are based, not only forms of matter and energy, but ideas, emotions, and beliefs as well.

Considering the definition from this expanded perspective, the Magus may be distinguished from the scientist, who seeks only to manipulate the forms of the created universe without acknowledging the Spirit of Light or the Unmanifest.

He may also be differentiated from the mystic, who seeks only a perfect union with the All and has no desire to manipulate the universe of forms beyond that goal.

The mechanical man, the scientist, denies heaven and revels in earthly delights. For him the furnaces of Vulcan are the be-all and end-all of existence. The mystical man, the saint, denies the forms of Earth and glories in the Spirit. Encased in flesh, he persists in pretending that his body does not exist.

On a stable platform between the two pans of this balance stands the Magus, who denies neither aspect of reality but seeks to unite them in harmony, as they were united before the great fall that led mankind to conceive itself as separate from the All.

The Magus has little admiration for the scientist trapped in the world of forms, who inevitably runs his head again and again into the wall of ignorance that surrounds materiality. He has little respect for the mystic, who selfishly seeks to leapfrog his way out of the universe before fulfilling his life purpose merely so he may luxuriate in the soothing rays from the Unmanifest.

Mankind was not placed on Earth to forget heaven and waste eternity rooting in the dirt. Neither was the race put here to despise the Earth and flee back into heaven. Man is an instrument whose sole purpose is the furthering, in its infinite complexity, of the desire of God as expressed in the evolution of the universe. Since man was created in the Creator's image, the desire of God is also the highest and best desire of man.

Mercury-Hermes, the messenger of the gods, is a symbol of the Magus. Prometheus, who gave the secret of fire to men, is also symbolic of the Magus. Odin, who snatched the runes of power from the roots of the cosmic tree Yggdrasil, is the Magus in yet another guise.

The Magus of five hundred years ago is now called Renaissance man, and pursued mathematics, art, and alchemy. Two thousand years before that he was the Pythagorean philosopher who traveled to Egypt and Chaldea to study the mysteries. A million years before that he was the shaman dancing around the campfire.

Today he has no class and is outcast from society. Educated, often successful, he cannot be satisfied with his imposed role. Even when social norms change like spring fashions he sees through the illusion of their novelty to their hollow centers. He is a leader without followers, a teacher without students. Only the perfect synthesis of the Light and Darkness can justify his life. He is seldom happy because supreme attainment is elusive, and there is no class for him to fall back on for support when he fails. He is never content, but is always moving, restlessly changing shapes to suit the circumstances in which he finds himself.

The guiding force in his character is balance. Any excess that tilts the scale of cosmic law is to be avoided. Too much asceticism is just as damnable as an excess of sensuality. Preoccupation with the body is as bad as complete physical disregard. The Magus strives to harmonize perfectly with the unfolding of the universe, which is the Will of the Unmanifest expressed through creation. He recognizes the natural supremacy of the Spirit over the body as akin to the rider's supremacy over the horse, but also knows that if the rider beats his horse to death he will get nowhere.

Yet the Magus is never content merely to balance his life at one level. He seeks to carry it to its final degree of perfection. His understanding of perfection stems from the Light and is a personal revelation. His twofold task is first to comprehend the best to which he may aspire, then to seek to realize that ideal.

He does not react to circumstances unthinkingly unless instant action is called for by the nature of the circumstance. Since his one desire is to attain his personal destiny—the Will of the All in his life— he is not easily diverted by the vagaries of worldly events. If a man curses him he will not curse the man back at once. If a man does him a service neither will he immediately open his heart. He serves the Light, never his own whims and vanities.

Whatever his social standing or material condition the Magus will rise above others. Physically he will tend to be more fit. Mentally he will be more acute. Morally he will be stronger. This does not mean he will never suffer hardship, for there will be times when he is forced to place what he knows to be right in the eye of God in opposition to the social currents of the world. However, he will always command himself and by extension all who come into his sphere of awareness.

He cannot be led by others. He may become a leader if it is his destiny, but he is never a follower. The will of the mob will not infect him. He is indifferent to fashion and social manners except insofar as these can be made to serve his purpose. Those in public positions will not inspire him with hero worship. He will not fall head-over-heels in love. He sees through even the most subtle attempts to deceive. Having found his true center he cannot be moved from it by the will of others.

Christ was the archetypal Magus. He struggled to fulfill the Will of the Unmanifest on Earth, accepting his destiny as leader and teacher even though in the beginning none wished to follow or learn, and he knew full well the anguish his role would ultimately bring him. Aware of the paramount importance of the Spirit, he nevertheless felt concern for the worldly sufferings of men and used his great Art to succor their bodies. He acknowledged no intermediate deity but recognized himself as the true Son of the one heavenly Father.

With his power Christ might have obtained riches and luxury for himself, but he placed cosmic law above personal pleasure. He might have retired in solitude and devoted himself to communing with the Light, but he accepted that he had been born onto the Earth for an earthly purpose. He was the supreme Magus of the Western world.

Not all are born to be christs. Seldom is the Magus perfectly balanced in all aspects. He is selectively blinded by his prejudices and desires. He progresses more rapidly in some wisdoms than others. But still he is Magus because always he strives toward his destiny, however far his feet may stray through ignorance and weakness from the path. He is no self-deceiver. Hardship will never cause him to call the Darkness Light. Should he fail in the end, he will know how and why he failed, and what he has failed—an attainment in itself.

Notes

1. Blake, "Auguries of Innocence," *Complete Writings* (London: Oxford University Press, 1972), 431.

2. Blake, "Auguries of Innocence," *Complete Writings*, 433.

3. Wilhelm and Jung, eds., *The Secret of the Golden Flower* (London: Routledge & Kegan Paul, 1962), 22.

4. Blake, "The Everlasting Gospel," *Complete Writings*, 753.

5. Mathers, trans., *Book of the Sacred Magic of Abramelin the Mage* (New York: Dover Publications, 1975), Book II, Chap. 4, 57.

6. Westcott, trans., *Sepher Yetzirah* (York Beach, Maine: Samuel Weiser, 1980), Chap. 1, Sect. 4, 15.

7. *Larousse Encyclopedia of Mythology* (New York: Prometheus Press, 1960), 328.

8. Nasr, ed., *Introduction to Islamic Cosmological Doctrines* (Boulder: Shambhala, 1978), 82.

9. Budge, *The Book of the Dead* (New York: University Books, 1960), 372-73.

10. Tennyson, "Sir Galahad," *Poems of Tennyson* (London: Oxford University Press, 1910), 205.

11. Browning, "Childe Roland to the Dark Tower Came," *Complete Works* (New York: Houghton Mifflin, 1895), 287.

12. Christian, *History and Practice of Magic* (New York: Citadel Press, 1963), 89-94.

13. Levi, *Transcendental Magic* (York Beach, Maine: Samuel Weiser, 1979), 29.

14. Myer, *Qabbalah* (York Beach, Maine: Samuel Weiser, 1974), 274.

15. Howard, *The Runes* (Northamptonshire, England: Aquarian Press, 1978), 25-6 ("Havamal," vv. 138-39).

16. Mathers, trans., *The Greater Key of Solomon* (Calif.: Health Research, 1978), 23-4.

17. David-Neel, *Magic and Mystery in Tibet* (New York: Dover Publications, 1971), Chap. VIII.

18. Patai, *Gates of the Old City* (New York: Avon Books, 1980), 636-42.

19. Mathers, *Book of the Sacred Magic*, 21.

20. Lane, *The Bronte Story* (London: William Heinemann, 1953), 79-80, 109-10.

21. de Kleen, *Mudras* (New York: University Books, 1970).

STAY IN TOUCH

On the following pages you will find listed, with their current prices, some of the books and tapes now available on related subjects. Your book dealer stocks most of these, and will stock new titles in the Llewellyn series as they become available. We urge your patronage.

However, to obtain our full catalog, to keep informed of new titles as they are released and to benefit from informative articles and helpful news, you are invited to write for our bi-monthly news magazine/catalog. A sample copy is free, and it will continue coming to you at no cost as long as you are an active mail customer. Or you may keep it coming for a full year with a donation of just $2.00 in U.S.A. ($7.00 for Canada & Mexico, $20.00 overseas, first class mail). Many bookstores also have *The Llewellyn New Times* available to their customers. Ask for it.

Stay in touch! In *The Llewellyn New Times'* pages you will find news and reviews of new books, tapes and services, announcements of meetings and seminars, articles helpful to our readers, news of authors, advertising of products and services, special money-making opportunities, and much more.

The Llewellyn New Times
P.O. Box 64383-Dept. 825, St. Paul, MN 55164-0383, U.S.A.

• • •

TO ORDER BOOKS AND TAPES

If your book dealer does not have the books and tapes described on the following pages readily available, you may order them direct from the publisher by sending full price in U.S. funds, plus $1.00 for handling and 50¢ each book or item for postage within the United States; outside USA surface mail add $1.50 per item postage and $1.00 handling per order. Outside USA air mail add $7.00 per item plus $1.00 handling per order.

FOR GROUP STUDY AND PURCHASE

Because there is a great deal of interest in group discussion and study of the subject matter of this book, we feel that we should encourage the adoption and use of this particular book by such groups by offering a special "quantity" price to group leaders or "agents".

Our Special Quantity Price for a minimum order of five copies of NEW MAGUS is $38.85 Cash-With-Order. This price includes postage and handling within the United States. Minnesota residents must add 6% sales tax. For additional quantities, please order in multiples of five. For Canadian and foreign orders, add postage and handling charges as above. Credit Card (VISA, MasterCard, American Express, Diners' Club) Orders are accepted. Charge Card Orders only may be phoned free ($15.00 minimum order) within the U.S.A. by dialing 1-800-THE MOON (in Canada call: 1-800-FOR-SELF). Customer Service calls dial 1-612-291-1970. Mail Orders to:

LLEWELLYN PUBLICATIONS
P.O. Box 64383-Dept. 825 / St. Paul, MN 55164-0383, U.S.A.

THE GOLDEN DAWN
by Israel Regardie

The Original Account of the Teachings, Rites and Ceremonies of the Hermetic Order of the Golden Dawn as revealed by Israel Regardie, with further revision, expansion, and additional notes by Israel Regardie, Cris Monnastre, and others.

Originally published in four bulky volumes of some 1200 pages, this 5th Revised and Enlarged Edition has been entirely reset in modern, less space-consuming type, in half the pages (while retaining the original pagination in marginal notation for reference) for greater ease and use.

Also included are Initiation Ceremonies, important rituals for consecration and invocation, methods of meditation and magical working based on the Enochian Tablets, studies in the Tarot, and the system of Qabalistic Correspondences that unite the World's religions and magical traditions into a comprehensive and practical whole.

This volume is designed as a study and practice curriculum suited to both group and private practice. Meditation upon, and following with the Active Imagination, the Initiation Ceremonies is fully experiential without need of participation in group or lodge.

0-87542-663-8, 744 pages, 6 x 9, illus.   **$19.95**

A GARDEN OF POMEGRANATES
by Israel Regardie

What is the Tree of Life? It's the ground plan of the Qabalistic system—a set of symbols used since ancient times to study the Universe. The Tree of Life is a geometrical arrangement of ten sephiroth, or spheres, each of which is associated with a different archetypal idea, and 22 paths which connect the spheres.

A Garden of Pomegranates combines Regardie's own studies with his notes on the works of Aleister Crowley, A.E. Waite, Eliphas Levi and D.H. Lawrence. No longer is the wisdom of the Qabalah to be held *secret!* The needs of today place the burden of growth upon each and every person—each has to undertake the Path as his or her own responsibility, but every help is given in the most ancient and yet most modern teaching here known to humankind.

0-87542-690-5, 176 pages, softcover.   **$6.95**

THE MIDDLE PILLAR
by Israel Regardie

Between the two outer pillars of the Qabalistic Tree of Life, the extremes of Mercy and Severity, stands THE MIDDLE PILLAR, signifying one who has achieved equilibrium in his or her own self.

Integration of the human personality is vital to the continuance of creative life. Without it, man lives as an outsider to his own true self. By combining Magic and Psychology in the Middle Pillar Ritual/Exercise (a magical meditation technique), we bring into balance the opposing elements of the psyche while yet holding within their essence and allowing full expression of man's entire being.

In this book, and with this practice, you will learn to: understand the psyche through its correspondences on the Tree of Life; expand self-awareness, thereby intensifying the inner growth process; activate creative and intuitive potentials; understand the individual thought patterns which control every facet of personal behavior; regain the sense of balance and peace of mind—the equilibrium that everyone needs for physical and psychic health.

0-87542-658-1, 176 pages, softcover.   **$6.95**

MAGICAL STATES OF CONSCIOUSNESS
by Melita Denning and Osborne Phillips

Magical States of Consciousness are dimensions of the Human Psyche giving us access to the knowledge and powers of the Great Archetypes.

These dimensions are attained as we travel the Paths of the Qabalah's Tree of Life— that "blueprint" to the structure of the Lesser Universe of the Human Psyche and to the Greater Universe in which we have our being.

Published here for the first time are not only the complete texts for these inward journeys to the Deep Unconscious Mind, but complete guidance to their application in Spiritual Growth and Initiation, Psychological Integration and "Soul Sculpture" (the secret technique by which we may shape our own character).

Here, too, are *Magical Mandalas* for each of the Path-Workings that serve as "doorways" to altered states of consciousness when used with the Path-Working narrations, and *Magical Images* of the Sephirothic Archetypes as used in invoking those powerful forces.   **0-87542-194-6, 420 pages, Illust.,softcover. $12.95**

THE LLEWELLYN INNER GUIDE TAPES

Because Path-Working has so many benefits to the Listener/Participant, we are making the texts of each of the Path-Workings in *Magical States of Consciousness* available on high-quality cassette tapes.

Each tape is accompanied by a booklet of necessary instructions, with the appropriate Magical Mandala for the path being worked.
All tapes are $9.95 each

32nd Path: Governing Intelligence, Development of intuition, enhance astral projection, and creative visualization.   **0-87542-151-2**

31st Path: Unresting Intelligence
30th Path: Collating Intelligence, 31st Path develops courage, enhances past life recall, arouses Kundalini, frees you from emotional conditioning. 30th Path enhances healing powers, develops discipline, assists in visualization operations.
0-87542-152-0

29th Path: The Bodily Intelligence
28th Path: The Perfecting Intelligence, 29th Path spreads harmony, heals family disputes, assists with helping animals, increases prosperity, enhances scrying. 28th Path disciplines the mind, helps in astrological analysis, planning career.   **0-87542-153-9**

27th Path: Awakening Intelligence, Courage to face fears, skill in avoiding quarrels, banishing in magical rites, increases debating skills, love.   **0-87542-154-7**

26th Path, Part I: The Renewing Intelligence
24th Path, Part 1: Image-making Intelligence, Preparing for transformation, the 26th Path asks why caution prosperity, sexuality, and goodness? The 24th Path queries Death.   **0-87542-155-5**

25th Path: Critical Intelligence, Strengthens the bonds with the Higher Self, promotes spiritual progress, develops self-confidence, assists in calling up God Forms, astral projection, invoking HGA. Protection while traveling.   **0-87542-156-3**

26th Path, Part 2
26th Path gives access to inner powers and outer control over tendency to domineer. Used for exorcism, rites of protection for home. Promotes generosity and tolerance.
0-87542-157-1

24th Path, Part 2
24th Path assuages grief, resolves inner conflicts. Used for Sex Magick, helps in understanding adolescents.

RAY BUCKLAND'S COMPLETE BOOK OF WITCHCRAFT
by Raymond Buckland, Ph. D.
Here is the most complete resource to the study and practice of modern, non-denominational Wicca. This is a lavishly illustrated, self-study course for the solitary or group. Included are rituals, exercises for developing psychic talents, and information on all major 'sects' of the Craft, sections on tools, beliefs, dreams, meditations, divination, herbal lore, healing, ritual clothing and much, much more. This book unites theory and practice into a comprehensive course designed to help you develop into a practicing Witch, one of the "Wise Ones". It is written by Dr. Ray Buckland, the very famous and respected authority on witchcraft who first came public with "The Old Religion" in the United States. Large format with workbook-type exercises, profusely illustrated and full of music and chants. Takes you from A to Z in the study of Witchcraft.
0-87542-050-8, 8½ x 11, 272 pages, illus., softcover.   **$12.95**

ENOCHIAN MAGIC—A Practical Manual
by Gerald J. Schueler
The powerful system of magic introduced in the sixteenth century by Dr. John Dee, Astrologer Royal to Queen Elizabeth I, and as practiced by Aleister Crowley and the Hermetic Order of the Golden Dawn, is here presented for the first time in a complete, step-by-step form. *There has never before been a book that has made Enochian Magic this easy!*

In this book you are led carefully along the path from "A brief history of the Enochian Magical System," through "How to speak Enochian," "How to Invoke," "The Calls," "Egyptian Deities" and "Chief Hazards" to "How to visit the Aethyrs in Spirit Vision (Astral Projection)." Not a step is missed; not a necessary instruction forgotten.
0-87542-710-3, 270 pages, 5¼ x 8, illus., softcover.   **$12.95**

MYSTERIA MAGICA
(formerly Volume V of the Magical Philosophy Series)
by Melita Denning and Osborne Phillips
No matter what your level of ability in Ceremonial Magick, this is one of the most important books you could ever own. Bringing together the best of the magical systems of Egypt, Ireland, Pre-Columbian America, the Mediterranian, Northern Europe and the Middle East, the authors lead us into new and profound areas of Magical Work. Knowledge is power, and the knowledge presented in these pages is some of the most powerful ever published.

This book offers you essential and profound magical knowledge, authentic texts and formulae of the Western Mystery Tradition which have hitherto been hidden in inaccessible libraries, in enigmatic writings, or in rarely-imparted teachings passed on only by word of mouth; and, in addition, it contains ample sections showing you how to use all that is disclosed, how to give potent consecration to your own magical weapons, how to build rites on the physical and astral planes with word and action, sound, color and visualization, to implement your own magical will.

The setting of the Wards of Power; The Setting of the Wards of Adamant (Sub Rosa Nigra); the Clavis Rei Primae and Orante Formulae; Banishing and Invoking; Identifying with God-forces; Astral Projection; Formula of the Watcher; Elementary Techniques of Scrying; The Constellation of the Worshipped; Principles of Ceremonial; The Dance as Instrument of Magick; Sigils; Conjurations of the Art; Enochian Studies Sphere-Working; Transubstantiation; Consecration of a Talisman; and much more—with tables, guidance to pronunciation of Enochian, workings with Elementals, formulae for integration, etc.
0-87542-196-2, 500 pages, 6" x 9", revised, softcover.   **$15.00**